B

ONE JESUS,
MANY CHRISTS

ONE JESUS, MANY CHRISTS

HOW JESUS INSPIRED NOT ONE TRUE CHRISTIANITY, BUT MANY

The Truth About Christian Origins

Gregory J. Riley

HarperSanFrancisco

A Division of HarperCollins*Publishers*

HarperCollins Web Site: http://www.harpercollins.com
HarperCollins®, ☙ ®, and HarperSanFrancisco™ are trademarks of
HarperCollins Publishers Inc.

Book Design by Martha Blegen

FIRST EDITION

Library of Congress Cataloging-in-Publication Data
Riley, Gregory J. (Gregory John)
One Jesus, many Christs : how Jesus inspired not one true Christianity, but
many : the truth about Christian origins / Gregory J. Riley.
    p.   cm.
Includes index.
ISBN 0–06–066799–0 (cloth)
ISBN 0–06–066798–2 (pbk.)
1. Jesus Christ—History of doctrines—Early church, ca. 30–600.
2. Church history—Primitive and early church, ca. 30–600.
3. Hero worship—Rome—History. 4. Christianity—Origin. I. Title.
BT198.R53   1997   270.1—dc21   97–3294 CIP

97 98 99 00 01 ❖ RRDH 10 9 8 7 6 5 4 3 2 1

For
Mark, Alex,
and,
Susan

CONTENTS

Chapter 1

Jesus and the Varieties
of Early Christianity

We take the existence of Christianity for granted today, but early in the first century it did not exist at all, and, after its inception, it long suffered the ridicule of both Jewish and pagan detractors that it was founded by a bunch of low-class types with bad grammar and bad accents. Yet it eventually won out over the richest and most powerful religious establishment in the world, with the best temple architecture, schools, and all the public money it could want. Why did it do so?

I have been interested for two decades in how to account for the rise of Christianity and have come to find the explanations given by religious partisans and scholars less than persuasive. Partisans are often content with purely theological answers, claiming that it was God's will, that God had prepared the ground of the first century, and that the world was yearning spiritually for some new message. Scholars, on the other hand, have concentrated on the more human aspects of the issue and, especially recently, have tried to understand the human Jesus, the "historical Jesus" as he is called. Sometimes widely different pictures have been drawn of who he was: Jesus was a Jewish eschatological prophet, a social revolutionary, a "holy man," or some type of philosopher. Each idea in its own way points to something genuine, but none seems to address directly the question we are asking here or make human sense out of the subsequent rise of the Church. There were lots of social revolutionaries and "holy men" in Jesus' time whose efforts are now all but lost, and no world religions arose around Amos the prophet or Socrates the philosopher. All of those figures were common enough in the world of Jesus centuries before and after his time and none set Western civilization in a new direction. Christianity certainly has a social message that in many ways draws on the prophets, and it is full of ideas inherited from "holy men" and philosophers, but it is not primarily a prophetic message or social program or a philosophy.

Christianity instead centers on a person, and the core of its message is a kind of biography of that person. So what in the culture of the ancient world and this biography of Jesus motivated people to choose to be eaten by lions in the local amphitheater? The point here is to understand what the draw was, what attracted people to the movement and message of Christianity in the first place. What could inspire such a high level of loyalty and commitment in the face of such dire threats and possible penalties?

It is not at all evident that the message would have the same appeal today. Our worldview and scientific understanding have evolved, expectations for life have changed, and models for behavior and ideals have been nearly reversed. It is no longer obvious that a message claiming that some foreign teacher was crucified in the middle of his life and then resurrected would capture the imagination of an entire civilization. It was not admirable to be either foreign or crucified in the minds of most Romans. Yet if we can understand the original appeal in its original context, we may begin to see why it had (and may still have for us) such a powerful ability to draw to itself not only the poor and disenfranchised, but also some of the most highly educated and highly placed members of ancient society.

Christianity was immensely successful. Eventually, this "superstition," as it was called by the Roman aristocracy, invaded the broad spectrum of society, including those upper classes who used their power to fight against it. Pliny the Younger, governor of the Roman province of Bithynia (on the north coast of modern Turkey), wrote to emperor Trajan (r. 98–117) about A.D. 110, a mere eighty years or so after the crucifixion of Jesus, describing the official trials he was conducting to find and execute Christians:

> The matter seems to me worthy of your consultation, especially on account of the numbers of defendants. For many of every age, of every social class, even of both sexes, are being called to trial and will be called.

Nor cities alone, but villages and even rural areas have been invaded by the infection of this superstition. (*Epistulae* 10.96, GJR)

Pliny was in a rather distant and out-of-the-way province, and he shows us that just a few generations after its beginning, Christianity had "invaded" every level of society. Another ninety years later, around A.D. 200, Tertullian, a Roman lawyer turned Christian, in his defiant open letter to the Roman magistrates defending Christianity against persecution, could boast proudly that "nearly all the citizens of all the cities are Christians" (*Apologeticus* 37.8, GJR).

This last statement, we suspect, is something of an exaggeration made for rhetorical effect, but both authors agree on at least two matters: the number of Christians was considerable, even alarming, and persecution was an important aspect of the "problem." For Tertullian and other members of the new faith, persecution was the height of injustice and barbarism. For Pliny and other Roman governors, it was a large part of the solution. Persecutions worked—they turned great numbers of Christians back to the traditional gods. Pliny continues in his letter that, because of his official trials, "the temples, up to now almost desolate, have begun to be crowded, and the solemn rites, long discontinued, are again being performed." Roman officials found that while they watched and did nothing, the whole world was turning away from the gods on which the empire was based to the new god Jesus. They also discovered that if they arrested the "guilty" and required them to denounce the Christian faith, then tortured and killed the obstinate, they could turn many back.

So the growth of Christianity was apparently quite uneven: it expanded rapidly in times of peace and contracted nearly as rapidly in times of persecution. But the persecutions never seemed to work well enough. In fact, they began in time to work in the Christians' favor. Eventually the Romans found what Tertullian was so proud of: "When we are killed, we conquer" (*Apologeticus* 50.3, GJR). Eventually the persecutions ceased to have any lasting effect, ceased to turn enough people away. Too many were obstinate; too many were willing to go to their deaths rather than deny their faith. Eventually the Christians won.

e⟩━━◆━━⟨ɔ

THESE ARE OBSERVATIONS and descriptions of historical events, but they are not explanations. To watch and describe the seemingly inexorable rise of Christianity is not to understand why it succeeded, why it was ultimately able to persuade the majority of members in an old and proud society to leave their previous way of looking at the religious world and "convert" to another hated and persecuted religious view. Christianity in time held strong attraction to all levels of society in the wider Roman world, but not for the reasons we today might think or claim for it. In fact, that it held any appeal at all is something of a surprise when one considers one of the more astonishing and least well known realities of the Christian movement—the movement centered on the person of Jesus, yet from the beginning Christians could not agree on who he was. At the very start, from the time of Jesus himself, his own disciples and followers were in fundamental disagreement about him.

After Jesus' death and resurrection, his disciples went out as missionaries. Some were more successful than others; a few went nowhere at all, but stayed in Jerusalem and their home areas in Palestine. But several went great distances, to Syria and Egypt, to Asia Minor, Greece, and the west, or east to Parthia and even India, if the story about the apostle Thomas is to be believed. All of this is standard Church tradition. What is not, but what is quite visible to scholars, is that they did not all preach the same message—they preached "many Christs." Even in the same geographical area and sometimes in the same cities, different Christian teachers taught quite different gospels and had quite different views of who Jesus was and what he did.

There does not seem to have been an original and coherent set of doctrines, even though the Church later tried hard to give the impression of an early unity. Disagreements among the Christians were an embarrassment and a point that the Romans could exploit in their criticisms. During the second and third centuries, doctrinal diversity was blamed on Satan-inspired heretics, and during the fourth century the Church invented, under pressure from the challenges of "heretical" groups within its own ranks, the legend of the Apostles' Creed.

That story tells of a meeting held among the apostles just after the ascension and just before their initial departure to foreign lands. They discuss the possibility of a potentially serious problem: that if they all go out and evangelize, they might be preaching in contradiction to one another. So they compose the Apostles' Creed, a common message to be taught by each of them wherever they might go. A version of that creed is used in churches all over the world even today, but it did not originate with the apostles. Creeds were a phenomenon of the fourth century and later, when the Church had taken over the empire and needed a common doctrine for all. The fact that the Church needed to compose the story illustrates the very point that the apostles did in fact go out preaching different doctrines.

Evidence for this disagreement is quite clear in the New Testament itself, let alone in the vast amount of Christian literature produced over the subsequent two or three centuries. Much of this literature is polemical in intent, arguing one side or another of a disagreement over the proper understanding of Jesus or his mission. The Gospels of the New Testament and the nearly eighty other gospels that were produced of which we have fragments or knowledge, present a picture of Jesus from the point of view of the authors and communities in which they lived and worked. Some of those pictures are more or less similar to each other, while some are quite different. Yet all were produced by one early Christian community or another generally with knowledge of and in contrast to the views of neighboring Christian communities. Again, sometimes those differences were friendly, and a new Gospel was meant to be complementary, merely drawing out some additional aspects of Jesus' person or teaching particularly important to one community. But often the intent was polemical; the aim was contrast and correction.

These differences are visible among the communities that left behind literature that has survived to the present. But few people could read or write in antiquity, only about 10 percent of the population, and most people left no record of their beliefs at all. We have, for example, little or no idea what the many Christians in the province of Bithynia whom Pliny encountered and persecuted believed. They were there in abundance and believed in some "superstition," as he called it, but what their beliefs precisely were has been lost to us. In a later chapter we will try to recover some of their ideas. In addition, we often read in the literature about "false teachers" and "wolves in sheep's clothing," but very seldom are their own writings preserved. One can hardly imagine that these

Christian teachers considered themselves "false" or "wolves," and in fact
would probably have said much the same about their competitors.

History is written by the winners, and heresy is defined by the theological victors. The "orthodox" of the fourth century were those on
whose side the Christian emperor stood, because ultimately he held the
power to appoint and exile bishops. But the emperors were alternately
Trinitarian or Arian, that is, by later standards alternately "orthodox" or
"heretical." Arianism became the most serious competitor to Trinitarian "orthodoxy" the church ever encountered. It was a theological system with roots in more than one of the earliest types of Christianity, but
it took its name from its most famous proponent, Arius (ca. 250–336), a
deacon and then presbyter in the church in Alexandria, Egypt. According to Arius, Jesus was the highest created being, something on the
order of the highest angel; "son of God" was only an honorific title.
Trinitarianism, on the other hand, understood the Father, Son, and
Spirit to be consubstantial, coequal, and coeternal.

What is humorous in hindsight is that those who were the "heretics"
kept changing, as a Trinitarian emperor was succeeded by an Arian
one, and then again by a Trinitarian. At the Council of Rimini in 359 a
group of Arian bishops came to power as the new emperor succeeded
the old and defined an Arian creed to replace the previous Trinitarian
creed defined at the city of Nicaea in 325. In describing the event some
years later, Jerome, translator of the Latin Vulgate, wrote, "The Nicene
faith stood condemned by acclamation. The whole world groaned, and
was astonished to find itself Arian" (*Altercatio* 19). Athanasius (ca.
295–373), bishop of Alexandria and champion of Trinitarianism during
most of the Arian controversy of the fourth century, without changing
his own position was alternately declared "orthodox" or "heretic" and
went into or was recalled from exile five times.

It is remarkable how narrowly Christianity escaped becoming a
rather different religion. Had politics turned out differently in the
fourth century, the Church might have defined "orthodoxy" as Arianism, instead of believing in the Trinity as the Nicenes did and the
Church does today. Non-Trinitarian Christianity survived in the East
long after the age of the creeds into the time of the Arab conquests in
the seventh century and later. We can see in the Qur'an itself evidence
for such conceptions among Christians whom Muhammad came in

contact with in Arabia. The consequences of such a difference, between the stricter monotheism that Arianism attempted to defend and Trinitarian monotheism, are remarkably important for the spirituality of the individual Christian, as we will explore in a later chapter.

One should keep in mind that no one in the first century was a Trinitarian in the sense defined by the fourth-century Church. Trinitarianism was a brilliant solution to the very difficult problems surrounding the many possible relationships among the Persons of the Godhead, and in the first century the questions had not yet been asked. Earlier Christians certainly believed in the Father, Son, and Spirit and were baptized in their names, normally by triple immersion, but they had no idea of the sophisticated definitions of the relationships among the Persons of the Trinity so important later on. Not even the language of the great creeds had yet been developed. The later formulation of the creeds was the result of a long process of debate and growth in understanding. Earlier, however, as the problems and difficulties became evident over time and Christians began to understand how remarkably at odds they really were with each other, they found that agreement on a doctrinal level was impossible. When questions about the relationship between Jesus and the Father, and then of both to the Spirit, began to become important, several very cogent but mutually exclusive solutions were offered, arising out of the traditions formed in the diversity of the several Christianities that had developed in the first century, right from the beginning.

Diversity of opinion about Jesus was original to the movement. The reasons for both the diversity and the fact that it was original will be explored somewhat later, but at this point it is important to consider these historical facts: (1) Christian missionaries who went out to preach the gospel and give their lives for their Lord and Master held (several) intelligent, defensible, and mutually contradictory views of who he was; and (2) Christianity nevertheless won over the Roman world. The obvious corollary to these facts is that it must not have been doctrines or doctrinal consistency that appealed to those who heard the message; the core of the appeal must have lain elsewhere.

It is not the purpose of this book to lay bare and trumpet the fundamental diversity of opinion among early Christians about God, Jesus, and the proper religious life and then "conclude" that there never was a true Christianity or, even worse, that there never was any truth in

Christianity. Something must have been true about it, or it would not exist today and we would not be able to account for its rise and obvious success. But the diversity must be faced if we are to clear the way to see where the real center actually was. It does not seem to me particularly remarkable to observe that the real center, the point, has been all but lost today. On the other hand, one positive effect of recognizing the original diversity in doctrines and conceptions is to understand that the power of the movement did not lay in doctrines, and especially not in unity of doctrines across individual church boundaries. Denominations, if one may use that word, were as much a part of Christianity at the beginning as they are today, although they were fewer in number as the scale was smaller. In spite of all the debate and acrimony over doctrines that was part of the early period, the Christian movement had the capacity to absorb differences and thrive among varieties of understanding because its real center was not compromised.

Variety in Christianity arose quite naturally out of the many differing religious and philosophical possibilities in the cultural environment in which it was born. We have often heard, for example, that Jesus was a Jew, but that identification has helped our understanding very little, and even obscured it, by pretending to say something meaningful while actually conveying almost nothing. There were nearly a dozen distinct brands of Judaism current in Jesus' day, each with its own leaders and partisans and opponents, yet he himself fit precisely in none of them. According to early Christian sources, he was to some degree in conflict or debate with every Jewish group he encountered and was killed by the Roman governor with the complicity of the main branches of the Jewish authorities. In other words, we do not know much about what being a Jew meant specifically in his case, and we do know that in some crucial ways he did not fit into conventional Judaisms of his day.

If we stand back a little further, we see something even more important and obvious: whether he knew it at the time, or meant to or not, Jesus became the founder of one of the world's greatest religions. He was what scholars in the field of religion call a "master figure," and master figures never fit in with the traditions from which they come. They are rare geniuses who are in conflict with their own religious inheritance and by their creative spirituality are able to set a whole culture on some new path. If the sentence "Jesus was a Jew" actually meant something like "Jesus was a Jew like other Jews we (think we) know of and are comfortable with," then we would not have Christianity today. He would not have qualified as a master figure; he would not have made any difference at all. But he made a huge difference, and something about him forever changed not only the Judaisms of his day, but all subsequent Western religious understanding.

And the fact of his appeal in the West is no small point. The story of Jesus attracted many Jews, though by no means all Jews. Recall that Jesus was opposed to many Jewish traditions and was opposed by many in authority. But it was in the Western, Greco-Roman world where Christianity flourished, that is, among the vast majority of people of the empire who were not Jews and had no reason to respect Jewish traditions, if they knew them at all. It was not primarily in Palestine, but elsewhere that his story found a hearing. A search for the heart of early Christianity must account for these facts also—that some Jews were attracted to the Christian message and some were not, while it found its real home and fertile ground for expansion among Greeks and Romans. Soon, and in the main, the Church was gentile.

Christianity began in Palestine among an originally Semitic people who had been dominated by foreign empires—Babylonian, Persian, Greek, and Roman—for most of six hundred years before the time of Jesus. This succession of foreign dominations produced a bewildering mixture of traditions and ideas about what a religious leader was supposed to be. Here lies the main source of the great diversity in early Christianity—the fact that it was accepted originally by individuals with competing ideas inherited from contrasting backgrounds, and then spread in the first generations into areas with widely differing religious traditions. Christian missionaries, to complicate the picture, took the message of the gospel not only into the several cultures of Greco-Roman and Semitic Palestine, but southeast to Arabia, southwest to Egypt and Ethiopia and across North Africa, northeast to Syria and Parthia and Mesopotamia, northwest to Asia Minor and Greece, and west to Rome and Spain and Europe. The gospel reached most of these areas in the first century or very soon thereafter, in the first generations after the crucifixion.

Not all of these many cultures and religious traditions had a place for someone like the Jesus of the Christianity of the creeds. The words "God" and "Son of God" meant different things in different cultures. "Christ" meant nothing at all like "Messiah" outside of the few Jewish sects dependent on Zoroastrianism; the Sadducean Judaism that ruled Israel held a very different concept. The very idea of a messiah, with its eschatological, religious, and political implications, did not exist at all in the rest of the world. Among the Romans and Greeks the word "Christ" sounded like the slave name Chrestus (meaning "useful"). "Lord" and "Savior" were common enough concepts in the Greco-Roman world, used especially of rulers and emperors, but these words had a temporal and this-worldly application to political peace, economic prosperity, and physical health. "Salvation," of course, referred normally to deliverance from disease. And it was "good news" (i.e., "gospel") when it was announced that the emperor was coming to town for a visit. Even relatively simple words like "prophet," "teacher," and "apostle" had different meanings in different cultural contexts. So as individual preachers began to found churches, teach, and construct their theological systems, those systems were distinct from one another not only according to the different backgrounds of the teachers, but also according to the cultures of the hearers. This was so not only where it might be obvious, in distant lands, but especially in Palestine, where the several cultures of East and West had mingled for centuries.

Perhaps the most well known of these competing "denominations" arose because of the traditional distinction between Jew and Gentile, really a bias against Gentiles inherited from Jewish antiquity among early Jewish Christians. One of the most noteworthy points of genius of the Christian message was the real recognition and application of the principle of equality of souls: that is, nothing having to do with the body or the material world—neither physical appearance, ethnicity, social distinction, nor gender—qualified one as superior or inferior in the eyes of God. So the apostle Paul quotes an early Christian saying in just such an argument over the acceptability of Gentiles in the Church, that "there is no longer Jew or Greek, there is no longer slave or free, there is no longer male and female; for all of you are one in Christ Jesus" (Gal. 3:28). Yet such high ideals were not held by all, and some Jews who became Christians resisted understanding the Law of Moses as having been superseded by Christ. Instead, they continued to follow the rituals and ceremonies prescribed by the Law and required all gentile Christians to do the same, essentially requiring them to first become Jews before becoming Christians. They continued to keep the Sabbath and other festivals, to observe food restrictions, and especially to require circumcision of all male converts. In the West, however, particularly in the churches founded by the apostle Paul, no such rituals and restrictions were seen to apply to anyone, and certainly not to Gentiles. So in protest against Paul and his allies and in continued adherence to Judaism, there developed over time a number of distinct expressions of what has been termed "Jewish Christianity."

These groups differed rather widely among themselves in many ways, so the term "Jewish Christianity" is something of an umbrella under which a number of distinct and quite ancient "denominations" are grouped. They are placed together in the main because of their location in Palestine and eastern Syria, their use of the Syriac or Aramaic language, and some level of continued use of Mosaic Law. The most familiar and "orthodox" of them by later standards is to be seen in the community of the Gospel of Matthew, which was heir to one of the earliest expressions of Christianity and formed many of the later Church's ideas. The Matthean Christians lived on the northern shores of the Sea of Galilee and looked to Peter as leader and founder. Recall that it is in the Gospel of Matthew that Jesus says, "You are Peter, and on this rock I will build my church" (Matt. 16:18), and that the traditional site of Peter's house is in the village of Capernaum. Matthew's community drew heavily on the Old Testament and Jewish tradition; it is the most "Jewish" Gospel in the New Testament.

But there were several other Jewish-Christian groups not so acceptable to later views. We know of some of these other groups from the angry reaction in Paul's writings, because they sent missionaries into his churches to try to subvert his teaching of freedom from the ritual law. In the Letter to the Galatians, these missionaries are described as "certain people from James" (Gal. 2:12). James was the brother of Jesus and soon after the crucifixion became the leader of the Jerusalem church, gaining an admirable reputation for personal piety. But the

Church held very much to Jewish ritual law, continuing to circumcise its male children and follow Jewish customs, and in this case even refusing to eat together with gentile Christians. This attitude can also be seen in the story in the book of Acts in which Peter brings the gospel to the Roman centurion Cornelius in the coastal town of Caesarea and upon his return to Jerusalem is accused by church members of eating with uncircumcised men (Acts 11:3).

Other Jewish-Christian groups we read about in the heresiologists, the Church writers who in the second century and later refuted the "heresies" that infected the Church. The word "heresy" is in quotes because it requires an "orthodoxy" to define it, and no such orthodoxy yet existed. Each Christian group, even the church at Rome, was at this time simply doing its best to follow its Master according to its lights. Typically, and probably less than accurately, there were said to have been seven Jewish-Christian "heresies." The groups that produced these theologies based them on their different inherited models and therefore held various views on God and the person of Christ. In general, however, they thought of Jesus as a "mere human" or at best as some lower-level spiritual being. Some rejected the virgin birth and saw in Jesus a mere prophet whose father was Joseph. Others saw a new incarnation of the true Prophet, who (in their view) had appeared in earlier times as Moses and Elijah and others. Still others thought of Jesus as an angel or some other type of divine being, a "son of god" lesser than the highest God. Other aspects of these groups and the effects of their views will be taken up in a later chapter.

On the other side of the issue of Jew and Gentile were those Jews such as the apostle Paul, and to a lesser extent Peter and others, who saw that Gentiles were entirely acceptable to God (recall the equality of souls) as long as they accepted Christ. These still respected the Old Testament law as an ethical guide and genuine revelation from God, but one whose time had passed; it had been superseded by the revelation in Christ. Herein lay the basis for the Pauline terminology of "new testament," the new covenant in the freedom of Christ that replaced the old regulations of Mosaic Law. The ethical rules found in the Jewish law were certainly maintained by all Christians worthy of the name, since they were the based on moral standards common to all ancient societies. It was never acceptable in any ancient society to lie or steal or murder or commit adultery. Greek and Roman religious philosophers had developed ethical standards to a very high degree, and one of the reasons for the great appeal of the message of Jesus among Gentiles was the high personal standards he required—the Christian message could in fact be shown to rival the best of Greco-Roman ideals.

Other groups of churches were founded by other apostles that began in Palestine and then moved into gentile areas. One "denomination" quite familiar is that of the churches of John, originating in Galilee and then centered on the west coast of Asia Minor, especially at Ephesus. They produced several writings under his name: the Gospel of John, the three Letters of John (1, 2, and 3 John), and the Revelation of John, all found in the New Testament, and other works such as the *Apocryphon of John* and the *Acts of John*. Characteristic of these churches is a very "high" view of Jesus as a divine being descended from heaven; he is the very Word of God in the opening of the Gospel. Associated with such a high view of Jesus was difficulty in understanding his earthly presence: the community held various views on whether or not Jesus had a real human body, and the argument can be seen going on in the New Testament itself. Traditions under the name of John split even further, and a significant element among Gnostic Christians used these traditions to understand Jesus, the "Man from Heaven," as the revealer of Gnostic spirituality.

Another, less familiar group looked back to the apostle Thomas as founder and head. It also arose originally in northern Galilee and then moved north and east into Syria. There arose literature under the name of Thomas, not included in the New Testament, among which are the *Gospel of Thomas*, the *Book of Thomas the Athlete*, and the *Acts of Thomas*. There are a number of similarities between Thomas and Johannine Christianity—and some fundamental differences. Characteristic of this group is the surprising claim that Thomas was the twin brother of Jesus, Jesus being the heavenly counterpart of the earthly Thomas. In the *Acts of Thomas* they are identical in appearance. For Thomas Christians, this symbolized the close relationship between the spiritual and earthly life of the believer. For this community, like that of John, Jesus was also a heavenly being descended to earth, but his mission was not to die for sins on the cross, but to enlighten those who would hear his words and understand their deeper spiritual meaning, thus awakening them to eternal life. Thomas Christianity borders on Gnosticism and was eventually basic to the rise of Manichaeism in the third century. Manichaeism was another "heretical" brand of Christianity with eventual worldwide significance: it spread rapidly and survived in China for a thousand years. Yet still other Christians of a more "orthodox" stamp looked to Thomas, and the movement became even further fragmented.

Perhaps these examples will be sufficient at this point—several more will be discussed in a later chapter—to illustrate the wide diversity of groups and doctrines that made up the early Christian movement. There really were several Christianities, each giving expression to something about the person of Jesus that it found to be essential, but none with the same conception or formulation. So we may return to our original observations: (1) Christian missionaries preached different and even contradictory doctrines about Jesus; and (2) they nevertheless eventually won over the Roman world. It therefore must not have been the doctrinal content that was at the core of the appeal of the message. So what was?

The story of Jesus was the story of a kind and righteous man, a man from God, the Son of God, whatever was meant by the phrase, who followed the will of God against evil to the death and thereby not only gained resurrection for himself, but could offer it to others who would do the same. And in so doing, the early Christians brought new meaning to the word "martyr." I think that Tertullian was right: the blood of the martyrs was the seed of the Church. That is the kind of energy necessary to start a world religion and call forth the commitment that requires one's whole life. That energy is found in only one place in the Greco-Roman world—in the tales of the heroes that had been told for a thousand years. The very culture was founded on them, and the people lived and died imitating them. For those who heard the story of Jesus in the ancient world, whichever doctrinal form it came to them in, Jesus was a hero. He was also, of course, many other things to his followers far more familiar to us arising out of the many doctrinal formulations. But why the story of Jesus was able to inspire so many people in the ancient world, why they imitated him and followed him to the grave, was that, in some way lost to us, he was their hero.

Chapter 2

THE WORLD OF JESUS THE HERO

A culture tells its members stories that embody its ideals and rein-force social norms and goals. We in the modern world tell our-selves consciously or unconsciously a story of success, the Horatio Alger story, that no matter what our circumstances, if we work hard and try our honest best, we will eventually climb the social ladder to wealth and status. Many forms of Protestant Christianity have been heavily in-fluenced by such ideas that if one be a Christian with strong faith, one will achieve by God's blessing health and prosperity in every endeavor. No such notion existed in the wider Greco-Roman world of the early Christians. People in the ancient world were far too close to the "sud-den changes of fortune," as Herodotus called them, to disease, poverty, and death. They lived short and often difficult lives in highly structured communities with little social mobility. They told each other very differ-ent stories from ours, tales of personal courage and ethical conflict in the face of overwhelming odds. Their favorite characters did not suc-ceed at all in the modern sense; instead they died in the midst of the very circumstances that showed forth the greatness of their souls.

We seldom think of Jesus as a hero, as though it were too obvious or not majestic enough to do so; Christians believe so much more about him. The long history of doctrinal development in Christianity has had profound effect on our views: high theological titles and honors have overtaken the more human story of Jesus and he has become almost ex-clusively the exalted Lord of history. In the three hundred years between his death and the Council of Nicaea in the fourth century, ideas sur-rounding his essence underwent a process almost unparalleled in the history of religions: theological conviction expanded the concept of the deity to allow his entrance into the Godhead as the Second Person of the Trinity. No one had yet conceived of the Trinity in Jesus' own day. The problem of the relationship among the persons of one trinity had not arisen; the terms and language necessary to discuss the issue had not even been developed. It is worth noting, for us who have the doctrine of the Trinity as an inheritance centuries' old, how remarkable this development was. It is worth understanding not only what we have gained, but what we have lost.

We have all but lost the most important and spiritually effective category of ancient religious experience, and the loss has left us to no small extent impoverished. We no longer recognize the essential aspect of the story of Jesus that caught the imaginations of those who first heard about him. He was not, for his earliest followers, the exalted Pantokrator, Judge of the World, as depicted in medieval art; that figure was far too distant and frightening to encourage anyone to imitation. He was not the healthy and successful business executive that miracle workers and religious charlatans of both past and present would have us believe; almost no one in his culture was either healthy or successful, and converting to Christianity in antiquity could make one even less so. He was not even the Good Shepherd watching out for his sheep as the concept is used today, although that was certainly an important image in the catacomb art of the early Christians. If these and other modern ideas were what there was of Jesus, if that was what Jesus was in fact, we would not have Christianity today. Few in his day, I assume, would have followed a modern Jesus very far, and most would never have followed him at all.

Yet, as we saw in the opening chapter, early Christians clearly did not follow Jesus because they agreed on who he was or what he taught. From the beginning they debated and argued over what he was—what could it mean to be Christ or the Son of God? The apostle Paul, for example, our earliest Christian writer, complained of more than one "different gospel" that other missionaries taught and even introduced into his own churches after he traveled elsewhere. By the second century, churches were so at odds that they were criticized by pagan observers for their contradictions, and the truth of the message was called into question: To which opinion was one to listen? How bewildered and divided they were has been largely forgotten by us because of the centuries of orthodoxy that have passed since such questions were decided. Beginning in the fourth century, the ecumenical church councils at Nicaea, Constantinople, and elsewhere produced the great creeds that defined the nature of God and Christ for all subsequent generations. The creeds were made necessary by the fundamental disagreements among major sectors of the Christian community. Unity of doctrines and orthodoxy became vital as the Roman Empire turned to Christianity and the government needed a definition of beliefs to which all could subscribe. But there were no creeds originally, and a unified set of doctrines was of little importance, even beside the point.

Seen from our modern point of view, Christians from before the time of the creeds, especially the earliest Christians, seem not to have understood Jesus at all. His very disciples founded churches often diametrically opposed to one another, giving rise to schools of thought that remained in conflict for centuries. Not even the questions they argued about are quite familiar to us. They disagreed on whether Jesus was a man, or a god, or an angel, or something else. They differed on his manner of birth, whether natural or divine; or perhaps he had not been born at all but descended full grown from above. They disputed whether he had a real human body, or a ghostly spiritual one, or one like that of the gods themselves. They argued, therefore, over what kind of resurrection he had, whether spiritual or fleshly. They could not even agree on whether he had actually died. The Christ was not supposed to die; perhaps he only appeared to do so, or some substitute made to look like him died in his place. And before that, what kind of a man was he? A philosopher? A prophet? A teacher? He certainly taught and his message was essential, but many of his words were curiously transformed by his own followers, placed in different contexts and given different meanings, while new sayings were composed and attributed to him. People, apparently, did not follow Jesus for his words. For all the attention given in the modern era to the sayings of the historical Jesus, his precise words seem hardly to have mattered at all.

In spite of this diversity and disagreement, Christianity in time won more adherents in the Roman Empire than all the traditional state gods and competing cults. It did so for a reason overlooked by all but a few scholars and lost to the modern world—the story of Jesus, even with its Jewish and Eastern content, fulfilled the most important cultural ideals in antiquity, those of the hero, from Achilles on down. The framework of this story was old and deeply embedded in ancient society. The life of the hero in its many incarnations was told and retold at gatherings, in plays, in literature, and in schools. It served as both entertainment and edification for more than a thousand years before and after Christ. Reverence for the heroes and later for the saints, who functioned as protectors and avengers in towns and countryside, was the most common form of religious observance in the ancient world. Their brave exploits and tragic fates gave the term "hero" its most important meaning: one who was an example for behavior, admired for courage and distinguished deeds. Their stories set the models of conduct for all levels of society. Emperors and slaves, philosophers and common folk molded their lives according to these stories that from birth had shaped their mental and spiritual universe. For all the differences of culture and tradition between Palestine and the Greco-Roman world, this was the pattern of the life of Jesus.

⊙═◆═⊙

We have become accustomed to think of two essential spheres of being, divine and human, divided by a vast and unbridgeable gulf. But in the world of the early Christians it was not so. The gods were not so distant or alien, so blindingly righteous, nor were humans as abjectly bankrupt, morally and spiritually, as later Calvinism would have us believe. Old stories were told everywhere of unions of gods and humans that produced children who shared in both natures. The divide between the divine and human spheres was not so vast that it could not be spanned. The gods at times made visits to humans for the purposes of instruction and guidance, deception and judgment, often changing their appearance into that of someone familiar or unremarkable; one might not discern their true identity at the time. Does not even the writer of the Letter to the Hebrews in the New Testament warn that we ought to treat strangers hospitably, since some had entertained angels unawares (13:2)? The gods could walk the earth unrecognized.

The children of the gods were also among us. Did not Achilles, Heracles, and Helen of Troy live among our ancestors? And how could Alexander the Great have been so great? He must have been the offspring of Zeus Ammon. And Homer must have been the offspring of one of the Muses. That Jesus the Son of God should teach among us with supernatural powers was not as exceptional as it may seem. Justin Martyr, in the middle of the second century, boldly notes this fact in his defense of the Christian faith to emperor Antoninus Pius (r. 137–61). He writes:

> When we say that the Word, which is the first offspring of God, was born without sexual intercourse, namely Jesus Christ our teacher, and that after he was crucified and died and rose up, he ascended into heaven, we are not saying anything new beyond those called among you the sons of Zeus. For you know how many sons of Zeus the authors honored among you speak of: Hermes the interpreting Word and teacher of all things; and Asclepius, who became a healer and after being struck by lightening ascended to heaven, and Dionysus, who was torn in pieces. . . . (*1 Apologia*, 21, GJR)

Likewise Tertullian, writing his defense of Christianity in the next generation, tells the Roman magistrates the story of Christ and then asks them, for the moment, to "accept this story—it is similar to your own" (*Apoloceticus* 21.15, GJR). So the stories of the children of the gods were paradigms for the early Church in its understanding of Jesus. For centuries among the Greeks and Romans into the time of the Christians and beyond, the line between gods and humans was narrow and easily crossed.

People from all walks of life knew these tales. Most visible to us is how consistently authors evaluated and described the lives of characters in literature according to them. The stories were told from dark antiquity right through the Christian period, becoming the basis for the Gospel narratives and the accounts of the apostles, martyrs, and saints on into the Middle Ages. They never ceased to have fundamental influence as models of human predicament and behavior. The pattern of the life of the hero was almost the only story line available and the only story with wide acceptance for serious literature in the Greco-Roman tradition. Nearly every biography and historical account sought to compare the qualities of its subjects against the standards of the heroic code. If famous people, and occasionally extraordinary common people, were themselves caught in fateful circumstances and acted as their models had done before them, they also could become heroes in the eyes of their

contemporaries, and stories could be told of them to succeeding generations. So Herodotus in the fifth century B.C. writes not only of the figures of myth, but also of remarkable normal people who were caught in
some overwhelming situation. Some of these who accomplished conspicuous deeds, who lived and died courageously, he includes among
the numerous protecting heroes who received reverence and prayers in
their local areas. Even for those who were not so honored, the stories of
the past embodied the expectations for anyone who wished to be held in
esteem in ancient society. So also the Gospel stories of the life of Jesus
were set in the mold of the tales of the ancient heroes.

The story of Jesus and those of the pre-Christian heroes is not of
course the same. Achilles is a Greek and Jesus a Jew. The specific content of their stories is different: Achilles, for example, is concerned
with honor and shame, with the gods and fate, and he fights as a soldier before the walls of Troy. Jesus is concerned with righteousness
and sin, with God and the Devil, and he fights a battle for souls in a
spiritual war. But the pattern of their stories, the structure of the world
in which they live, and the larger issues they face match remarkably
well because of the cultural influence of the Greco-Roman world on
Palestine during the nearly eight centuries that separated Homer from
Jesus. Their venerable cultures, languages, and religions were distinct
originally, but much occurred to transform the Israelite religion of the
Old Testament, roughly contemporaneous with Homer, into the
Judaisms inherited by Jesus.

❦

MOST IMPORTANT IN THE TRANSFORMATION of Israelite religion and culture were the successive conquests of the Persians, Greeks, and Romans that began after the Babylonian Exile in the sixth century B.C.
These were great and sophisticated empires that occupied and ruled the
small land of Palestine for most of the six hundred years before the
founding of Christianity. Their superior cultures brought fundamental
changes to all aspects of society in every country they governed. Any
attempt to understand the thought world of Jesus' day from the Old
Testament alone without reference to these dominant empires, as is so
commonly done, is doomed to essential misconception. Israelite reli-

gion and society as it was before the Exile, when most of the Old Testament was composed, no longer existed.

The vast majority of the texts of the Old Testament were written in a time when conceptions of God and the spiritual world were quite different from those current in the days of Jesus and the Church. The differences must be understood to appreciate the content of the message of Jesus and the appeal of his story to the Roman world. The religion of the Israelites and the religion of Jesus were quite dissimilar, despite the impression gained that they are in some basic continuity. The assumption arises, first, from the fact that the Old Testament is most commonly bound together into a single book with the New Testament and serves as an apparent preface and introduction and, second, because we call both those of Moses' time and those of the Roman era "Jews" with little discrimination. The point is an important one for this discussion, for in the Israelite worldview there are no martyrs, no blessed poor, no heroes of the sort that would later become so significant in Christianity.

Consider the career of the righteous and chosen ones of God in the Old Testament. Abraham "died in a good old age, an old man and full of years" (Gen. 25:8), at 175 years old. Isaac lived to an age of 180 and Jacob to 147. All were enormously wealthy, at peace, and surrounded by their children and grandchildren. When Moses died at 120 years of age, "his sight was unimpaired and his vigor had not abated" (Deut. 34:7), after a stellar career as prophet, miracle worker, and military general whose enemies are destroyed at every step. In one case the earth even opens up and swallows his rival Korah and his followers, together with their families, so that "they with all that belonged to them went down alive into Sheol" (Num. 16:33). King David reigned for forty years and died in his own bed "in a good old age, full of days, riches, and honor" (1 Chron. 29:28). Note that although Jesus is called "the son of David, the son of Abraham" in the opening sentence of the Gospel of Matthew, the pattern of his life was nothing like theirs.

For the Israelites and other cultures in the ancient Near East, there was a symbiosis, an interdependence, of gods and humans. Gods provided humans with knowledge of agriculture, metallurgy, writing, medicine, and the means of survival by granting seasonal rains and crops. Humans sustained the gods with ritual and cult; the worship of the gods was the very function of humanity. People were created for the cultivation and service of the gods, to build them temples, offer them sacrifice, and obey their dictates. The requirements for successful human life may be summed up as "life and prosperity" for faithfulness to the divine laws and "death and adversity" for disobedience (Deut. 30:15). Those who follow the will of God find long life, prosperity, and success (Josh. 1:8), for "the blessing of the Lord makes rich" (Prov. 10:22). On the other hand, for those who disobey, "The Lord will send upon you disaster, panic, and frustration in everything you attempt to do, until you are destroyed and perish quickly" (Deut. 28:20). The penalty for the unrighteous is poverty, disease, persecution, homelessness, and early death. The ideal figure is righteous and faithful in matters pertaining to religion and as a result lives long and well among children and grandchildren, honored by all in both life and death. Such blessings and curses are experienced during earthly life, since all people, both good and evil, descend after death into the land of the dead under the earth, called Sheol by the Israelites. There is no judgment of the dead, no blessed eternal life or fiery hell, for people do not have eternal souls in the later sense—recall that Adam is but a clay vessel with air in it, the breath of life, which is exhaled finally at death, dust to dust. What survives death is a mere shade, a ghostly image in the underworld.

The physical universe of the Israelites and most other ancients was small, much like a sphere half filled with water, upon the surface of which floated the disc of the earth. Heaven was a hard expanse only a few hundred feet above the earth, upon which dwelled the gods in their homes. It could be reached on a high mountain or high tower—recall that the Tower of Babel was to have reached heaven. A later Jewish text tells us that the motivation for building the tower was that humans wanted to find out whether the firmament of heaven was made of clay, copper, or iron (3 *Baruch* 3:7). So we are told, "Can you, like him, spread out the skies, hard as a molten mirror?" (Job 37:18). There was water everywhere else, above the heavens, around the earth, and below surrounding the underworld with rivers. The underworld itself was a kind of kingdom fortress with gates and bars, ruled over by personified Death, conceived of as a great and insatiably hungry monster. All people "are handed over to death, to the world below" (Ezek. 31:14), from which there is no return.

The most common political structure of the time was the city-state surrounded by its associated villages and farmlands. Each city had its own protecting deity often chosen from among the gods of the pantheon shared with other cities in the area related by language and ethnicity. So Athens worshiped Athena in particular, though it shared the pantheon headed by Zeus and Hera with other Greeks, and Ugarit worshiped Baal, though it shared with other Canaanite peoples the pantheon headed by El. This system is known as henotheism, the worship by a city-state of one particular god chosen from among the recognized and shared pantheon of gods worshiped by neighboring states. So Israel worshiped Yahweh, while its neighbors worshiped Milcom or Chemosh or Dagon or Baal, all deities of the shared pantheon of the Canaanites. It was customary for each city to exalt its god above that of its neighbors and to tell common stories of divine adventures with its own god as main actor. So Israel calls its God great among the gods (Exod. 15:11), who is jealous of Israel's worship of neighboring gods: "You shall have no other gods before me." (Exod. 20:2). One city or another would from time to time extend military control over its neighbors, forming a larger political unit, and exalt its main deity over those of its subjects. Occasionally, one such city would rise to the status of empire, with wide influence over its geographical area, imposing its god on many subcultures and subsuming the qualities of other gods into its own. This was the genesis and mechanism of the rise of monotheism, achieved first in Egypt, but developing also in Mesopotamia, Persia, and Greece in widely variant ways.

The spiritual world was conceived as a unified system, with every part holding an honored and proper place. It may be termed a "monism," as opposed to a "dualism" of God and the Devil, warring camps of righteous and evil spiritual beings. In the monistic universe, there are gods of the upper world of light and those of the earth and underworld, good spirits and destructive spirits, each with its own proper function. Everything that happens is overseen by and occurs through the will of the higher deities and is accomplished on the human level by some lesser spirit: rain is brought by one and drought by another of the numerous spiritual beings that run the cosmos. Righteousness and sin are an individual's choice and responsibility; good spirits bring the blessings the righteous merit, while spirits of calamity bring disease and destruction to the wicked. There is no Devil or army of demons with whom to contend, enticing one to sin for the destruction of one's soul. People have no souls as such, and spirits of calamity cause arthritis, not adultery. The cosmos is more or less at peace with itself, and history is merely a long succession of events without deeper meaning. The cosmos is eternal; we are told of the heaven and earth that "He established them forever and ever" (Ps. 148:6). The world has no reason to end in cataclysm or apocalyptic judgment—there is nothing fundamentally wrong with it.

But in Israel something did go wrong. The monistic view of the world throughout its history was never able to explain why innocent people suffered. The contract between the divine and human realms throughout the ancient Near East had always been that the faithful and just individual or city would enjoy the protection and blessings of God. Occasionally we hear of one or another wise individual complaining that the righteous do indeed suffer when they are not supposed to, that the contract is somehow flawed and the gods are more capricious than they claim to be. So argue the wise in compositions from Mesopotamia and Egypt and in the central chapters of the book of Job; they protest the innocence of the sufferer and demand an explanation, only to hear in reply the divine command to remain silent, or to hear no reply at all.

Basic to the contract between the Lord and Israel were a series of covenants, one with Abraham, another the Law of Moses, and a third the promise to king David and his descendants. The covenant with Abraham granted to his descendants the land of Israel as their possession. The Law of Moses defined in terms common to Near Eastern culture the divine requirements for human behavior and the balance of blessings and curses for obedience and disobedience. The covenant with David promised that a descendant of his would forever sit on the throne of Israel. But by the beginning of the sixth century B.C., the contract between God and his people began to disintegrate. More than a century earlier, in 721 B.C., the small northern kingdom of Israel had been conquered by the Assyrian Empire and a significant portion of its population deported to Mesopotamia. The great Deuteronomistic history, a work that spans the biblical books of Deuteronomy through 2 Kings, explained the reason for the calamity according to the classic theory that the disaster was divine retribution for apostasy and sin (2 Kings

17:7–41). Written in the surviving southern kingdom of Judah under the reign of Josiah (2 Kings 22), it was also meant to glorify this devout king, this new David. For his piety and zeal, Josiah was described as the most righteous of all the kings of the nation (2 Kings 23:25). He began the restoration of the henotheistic worship of Yahweh, which had by his time been melded with and nearly submerged in the pantheon of Canaan. There was hope that he would reunite the Northern and Southern kingdoms and restore the fortunes of all Israel. Yet he lost his life in a battle against Egypt at Megiddo (2 Kings 23:29), and the program of restoration was frustrated.

Inevitably, the tiny southern kingdom of Judah was conquered in turn, this time by the Neo-Babylonian Empire in 586 B.C., and its population was to a large extent exiled to Babylon. The hopes of the Deuteronomistic history were dashed and the work had to be revised. The author of the second, postexilic, edition attempts to account for the loss of Josiah and the subsequent Exile by declaring that Manasseh, the grandfather of Josiah, had sinned to such an extent that the Lord could not forgive him even generations later (2 Kings 23:26–27). The old theory was that military defeat was divine retribution for apostasy and sin, yet the national catastrophe of the Exile was not easily reconciled with such a conception. Many who lost their homes and families had been righteous in their own opinion and had followed the law of God, as one may easily see from the psalms of lament composed during this period (e.g., Ps. 44:9–26). No answer to this contradiction and failure of the original covenants was possible or forthcoming. There was no provision for the suffering of the righteous on such a scale as national destruction. All that was left was depression and anger: "By the rivers of Babylon—there we sat down and there we wept" (Ps. 137:1). The land promised to Abraham had been lost and was now ruled by foreigners. The balance of rewards and punishments for good or evil seemed completely overturned, even reversed; the innocent had suffered for the sins of earlier generations. And the promise to David had failed; there was no throne, no country to rule, and the heirs to the throne had been executed or exiled. So a bitter saying was spoken among those who had suffered in innocence: "The way of the Lord is not just" (Ezek. 18:25, RSV), and a cynical proverb was often heard that "the parents have eaten sour grapes, and the children's teeth are set on edge" (Jer. 31:29–30; Ezek.

18:2). The idealistic covenants assuring long and pleasant life had failed, as they must in the real world of death, suffering, and loss. The Lord who had ruled the small land of Israel, caught in the path of great empires, had apparently been defeated.

Yet new hope and new understanding were soon to appear. Two generations after the exile, the Persians under their king, Cyrus, in 539 conquered the Babylon that had conquered Israel and took over the rule of the exiled Israelites and Palestine. Within a year, Cyrus decreed that the exiles were free to return to their own land, and Cyrus himself appeared to them to be the very anointed one of God, the savior of the nation. Yet Cyrus brought not only a release from the Babylonian oppressors, but also a very old and highly sophisticated religious worldview drawn from the Indo-European cultures of central Asia and based on an entirely different principle from the monism central to Israelite religion: cosmic dualism. The Persians introduced to Israel a new type of monotheism, different from the types found in Egypt and Mesopotamia, that postulated a single One standing before and behind all else and the source of not only creation, but even of good and evil. The Israelites' acceptance and melding of this remarkable idea into their own traditions may be seen just a few verses later in the passage in which Cyrus is called the Lord's anointed ("messiah" in Isa. 45:1): "I am the Lord and there is no other, the one who forms light and creates darkness, who makes good and creates evil" (Isa. 45:6–7, GJR).

But the Persians brought much more, for this was but one element in a much larger and radically new set of ideas that inevitably and over time recast the view of the spiritual world for subsequent Judaism, Christianity, and eventually Islam. Foremost, God gained an enemy in the Devil, and these two were seen to be locked in a bitter and protracted battle for survival that involved all of creation. The Persians taught of righteous angels and wicked demons, the judgment of the dead, heaven and hell, the resurrection, eternal life, and an eschatology of the coming end of the world. They understood why the righteous suffered. A reflection of that idea in Israel may be seen in the first two chapters of the book of Job, which were added to the original book after the Exile. Job, the most righteous man on earth, suffers precisely because he is righteous; his faithfulness must be tested as a player in the battle between God and the Devil. As a consequence of these dualistc ideas, the concept of history changed dramatically—time itself was seen to be moving forward toward its appointed end and the final defeat of the forces of evil and vindication of the righteous.

One must recall that none of these concepts are to be found in the Law of Moses or other texts of the Old Testament written before the Babylonian Exile. In the old Mesopotamian East and the cultures dependent on its traditions, history had no reason to end; the world was at peace with itself and everything including the destructive powers had an honored place and proper function. There was no ongoing war in the heavens, no competition between spiritual forces for the loyalty of souls to be sent to heaven or hell. In fact, there were no souls at all in the later sense. The gods had created humans out of clay and breathed air into them. When they died, their bodies returned to the dust and their ghostly shades descended to the shadowy underworld.

The conceptions of cosmic dualism and eschatology encountered by Israel slowly but inexorably transformed much of its religious world. The old models of king and prophet and law, opposed by neighboring states and rival gods, had been overwhelmed by new political realities. Israel had been conquered and no longer had kings, no longer ruled its own land, and soon ceased to have prophets. The rival gods were now the conquering gods. The old political realities on which the covenant with Abraham, the Law of Moses, and the kingdom of David were based were lost and the ideals that undergirded them were transformed. They were replaced among some by a new view of a real spiritual world behind the material: Jesus was indeed a king, but in the spiritual kingdom of God; he was indeed a prophet, not of the Law but of the mysteries of God hidden from the wise and powerful; and he was a warrior, but against the Devil and the world forces of darkness.

ALEXANDER THE GREAT brought his Greek army into Palestine as conqueror in the later part of the fourth century B.C., taking control in turn of Israel and its neighboring states and beginning the spread of the most influential culture in the Mediterranean world east to India. The Greeks taught an even more sophisticated monotheism based on centuries of philosophical discussion and scientific observation. They could prove that the earth was not a disc floating on water, as in the Semitic worldview, but part of a vast universe ruled by laws of nature that also governed the spiritual life. They brought mathematics and science and art and athletics. And they taught to all who would listen the exaltation of reason, the love of philosophy, and the ideal that the spiritual was qualitatively superior to the material. Like the Persians, they were also heirs of Indo-European dualism. The Greeks had always lived in an ambiguous universe, where Fate and the jealousies of the gods had functioned as did the Devil among the Persians. So they brought their own related version of why the righteous suffered and celebrated that story in some of Western civilization's greatest literature.

They brought not only their ambiguous universe, but also and most importantly a dualism of body and soul. People came to be seen as composed of two separable entities, the fleshly clothing of the body over the real spiritual essence of the soul, the one perishable, the other eternal. The soul, which had originally been merely the air in the lungs as the breath of life, became the substantial carrier of personal identity, the real person clothed in the body of flesh. While the body was seen as a temporary dwelling, even a prison, the soul was eternal because it shared in the divine nature—it was made of the same spiritual substance as God and in the opinion of some had even come from God. Here was the "treasure in clay jars" (2 Cor. 4:7) so important to the apostle Paul. This view of human nature granted people a new dignity and sense of personal worth, and especially a future beyond the grave.

Greek philosophical and theological ideas became the most pervasive influences in antiquity. Upper-class Romans raised their children to speak Greek as their first language. Mesopotamians studied in Athens. Samaritans became Stoics and Cynics. Jews studied Greek language and literature and labored in imitation of the Greeks to present Abraham and Moses to the world as philosophers. North Africans became lawyers by studying Homer and the classics. Egypt became a leading center of Greek thought. Groups in Palestine adapted the new concepts of Persia, Greece, and Rome variously to old images found in the Hebrew Bible and its traditions and became the Samaritans, Sadducees, Pharisees, Essenes, Hellenists, Zealots, and many other sects who comprised the melding of Indo-European and Semitic traditions in Roman Palestine. Fundamental to that melding was a new way of understanding one's place in the universe, based on the dualism of God and the Devil and the dualism of body and soul, both almost entirely absent from the Old Testament and both fundamental to the life and teachings of Jesus.

HERE ONE ENCOUNTERS a basic spiritual insight of Jesus that set Christianity apart. These two sets of ideas, the dualisms of God and the Devil and of body and soul, when coupled as they came to be with stories of the heroes, placed unprecedented value on the individual, regardless of one's social class or status. In reality, however, they heavily favored the ill-fated and suffering. The universe had a dark side: Fate, the jealousies of the gods, and the Devil and the dark powers all conspired against the innocent and brought them to ruin. Those who were in such difficulties could be seen as having in some way been especially notable and therefore as having actually merited such circumstances by inner greatness. The stories of the Greek heroes were of just such a type, in which destiny or the envy of one god or another often brought the downfall of an otherwise blameless victim. The new concepts from Persia produced similar stories among the Jews, but with the Devil as adversary. Job after the exile, one may recall, "deserved" the loss of his children, wife, property, and health because he caught the attention of God and the Devil as the most righteous man of his generation.

Jesus and the early Christians were able to meld these ideas into a worldview that made such suffering and opposition by superior powers not only a virtue, but the very point of human life. All were locked in the cosmic drama: the role of the suffering but righteous individual, of the hero, was to be lived by everyone regardless of social class. The mighty struggles with fate and injustice and the dark powers became the struggles that all were asked to face: "Take up your cross and follow me." The short and difficult lives of those who heard him were such because that was how the very universe was structured: the poor were blessed not as objects of pity or charity but as central players in the cosmic drama. For those who would follow Jesus, this gave unprecedented value to the life of even the basest individual. The rich and powerful were in real danger, for in his words, "What does it profit to gain the whole world and lose one's soul?" Now the blessed afterlife, the eternal reward for perseverance and integrity, was opened as heaven to all, but especially to the poor. Humble people everywhere, who made up the vast majority of people in antiquity, heard his message and found themselves valued members of a new kind of kingdom in which quality of soul, not social position, was the measure of greatness. Many chose to live in imitation of Jesus even at the cost of their own lives and became in turn the martyrs and saints who themselves received honors from their contemporaries and succeeding generations. This was what inspired the disciples of Jesus to imitate him and bring his gospel to the Roman Empire, and what inspired the poor of the empire to leave their traditional religions and turn to Christianity. Jesus was their leader, their Lord, as they called him, whose pattern of life they themselves were bidden to follow and whose victory over death they would share.

Chapter 3

THE STORY OF THE HERO
AND THE IDEALS OF ANTIQUITY

Plutarch, a contemporary of the early Christians, tells us in the early second century that there are five classes of living beings: gods, *daimones*, heroes, humans, and last of all animals (*E at Delphi* 390e). The types are ancient already for Plutarch and well fixed in tradition. To begin at the end of the list, we find in the philosophers and for antiquity in general that the fundamental difference between animals and the remaining classes was the absence among animals of speech, and therefore the lack of the power of rational thought. So animals are the *aloga*, a Greek word meaning both "without speech" and "illogical," without the power of reason. For the remaining four types, Plutarch points to Hesiod, who lived some eight hundred years earlier, as the first to describe these divisions of the living.

Plutarch is correct in his assertion that Hesiod was the first Greek to describe these four, but Hesiod did not invent them; he too, it appears, inherited this classification, and its actual source may be entirely lost to us. In his famous poem entitled *Works and Days*, Hesiod constructs an account of the origins of these divisions (106–201). He melds the four classes with another story, inherited from the Indo-Europeans, of the Four Ages of humanity identified with four metals: gold, silver, bronze, and iron. The Four Ages are known to us elsewhere, notably in Daniel 2 in the story of the statue of gold, silver, bronze, and iron in Nebuchadnezzar's dream. The text of Daniel stems from a time long after Hesiod and clearly reflects the influence of the Persian and Greek cultures that had ruled Palestine by that time for centuries.

According to the scheme of the Four Ages in Hesiod, human history begins in the blessed Golden Age and then literally degenerates down through the Silver and Bronze ages to the present Age of Iron, a harsh time of labor and sorrow. Each of these ages is peopled with a generation that is characterized by a metal associated with it that lessens in value and increases in harshness. The end will come when bad goes to worse and lawlessness engulfs our present Age of Iron, prompting Zeus to destroy this last race; the end will signal again, it is implied, the return of the Golden Age (*Works and Days* 175).

Hesiod's purpose is to explain how human and spiritual life in its various classes originated, and his melding of these two separate inherited ideas, the Four Classes of Beings and the story of the Four Ages, is poetically brilliant and effective, yet its very artistry hides the fact that it is not wholly successful. The two stories do not fit comfortably together. One is an apocalyptic tale from the East of the degeneration of humanity into arrogance and criminality and its eventual judgment at the end of time as we know it. The other is a description of the natural and cosmic divisions of life without any such negative overtones. The Four Ages require that God be a distant and entirely righteous judge and present-day humanity be hard-hearted and almost entirely evil, like iron. In the use of the scheme in the book of Daniel, the fourth kingdom of iron is greater and harsher than any preceding it, as iron is harder than any of the other metals. Not so with the Four Classes descending from gods through *daimones,* heroes, and humans—the order is curiously reversed. Humans are again the least of the four, but the "softest" if you will, and in Greek tradition in general it is without question the race of gods that is the harshest, a point to which we will return.

Hesiod begins with one of the more remarkable and characteristically Greek ideas of antiquity: "Gods and mortal humans arose from the same source" (*Works and Days* 108). We are told that the gods first made a Golden race of mortals who lived at the time of Kronos, Father Time. Kronos had overthrown his father, Sky, and ruled the second generation of the gods. His was the generation that both made the first humans and gave birth to Zeus and the Olympian gods of classical Greece. Zeus and his third generation in turn overthrew their forebears and succeeded to their rule. Thus the generation of Kronos made both the gods who now rule the cosmos and the original humans—we and the Olympian gods are siblings, having arisen from the same source.

To make an important digression here, one should note the radical dissimilarity between this Greek idea and how humans originated in the thought of the Mesopotamian and Canaanite East. There the gods make humans after all the divine generations are completed, creating them out of clay as servants and blowing spirit into them for animation. So God makes Adam of the dust of the earth, breathing into him the breath of life. Adam later, as something of a clay pot with air in it, eventually breathes his last and returns to dust. In old Semitic tradition the divide between gods and humans is vast; among the Greeks it did not originally exist at all.

Hesiod describes the Golden race as happy and beloved of the gods, living without sorrow or difficulty, beyond the reach of evils. When they died, their souls became the *daimones*, agents of Zeus who now invisibly watch over human affairs, kindly spirits who guard and deliver us from harm (*Works and Days* 122–24). Hesiod is composing a beautiful and influential tale, giving genealogy to an old idea. The original meaning of the term *daimon* was "divinity," and it was commonly used to designate the class of lesser divinities arranged below the Olympian gods, something on the order of the angels in Zoroastrian and later in Western tradition. Since nearly all deities in the classical period were morally ambiguous, the *daimones* could be described as either good or evil, and the same *daimon* could bring both good or ill according to one's piety or fate. These were the lower divine beings "between gods and mortals" who mediated between the human and divine spheres (Plato *Symposium* 202e). Not until after the Exile in intertestamental Jewish literature, with the rise of dualism and the concept of the Devil, did the term begin to display the meaning "evil demon in league with the Devil" and take on an entirely negative denotation. Christian writers use it almost exclusively in this later sense and employ the term "angel" for beings with the function described by Hesiod.

Next in Hesiod's scheme come the Silver and then Bronze ages, during which the world begins to devolve. The Silver Age is much less pious than its Golden predecessor, and violence begins to arise among the people. They foolishly wrong each other out of *hubris* (arrogant pride) and refuse to give the immortal gods their proper reverence and sacrifices. Thus they anger Zeus and come to their end, having lived a much shorter time than their predecessors. Still they are worthy of honor and after death pass under the earth to become the underworld *daimones*. The Bronze race is much worse; the violence that had begun in the Silver Age overtakes them. They are likened to ashen spears, "terrible and strong." They are powerful, dressed for battle in bronze armor, and are lovers of war. They are in fact so violent that they destroy themselves and leave no descendants at all, dying, as we are told, "nameless" (*Works and Days* 156).

Hesiod ought next to describe the Iron Age, but instead turns to the class of heroes. To the reader's surprise, the heroes are not a degeneration at all. Instead they are a return to the moral qualities of the Golden Age and are described in like terms. They are noble and righteous, "a divine race of hero-men who are called demigods, the generation before our own" (*Works and Days* 159–60). This is a remarkable description, somewhat astonishing to one who would expect Hesiod to be following his model of the Four Ages with its four metals. First of all, the insertion of the Age of Heroes requires that the number of ages be increased by one, so that the final Iron Age of our own time becomes number five. In addition, since there is no place for the Age of Heroes in the scheme, it has no metal associated with it. Most important, the Heroes contradict the litany of moral decline: they are not degenerates, but righteous demigods, literally *hemitheoi*, "half gods," again to be ruled over by Kronos in his new capacity as sovereign of the blessed afterlife. Yet they are curiously human like ourselves; they fight the battles and suffer the pains and death of the famous epics of Greece, the battles of Thebes and the Trojan War. These are the classical heroes of antiquity.

Last of all, of course, he reaches our own Age of Iron: "Would that," he moans, "would that I were not among the men of the fifth generation, but either had died before or been born afterwards" (*Works and Days* 174–75). Ours, this fifth generation, is the age of injustice, in which signs of decay and impending doom are everywhere visible. Ours is the age that will face the final cataclysm of divine judgment that our own lawlessness and *hubris* will draw down upon us. Yet Hesiod in his artistry has given the melded tales both example and hope: the previous

race had been that of the righteous heroes, and the one to come a return
to the Golden Age.

I HAVE NOTED HOW ILL-SUITED the stories of the Four Ages and the Four
Classes of Beings are for each other. The main difficulty is the contradiction between the low view of human history in the apocalyptic story
of the Four Ages and the high view of human lineage and potential in
the story of the Four Classes. This is no idle conflict; it is also one of the
more important tensions in the message of Jesus and the early Church.
In fact, what Hesiod here attempts is our earliest example of an issue
that will become fundamental to the Christian gospel: How is one to live
righteously in a dark and inimical world? How does one win one's soul?

The story of the Four Ages is a joyless tale of the devolution of history into this present evil age, which itself will descend into chaos when
the signs of the end become clear. The majority of people will follow
their own selfish and lawless ways and will finally meet their end under
divine judgment. The Four Classes of Beings, on the other hand, offer a
rather positive assessment of humanity. They grant us a certain close-
ness to the divine nature, a kinship and common lineage. Human history begins with the *daimones*, the generation of the Golden Age, who
after death become lesser divinities and guardian angels for the earthbound. The following race of heroes is half divine and half human by
actual parentage and lives in ways clearly praiseworthy. Mere humans
for their part stand in a very honored line and are the final stage of an
exalted genealogy. They are watched over by Zeus and the *daimones* and
have the examples of courageous and just behavior set by the heroes.
They are given the task of following the dictates of piety toward the gods
and justice toward others.

The tale of the Four Ages is clearly an early expression of what would
become in Jesus' day the eschatological expectation of final judgment
so important in the New Testament. In this view, as in Hesiod, the
world devolves toward its appointed end, determined long before by fate
and divine forces beyond human control. Finally lawlessness increases,
and the "signs of the times" show that divine judgment is imminent.
The mass of humanity is seen as following the wide and easy path to

ruin and is destined for destruction. Yet in the midst of this dark vision, those who have the character to hear and understand the gospel are called to a life of faithfulness and justice. There is amid the darkness a hope in the ability and dignity of those who would listen and follow. There are, just as in the life of Jesus, the ministering of angels and the guidance of wise words for the new children of God. As had Hesiod, Jesus and the Church in their own ways succeed in combining the two stories, the apocalyptic tale of the imminent end of the world with the high valuation and expectation of those who would be able to hear and respond to their gospel. What the message called the early Christian to do and to become was for Hesiod and the following thousand years of Greek and Roman history personified in the stories of the heroes.

THE BALANCE OF JUSTICE AND THE HEROIC CODE

The English word "hero" is a transliteration of the Greek original. By it we designate two related ideas: a person of distinguished courage, admired for bravery and noble character; and one of such qualities who stands as an ideal and an example. Both aspects of the term are true in the ancient Greek concept and the Christian appropriation of it. The heroes lived out in story all the many possibilities of life, failing and succeeding according to their adherence to or transgression of *dikê*, the Greek word for "justice," in the form of balance and imbalance in a world controlled by the Fates and the often ambiguous gods.

The fundamental relationships between the human and divine spheres were governed by this concept of justice and balance, the proper respect for divine prerogatives and the limits of human action. In the *Iliad* of Homer, for example, Agamemnon, the ruler of the Greek forces who went to conquer the city of Troy, arrogantly mistreats his most important soldier, Achilles. This pretentious overstepping of his proper limit was perhaps the most famous instance in ancient literature of *hubris*, excessive pride and insolence. *Hubris* by its nature is out of proper balance; it is "too much." It is claiming more for oneself, exalting oneself higher, than is just. *Hubris* inevitably brings down from the gods upon one *atê*, delusion of mind, the twisting of judgment that leads to some fateful misstep that is the beginning of one's downfall. The downfall is *nemesis*, the divine judgment that humbles the arrogant one and brings the scale of *dikê* back into balance. In the words of Aeschylus, "*Hubris*, when it flowers forth, bears a sheaf of *atê*, from which one reaps a harvest wholly of tears" (*Persians* 821–22). Agamemnon in his arrogance (*hubris*) takes from Achilles his beautiful lady Briseis, "that you may learn well," he says, "how much better I am than you" (*Iliad* 1.185–86). This act of *atê* causes Achilles to withdraw in anger from the fighting and the Greeks very nearly to lose the war (*nemesis*). The imminent failure of the Greek expedition in turn brings the wounded and humbled Agamemnon to admit his error and apologize publicly to Achilles (the return of *dikê*). The cycle of *dikê*—*hubris*—*atê*—*nemesis*—*dikê* governed the moral and spiritual lives of antiquity and was the framework within which the stories of the heroes were told. How one reacted in the situations of life set by the Fates and gods, how one faced the *hubris* of others or endured the penalties for one's own, showed one's quality of soul.

The proper balance of conduct among people and between people and the gods constituted the ideals of classical culture. Those ideals were determined by custom and tradition and, while not written into law, are often termed the heroic code. The heroic code included among other virtues prowess in battle, wisdom in the forum of public council, due honor for others of every rank, hospitality to strangers and visitors, and courage in difficulties and especially in the face of death.

The first two are symbolized by the main characters of the greatest surviving epics of antiquity, Achilles of the *Iliad* and Odysseus of the *Odyssey*. Achilles is the most skilled warrior on the field of battle before Troy, and the outcome of the battles and ultimately the war is determined by his presence or absence in the fighting. He is not without ability in speaking in the assembly, but his military prowess brings him the title "best of the Achaians" (i.e., "best of the Greeks"). Odysseus on the other hand, while a great fighter and brave soldier, earns his reputation for cunning wisdom. He is described as being "like Zeus in counsel" and acquires the epithet "wily Odysseus."

The third and fourth virtues are also at the base of these two epics. The plot of the *Iliad* turns, as noted above, on the violation of the honor of Achilles and its consequences, while the *Odyssey* is a tale of the abuse of the hospitality of the house of Odysseus and the dishonor done him as he returns to his home in the guise of a beggar. Honor in this early period was perhaps the single most significant aspect of the code, for violations of *dikê* ("justice") are most often understood in terms of a breach of another's honor. For example, Oedipus, after his innocent but fateful fall into the horror of patricide and marriage to his mother, is dishonored by his city of Thebes. Thus, according to Sophocles, Thebes loses its place to Athens, which accepts him graciously. The house of Atreus, the ancestor of Agamemnon, king of Mycenae and leader of the Greek forces at Troy, is beset by a long string of dishonorable acts that lasts for generations, costing Agamemnon his life and ending finally only with the intervention of the gods.

The duty of hospitality was the basis for the famed guest-host relationship that governed the reception and protection of the visiting stranger. One of the epithets of Zeus was Zeus Xenios, "Zeus the guardian of the visiting guest," and any violation of the relationship expected of either host or guest would lead to divine punishment. The Trojan War itself, as complicated as its causes were, was brought about because of the transgression of the rights of the household of Menelaos by a visitor. Paris, the son of Priam, king of Troy, visited the home of the absent Menelaos and took his wife, Helen, back with him to Troy. Although there were divine and fated causes behind the conflict, the war was fought on the human level to recover her and to punish the transgressors.

Underlying and foundational to all these virtues is the necessity for courage in the face of whatever the Fates have determined. It was one's deeds of courage and brave constancy in suffering that were remembered by one's family and city, even sung by the bards, and that kept one's name alive after death. When the ideals of classical culture were developed, there was as yet no heaven or hell, no immortal soul, no spiritual "life after death." There were but two kinds of immortality for humans: the leaving of progeny to carry on one's name, and being remembered by others for one's character and brave deeds. But in the world of story and epic, the tradition that expressed the ideals of antiquity, there was no question of the relative value of the two. The word in Greek for fame is *kleos*, and to win "unwilting *kleos*" was the ideal of every worthy epic character. Socrates is told of humans by his counselor Diotima: "For the sake of this, they are ready to risk any dangers, even more than for their children, and to spend their money and suffer whatever pains, and to die for it." (Plato *Symposium* 208c, GJR). One's fame for bravery and constancy was what kept one alive among future generations.

THE GENETICS OF THE HERO AND VIRGIN BIRTH

Hesiod uses the word *hemitheoi*, "half gods," to describe the class of heroes. Socrates, in Plato's dialogue *Cratylus*, discusses the etymology of the Greek word *heros*, which, according to his fanciful etymology, is but a form of the word *eros*, the Greek word for "love." He says:

> Do you not know that the heroes are half gods (*hemitheoi*)? . . . All to be sure were born when a God loved a mortal woman or a goddess loved a mortal man. (398c–d, GJR)

The heroes as a class were properly the offspring of the union between divine and human parents. Stories of the liaisons between male deities and human females were often told in the epics and poetry of antiquity. Female deities could also mate with human males. Aphrodite loved Anchises and bore Aeneas, the future founder of Rome. Thetis the sea goddess married Peleus and bore the best of the Achaians, Achilles. All of the most remarkable characters had divine parentage on one side or the other. Most often, however, the liaison was between a male god and a virgin human female. So Perseus was the son of Zeus by the virgin Danaë; Dionysus, the son of Zeus by the virgin Semele; and Sarpedon, son of Zeus by the virgin Europa. Zeus in fact fathers more than a hundred children by human women, most often, though not always, by virgins. One dark reflection of this nearly ubiquitous motif may be found in the book of Genesis: the sons of God mate with human females and their offspring were "the heroes that were of old, warriors of renown" (Gen. 6:4).

Such stories were forever an embarrassment to pagan philosophers because they seemed to ascribe immorality to the divine nature. Plato in fact banned such literature from his concept of the ideal republic. Philosophers and moralists rejected these motifs as mere inventions of the poets, and a long discussion ensued on how to use poetic literature by rejecting such foolishness but learning from what was good. Christian writers, centuries later after the time of Constantine and the rise of the Christian empire, used the analogy of the bee, which goes to each flower in the garden but takes only what is good from each one. So the wise reader goes to each poet, but takes only what is profitable for the soul, leaving behind the myths about the passions of the gods.

Earlier, when Christianity was locked in a struggle for survival against the intellectual forces of the pagan empire, Christian apologists never tired of pointing to the stories of the immoralities of the gods as evidence for the decadence and therefore falsity of pagan religion. Yet the stories pointed to a deeper truth for those who could see it, and religious thinkers used allegorical modes of interpretation to understand in a new light the traditional themes of the loves of the gods for humans. Pausanias, a geographer and traveler, wrote of the story of Kronos in his *Description of Greece* in the second century. He says:

> When I began my composition, I thought that these stories of the Greeks were mostly silliness, but . . . I later gained this understanding of them: those of the Greeks who were thought to be wise long ago told the stories by means of enigmatic riddles not straight out, and therefore the things said about Kronos I guess to be some wisdom of the Greeks. (8.8.3, GJR)

One of the most famous love stories was the allegory in the story of Cupid, the god of love, and Psyche, a beautiful young and innocent virgin. Psyche first meets the invisible god in his invisible castle and, falling in love, becomes obsessed with seeing him, against his direct command. Surreptitiously, she lights a candle to gaze at him at night while he is asleep and visible and is so awestruck by his beauty that she stands transfixed; soon hot wax from the candle drips on him and he awakens. For this disobedience, she is banished; she wanders the land suffering many toils and trials until finally she is reconciled, a chastened and much wiser person. While the story itself is full of adventure, suffering, and final enlightenment for Psyche, the very names of the characters tell listeners that it is an allegory of the love of God for the soul, the meaning of the word *psyche* in Greek.

Not all heroes are direct offspring of gods; they may be grandchildren or great-grandchildren, or even later descendants of divine and human parents. So Hippolytus is the grandson of a god, son of Theseus who was son of Poseidon; and Pentheus is great-grandson of Ares and

Aphrodite, grandson of Harmonia (their daughter) and Cadmus, founder of Thebes. Some heroes have no divine ancestors at all, so far as we know. Eumaios, the swineherd of Odysseus, for example, is merely a swineherd, but is classed among the heroes for his justice of soul and the pious hospitality he gives to Odysseus the beggar. His case is of great moment for subsequent meditation on heroes, a point to which we will return. Nevertheless, the norm, if there is one, is that of divine lineage. Recall that for Hesiod, gods and humans are of the same stock, and sexual liaisons between them are not impossible, even though they are not common.

REMARKABLE TALENTS

The offspring of divine-human unions took from the divine parent remarkable prowess or strength or beauty or wisdom. Helen of Troy, the most beautiful woman of antiquity, was so because her father was Zeus. She inherited other talents as well, becoming known for skill in the use of medicinal drugs. Asclepius, eventually elevated to the divine sphere, was the founder of the medical profession because his father was reputed to be Apollo, the god of healing. Asclepius was the most formidable alternative to the claims of Christians for Jesus as a miracle worker and source of divine healing. The inherited talents constituted the heroes as a class above normal mortals, and as such they were the storied kings and queens, generals and leaders, and founders of cities and dynasties. Cities and towns had their traditional founders and first rulers: Theseus was the first ruler of Athens; Cadmus, the founder of Thebes. Clans everywhere, the larger family units that made up the political landscape of ancient city life, had their eponymous heroes, the traditional founders after whom the clans were named.

Divine lineage was always suspected for "normal" but notable people in historical times who performed great deeds, displayed miraculous powers, or possessed remarkable wisdom. If divine lineage could not be proven—and how could it be?—then it would be invented and attributed to the one in question. How could Alexander the Great have been so great? In 331 B.C. he was proclaimed to be the son of Ammon by the desert oracle of this major Egyptian god, and he appears to have consciously emulated the sons of Zeus, Heracles, and Dionysus. Homer, it was thought, must have been the offspring of one of the Muses. And Demaratus, the Olympic champion and ruler of Sparta, must have been the offspring of at least the hero Astrabacus (Herodotus *Histories* 6.69). Stories of divine parentage were told of city founders, great soldiers, philosophers, great athletes, and poets. Later we see an appropriation of the cult of heroes by the cult of the emperors of Rome, who routinely claimed some divine descent to make their acceptance of divine honors, the status as *divus*, more believable.

Yet each of the heroes also inherited from the human parent the archetypal aspect of the human condition—mortality, the human fate of suffering and death. The one great difference between gods and humans was that humans died. The single most common epithet for the gods was the "immortals." Everything about them was immortal, even their food—ambrosia is from a Greek compound word meaning "not mortal."

For all the differences in power and perspective, however, gods and humans shared the same moral sense, the same standards of justice, the same "code." And while humans at times violated justice, the gods too were an ambiguous lot, often participating in the exaltation or downfall of one or another of their favorites. Somehow the world did not seem fair. The struggles against the injustices of the gods and the suffering caused by fate is what brought human life such *pathos*, what showed forth the greatness of character. These struggles are the subjects of Greek tragedy and what make such literature so alluring. But the stories of the liaisons between gods and humans that gave birth to heroes served another purpose.

INTERWOVEN DESTINIES

The genesis and inheritance of the ancient Greek hero are significant. As heir to both the divine and human worlds, the hero stood as a kind of bridge and point of focus between the two. Heroes became central players in the divine plan to control the balance of *dikê* among humans. The fates of individuals, cities, even whole peoples were often controlled by the gods through the agency, witting or unwitting, of their half-divine children. They were frequently involved in critical circumstances interwoven among the destinies of many other people. It is as though their very genetics placed them in the midst of destiny on a larger-than-human scale.

The most famous examples of such interlaced fates are to be found in the great cycles of epic stories, the stories that tell of the fall of Troy, known as the Trojan cycle, or those surrounding the destiny of the city of Thebes, known as the Theban cycle and containing the tales of Oedipus and Antigone, or again, those of the voyage of Jason and the Argonauts. These tales spawned literally hundreds of plays and tragedies, poems of all types, works of art, memorial athletic contests, and local cults, all with their associated architecture and public festivals. The plays and poetry were performed and recited right through the Christian period and beyond. They were the basis of education and Greek learning, a point of great importance for the manner in which the gospel story was told. In all of them the destinies of individual heroes were seen as part of a larger plan determined by God for the rise and fall of whole peoples. In these tales the life story and fate of the individual is subsumed by the larger divine plan, in which the individuals are important, yet still only a part of the whole.

The most influential cycle of tales was that surrounding the fall of Troy. The central surviving work in the cycle is the *Iliad* of Homer, which describes a short period of less than two months during the tenth year of the war. The entire story, however, begins long before the *Iliad* opens and continues long after its final lines. It involves the whole Greek world—cities and districts from every part of Greece are involved in the events and send contingents of soldiers to fight on one side or the other. Scores of heroes from all over participate in the action, each playing a significant part and contributing to the whole. It is in this sense an epic for the whole world as perceived from the Greek viewpoint. Fate and destiny determine the events and outcome, and all is overseen and pushed along by the gods. But the *Iliad* focuses primarily on the actions of one character, Achilles. I bring this point up because the story of Jesus in its context as part of a larger divine plan bears a certain similarity that we shall later examine.

For those in historical times who fulfilled a larger than normal destiny the genealogy and status of hero could easily be invented and attributed. Such was the case, as we have seen, with Alexander the Great, or any number of lesser but still remarkable individuals. A most notorious example is to be found in the work of the Roman poet Virgil. Writing in the first century B.C., Virgil uses his poetry to extol the virtues of Rome and especially of Augustus, the founder of the new political system that marked the change from republic to empire. In his *Aeneid*, the epic of the founding of Rome modeled after the Homeric epics, the soul of the dead hero Anchises speaks with his son Aeneas, who has visited him in Elysium, the place of the blessed dead under the earth. Aeneas had rescued his father from the burning city of Troy after its fall to the Greek forces and brought him to Italy, where he eventually died. Aeneas is on his way to become the founder of the new city of Rome and seeks advice from his father. Anchises, living now among the souls of the dead, points out a series of remarkable souls who will return to live again in new bodies on the earth and accomplish great things. After indicating one and now another future great Roman, he points dramatically to a particular man: "This man, this is he whom you have often heard promised to you, Augustus Caesar, offspring of a god, who will again found the Golden Age" (6.791–93, GJR). The Golden Age is familiar to us from Hesiod. Augustus is to end the Age of Iron and remake the world into a paradise. He is called the son of (a) god, as he was the adopted son of the divinized Julius Caesar. This is remarkable praise, written as a prophecy ages old, for a living man.

THE TRAP OF FATE AND FREE WILL

The hero, as heir to a more-than-human destiny, is often caught by fate, trapped or ensnared by something out of individual control, determined by higher powers. All human life was determined by the gods, symbolized by the goddess Anankê ("Necessity") and her daughters, the three Fates, named Atropos ("Unchangeable"), Klotho ("Spinster"), and Lachesis ("Disposer of Lots"). These daughters of Zeus weave a tapestry that contains a depiction of everything to occur on earth, but especially the thread of life for each individual. As one cannot change the pattern of a tapestry, one cannot change one's destiny. So innocent Oedipus is trapped, no matter what he devises to avoid it, by one of the most horrifying of all destinies, to kill his father and marry his mother. Unknown to him, he had been abandoned as a newborn by his real parents, the king and queen of Thebes, because they had heard a prophecy that their son would be their doom. He was rescued by a shepherd and taken to Corinth, where he was raised by the childless king and queen. After hearing the prophecy about himself, he left Corinth forever so as never to become the bane of his supposed parents and ran right into his own real, but unknown, father and mother, thus fulfilling his fate. His story of innocent suffering at the hands of harsh fate is very much in structure like that of Job, who suffers innocently at the hands of the Devil. Both find their lives and families ruined, yet both are eventually vindicated. Many other such stories are to be found: Helen is trapped by Aphrodite, deluded into leaving the husband and home she loves to follow Paris to Troy, a choice she learns bitterly to lament; and Agamemnon, ruler of all the Greeks, is caught by his fate, literally ensnared in a net and killed.

The vicissitudes of fate was a topic of importance among the ancients. How quickly life could turn from prosperity to ruin, or much less often from low station to high, was a problem discussed in many works or played out in drama over and over. The Roman poet Horace calls the goddess Fortune "ready to raise our body from mortal state or to turn our proud triumphs into funerals" (*Odes* 1.35.2–4, GJR). The lives of the members of Oedipus's family, for example, one by one all turn in a short moment from happiness to curse as part of the larger fate of the city of Thebes and its ruling house.

In the *Histories* of Herodotus, one finds a famous though fictional description of the meeting of Solon, one of the seven wise men of Greece, with the fabulously wealthy king of Lydia, Croesus. At the beginning of the tale, Herodotus tells us that the Greeks have for centuries been regarded as the wisest of all peoples, and that among the Greeks the Athenians are the most intelligent; of these Solon is the wisest and the one chosen to give the city its laws. Thus Herodotus frames a story of a meeting between the wisest of all men and an oriental despot, a good man famed for wealth but encumbered by an inflated view of his own blessedness. We are to expect some foundational wisdom from Solon basic to the ideal ancient worldview, and we are not disappointed. Solon has just instituted the law code of the Athenians and left town lest they entreat him to change it. In his travels he goes east to Lydia (in what would today be central Turkey) and is received hospitably by Croesus. After a few days, Croesus shows him his fabulous wealth and asks who he thinks to be the happiest man in the world. To his surprise, Solon answers with examples of individuals of normal resources and station who lived having escaped tragedy and who died bravely and with honor. No one is to be called blessed until after death; before that, one who is apparently happy has only been lucky, for fortune changes rapidly and is out of one's own control. "I know," says Solon, "that every divinity is envious of human prosperity and troublesome. . . . For indeed, after showing a glimpse of happiness to many, God utterly ruined them" (1.32–33, GJR). Croesus dismisses him as a fool, but Solon has declared a fundamental truth of ancient wisdom; the very next sentence is, "*Nemesis* fell upon Croesus." Croesus foolishly attacks Cyrus and the Persian Empire to the east and loses his kingdom. In his pain and loss he requests of his new master, Cyrus, that he be allowed to send his leg chains to the oracle at Delphi to complain that he had been encouraged to fight the Persians by Apollo himself. The oracle replies that "not God himself could escape destiny" and his fall was his fate.

Some are presented with a choice of fates, giving them some latitude in the face of the inevitable. The most famous such case is the celebrated choice of Achilles. He is told by his mother that he carries two destinies, to abandon his role at Troy and return home to a long and peaceful but anonymous life, or to fight and die at Troy, never to see his son and dear father again, but to be Achilles, the greatest of all Greek warriors. The choice is his own, and in the middle of the story of the *Iliad* he appears, in his anger against Agamemnon, to choose the homeward journey and recommends that others do the same (*Iliad* 9.410–16). Yet eventually his closest friend, Patrocles, is killed by Hector, the champion of the Trojans; Achilles resolves to avenge his friend and seals his own fate at Troy. In his vengeance Achilles become a veritable superhuman soldier, ravaging the enemy like a lion among sheep, yet time and again Trojan soldiers choose certain death rather than turn cowardly away and live. The narrator tells us that they have met their fate.

One such case is remarkable for its opposite outcome: Aeneas faces Achilles and, after trading insults and challenging words, initiates the contest with him. All know that Aeneas has chosen certain death, and he is called a fool for the challenge. Yet in the midst of the fight Poseidon intervenes, declaring that "It is destined that he be a survivor" (20.302).

Poseidon lifts him off the ground and flings him through the air, over the heads of the opposing armies to the outskirts of the fighting, out of harm's way. There Poseidon rebukes him, telling him that he should give way, "Lest, beyond your fate, you go down to the house of the death god" (20.336). One can, apparently, neither try to live nor try to die apart from one's fate.

This choice to die for principle and with honor became one of the most famous heroic events to be imitated in the entire tradition. Many historical individuals, when faced with a choice between what would clearly lead to their own deaths and some safe but ignominious alternative, made a similar choice: death with honor over life and disgrace. Certainly one of the most important of these figures was Socrates, one of the most influential philosophical and heroic figures in history. Socrates had been declared by no less an authority than the oracle at Delphi to be the wisest man in the world. His own explanation for such an unanticipated and unprecedented title was that in one thing only did he have wisdom, that he understood that he was not wise at all. As a result of this oracle, he spent his time in Athens, as Plato tells us, "searching out according to God's will who of both citizens and strangers I think to be wise. And whenever someone seems not to be, assisting God I point out to him that he is not" (Plato *Apology* 23b, GJR). This occupation of pointing out to his neighbors their stupidities, as one might well imagine, brought him no small amount of animosity, and at seventy years old in 399 B.C. he was finally brought to court on false charges of atheism and leading the youth of the city astray.

His famous defense at the trial, related by Plato, is not really an attempt to defeat the charges but to justify his life as pious and righteous in the face of prejudice. He is condemned, and finally the court sentences him to death. After the vote for condemnation, Socrates addresses those jurors who voted against him and for his death:

> I did not want to say to you the things sweetest to you to hear—me wailing and crying and doing all the other things unworthy of me, as I think, but indeed the sort of things you are used to hearing from others. . . . I much prefer, having given this defense, to die, than to live with that sort. For neither in court nor in war is it right for me or anyone else to contrive some means to escape death by doing just anything. For in fact often in battles it becomes clear that one might escape

death by throwing away one's weapons and turning to the mercy of the
pursuers. . . . This is not the difficult thing, gentleman, to escape death,
but it is far more difficult to escape evil, for it runs faster than death.
(*Apology* 38d–39a, GJR)

He is taken to prison, but there follows by chance a month's delay
until the execution because of an unrelated religious ceremony. Yet all
the while he makes choices to go ahead toward death. His friends plead
with him, make arrangements for exile, in short do everything possible
to give him any number of means of escape, yet he refuses. He had
lived his life in obedience to God and saw his trial as God's will. Many
who loved him tried to save him; he had many opportunities to change
the course of events, but he chose death with honor. The list of names
of those in subsequent centuries who followed the examples of Achilles
and Socrates in also choosing death is long and distinguished.

DIVINE ENEMIES

The issue of destiny, often fatal destiny, points to another aspect of the
heroic career—heroes have divine enemies. The gods have never been
particularly friendly to the earthbound and mortal; they often stand in direct inimical relationship to their offspring, especially to the ones most
like themselves. In the story of Troy, for example, the life of Helen, the
world's loveliest woman, is ruined by Aphrodite, the most beautiful of
the goddesses. At a banquet of gods and humans that began the events
leading up to the Trojan War, the goddess Strife threw into the midst of
the assembly a golden apple inscribed with the words "For the loveliest."
Hera, queen of the gods, Athena, and Aphrodite vied for the prize and
decided that Paris, son of Priam, king of Troy, should choose one of
them in a beauty contest he could not judge successfully in more ways
than one. Each goddess promised him something, but he chose
Aphrodite, who promised him Helen as his reward; thus began the visit
of Paris to Helen's home and her flight with him to Troy. Near the end
of the war she learns to despise her handsome lover and upbraids
Aphrodite for the delusion that made her lose her home and family and
brought the accusation of adultery against her. Likewise, during the war
the highest ruler of the Greeks, Agamemnon, famed for spear throwing,

is opposed by Zeus, highest of the gods and famed for his lightning bolts; the two greatest kings, human and divine, are in competition. Achilles is opposed by Apollo, to whom he bears an uncanny physical resemblance. Heracles, whose very name means "praise of Hera," is in another cycle of tales opposed by Hera herself. It is this competitive relationship that produces the tragedy, the famous trials, and his death.

The gods are jealous of human prosperity, as we were taught by Solon in his conversation with Croesus. This is not the whole story: humans are remarkably like the gods in every culture of the ancient world, and there is an old tradition of competitiveness between the two that needs some emphasis. Recall that in the book of Genesis humans are made in the image of God, and in the time of its composition, this did not mean in the spiritual parts of the soul. All over the ancient world humans and gods looked alike, except for the fact that humans were smaller and made of nonspiritual, and therefore mortal, materials. But humans are forbidden to be like gods in knowledge or power, and especially in pride of heart. God does not want Adam and Eve to eat of the tree of the knowledge of good and evil. In Greece, Prometheus is punished for providing humans with fire, the knowledge of agriculture, and the means to survive. In the story of the fall of the angels found in 1 *Enoch* and the book of Genesis, the angels sin not only by mating with humans, but by teaching them the secrets of heaven along with the arts of survival.

The point at issue is especially critical surrounding the issue of *hubris*, arrogant human pride—arrogance brought divine judgment. This is a very old idea, found throughout ancient literature. Again in Herodotus, when Xerxes, king of Persia, prepares to invade Greece in 480 B.C., his counselor Artabanus cautions him as follows:

> You know, my lord, that among living creatures, it is the great ones that God smites with his thunder, out of envy of their pride. The little ones do not bother him. It is God's way to bring the lofty low. . . . For God tolerates pride in none but himself. (*Histories* 7.10e)

Later, envy is banished from the divine nature by the philosophers as unworthy of deity, and the role it used to play is taken up by the evil and envious lesser spirits that begin to grow in importance after Plato's time. The role is played in the world of the Christians, of course, by the Devil and demons.

RULERS AS HUMAN ENEMIES

Behind the tragedies of the heroes are the gods and fate, the very character of the heroes themselves, full of talent and possibilities, and often pride of achievement and an unshakable sense of just principle. But on the human level, their major enemies in general are those in authority above them, the rulers and kings. A few, like Agamemnon, ruler of the Greeks, and Priam, king of the Trojans, have no higher authority but the gods and find their tragic ends through the agency of the less highly placed. But in the main, the hero is a subversive element, refusing to be subject to the unjust dictates of authority or in some way standing as a symbol of the abuse of power by the unrighteous. In the *Iliad*, of course, it is Agamemnon who is the cause of the tragedy of Achilles by his arrogant abuse of this his most valuable soldier. Antigone is murdered horribly by the king, who declares that no one may bury the body of her brother. Her sense of piety and love for her dead brother bring upon her the fate of being buried alive. Hippolytus is cursed to death by the king, his own father, though he is entirely innocent of the charges against him. Heracles, the most popular and widely worshiped hero of antiquity, is charged with his twelve labors by Eurystheus, ruler of Argos.

The gods are responsible for the birth of the heroes as their offspring and, through the agency of human rulers, also for the trials and testing that lead to their tragic demise. The gods stand behind everything, and the unwitting human rulers who persecute and kill these subversive children of the gods are only performing a part of a larger plan to complete not only the fate of the heroes, but their own fates as well. To be the agent of destiny bringing down upon a hero his or her own fate is itself a dangerous and often deadly function. This is true not only for unjust rulers, but for agents of fate on nearly every level. Within the *Iliad* is a great chain of fated deaths. Sarpedon, son of Zeus, is fated to die and is killed by Patrocles, best friend of Achilles. Patrocles is then killed in turn by Hector, greatest fighter among the Trojans. Hector is killed by Achilles for his killing of Patrocles. Achilles' choice to avenge his friend and destroy Hector seals his own fate; Achilles is eventually killed by Paris outside the story of the *Iliad* itself. Eventually Paris and Troy are destroyed by the Greek army of Agamemnon, who is then himself killed by his wife and her paramour on the very day he arrives home, and on it goes. Yet in the larger world of epic and tragedy, it is the rulers who abuse the innocent hero, and then both they and their cities suffer. This is no small observation—not only did Troy and Thebes suffer for their abuse of righteous individuals, but the Christians understood the destruction of Jerusalem as just such a punishment for its crucifixion of Jesus.

THE TEST OF CHARACTER

Common to all stories of heroes is the test of character—the critical situation that is the hero's destiny and shows forth the true character of the soul. The problem set by the stories is really a framework to display the inner choices made and the integrity of the hero in the face of the injustices of life. Favorite tales were sung by bards of the great struggles of these divine-human beings against fate and the seeming injustices of the gods that invariably test the quality of their souls and often end in their tragic deaths. They perform remarkable deeds and suffer horrible fates, arousing "pity and fear," according to Aristotle, in those who hear of their exploits and destinies. Not all heroes pass the test. The trial sometimes brings forth the reaction of *hubris*, the arrogant abuse of others inherent in their characteristic greatness. But *hubris* or not, the combination of fate and character brings the inevitable downfall, suffering, humiliation, and often death, producing for us the tragedy that makes Greek literature so full of pathos and so captivating. The test educates one by suffering, leading to humility and fulfillment of one's destiny, the will of Zeus and fate, with courage. *Pathei mathos*, we are told by the chorus in Aeschylus's play *Agamemnon*, "by suffering comes learning" (177).

Agamemnon had learned the lesson of humility in the face of his abuse of Achilles, but his suffering was not over, nor the penalty he deserved for other acts of *hubris*. He had, just prior to the Trojan War, killed the favorite stag of the hunting goddess Artemis, as a result of which she demanded the sacrifice of his daughter Iphigenia. The penalty for disobedience was that contrary winds would not allow the huge Greek fleet that Agamemnon had assembled at the port of Aulis to sail to Troy. He failed the test of character and decided to sacrifice his daughter.

As in the story of the sacrifice of Isaac in the Bible, at the last moment a stag is substituted for Iphigenia, unbeknownst to Agamemnon and the Greeks, however, and she is spirited away to become the priestess of Artemis in the eastern city of the Taurians. After the deed, the winds turn favorable, the Greeks sail to Troy, and eventually the war is won. But just when Agamemnon arrives home in triumph, he is murdered by his wife and her lover in revenge for the sacrifice of Iphigenia. *Pathei mathos,* but too late.

The most famous test of character by suffering were the labors of Heracles. Heracles was the son of Zeus and the most popular and commonly worshiped hero in antiquity. His implacable enemy was Hera, the wife of Zeus, jealous of her husband's dalliances and therefore angry with his pride in remarkable human offspring. Hera seeks several times to kill Heracles and ruin his life by various means and succeeds eventually in causing him so much physical pain that he casts himself on a pyre and burns to death. When visited by Odysseus in the underworld, the shade of Heracles asks, "Are you too leading some evil fate such as I endured? For I was a son of Zeus, but I had endless suffering" (*Odyssey* 11.618–21, GJR). Heracles was forced to perform twelve famous labors in the service of his wicked uncle, again as the result of Hera's ire: she sent a fit of madness upon him and he, in an insane rage, killed his wife and children. In expiation he sought out the advice of the Delphic oracle and was advised to serve his unworthy uncle for twelve years, but as a prize he would win immortality.

Associated with and in addition to these labors were many acts performed to help others, ridding their lands of ferocious beasts, brigands, and other horrors. An early story attributed to Prodicus, a philosopher and contemporary of Socrates, claims that as a young man Heracles was approached by two women, personified Vice and Virtue. The first was voluptuous and seductive, promising him a life of ease and pleasure if he would follow her. The second was of cultured bearing and modest, promising him all the labors and difficulties life must offer one who wished to earn and deserve a reputation for virtue. He chose, of course, the latter path. His help for others in need and his reputation for rugged strength, simple living, and courage in the face of suffering made him an example for the Stoic and Cynic schools of philosophy of the ideal individual.

BAIT IN A TRAP

The fate in which the hero is bound while alive often forms a complex pattern of divine justice in which the gods themselves are partners: the hero suffers humiliation, privation, and even death as a kind of bait in a larger divine trap designed to catch and destroy the wicked. There is more than one story line being played out, as we saw above concerning interwoven destinies. This role as bait is itself a test of character for those who encounter the hero, and the bait comes in deceiving forms.

Odysseus, king of Ithaka, had gone off to fight at Troy, and then because of a sacrilegious invasion of the main temple there incurred divine anger that cost him his homecoming. He wandered far and wide during his attempts to return, but was always prevented from succeeding and repeatedly cast away. He lost his ships and all his men, then struggled on alone. His wife despaired of his ever returning and, supposing him dead, began to entertain suitors for a remarriage. More than a hundred suitors besieged their house as freeloaders, daily feasting and acting grossly against all propriety, consuming for free the substance of Odysseus for more than three years. Finally, after ten years of wandering—we get our English word "odyssey" from these wanderings—he returned home. Yet his fate, to suffer so much and so long in trying to return, became the window of fate for the suitors. He became bait in a trap to destroy these wicked souls. He returned home unexpected and unrecognizable as a wrinkled old beggar seeking hospitality from those who had invaded his own house. The few members of his household who received the beggar hospitably survived the test and were eventually rewarded. The suitors and their friends treated him with contempt and abuse and, although they were arrogating to themselves the hospitality of the house of Odysseus, refused its hospitality to him. Eventually they were destroyed.

In another example, Oedipus, after the revelation that he had killed his father and married his mother, put out his own eyes and was exiled as a parricide, forced to wander for the rest of his life as one of the most horrifying of mortals in both appearance and reputation. Thebes, his home city, where he had once been king, rejected him and refused any assistance. Yet at the end of his life he was received hospitably by Theseus, king of Athens, becoming in death a curse on his own home of Thebes for its abuse and a talisman of protection for Athens, which had received him. The hero could be a kind of unlovely mystery, an enigma, that sound character alone could properly perceive and a test that righteousness alone survived.

The idea itself, that God should test the character of humans by some unlooked for and even despised means, is an old and common theme. The reason for the flood in Greek tradition was that Zeus himself had come to earth as a beggar seeking hospitality, as a test of the righteousness of earth's inhabitants, and had been so wickedly treated that he decided to destroy them. Only Deucalion and his wife survive. The writer of the Letter to the Hebrews tells us that we should be careful to show hospitality to strangers, for some have entertained angels unawares (Heb. 13:2). The reference is of course to the three strangers who visit Abraham and seal the fate of Sodom and Gomorrah (Gen. 18:2). Abraham and Lot pass the test, while all others in these cities fail. And in the tradition of Jesus, at the final judgment and the separation of the sheep and the goats, it is how one has treated the least important, the least lovely, the least successful, that determines whether one enters heaven, for in some spiritual way it is Jesus himself who is so disguised in them (Matt. 25:31–46).

EARLY DEATH IN THE MIDST OF LIFE

Heroes do not often live long. They commonly die painfully in the prime of life, in the midst of the very test, the crisis for which they were destined. The list of those who die in the midst of their lives, at the peak of their powers, and before fulfilling their dreams is long, in fact one of the defining characteristics of the hero story. It is this aspect that brings forth the pathos and makes their stories the inspiring tragedies that have been preserved to the present day. The exceptions, those heroes who live to old age, are those who have suffered remarkably, such as Oedipus and Odysseus, or who for reasons of fate have survived only to be destroyed as elders, such as Agamemnon and his counterpart, Priam, king of Troy.

But almost no one lived very long. Statistics from tombstones give an average age at death for people in the ancient world at around twenty years old, slightly longer for women than for men. These statistics do not include infants, for infants were only rarely buried in formal graves. The tomb and its gravestone was a *sema*, a marker and remembrance of the person within that was meant to be read and to bring *kleos* ("fame") to the deceased. Its significance was great in antiquity; consider the pyramids and monumental tombs found all over the ancient Mediterranean world. Even small tombs were expensive, and the statistics that we have come only from families who could afford them. One surmises that the abject poor would have died even sooner, with even fewer resources to ward off starvation and disease.

There were people who died in old age, but they were far fewer than we are used to seeing. In the Homeric works, every significant thing or person carries one or more poetic epithets that are repeated at nearly every mention: "swift-footed Achilles," "lord of men Agamemnon," "the wine-dark sea," "rosy-fingered dawn." The epithet for old age is "hateful old age." Almost all people in antiquity who were not first killed by accident or war died early of disease. There was no effective medical care, no dentistry, no means of controlling pain. The only available means of healing diseases were those that ancients were able to invent based on a mixture of observation, magic, and various types of tradition. "Medicines," such as they were, often harmed the patient as much as helped, and most did nothing. Many were simply magical, for example, a foot-shaped root made into a plaster and applied to the skin to cure a foot ailment. Some procedures could prove fatal, for example, phlebotomy ("bleeding"), which was used to balance "bodily humors." Surgery, cautery, and amputation were common means of fighting the deadly spread of infection. The saying of Jesus, "If your hand causes you to stumble, cut it off . . ." (Mark 9:43) is a spiritual lesson drawn from common medical practice; cutting off one's hand is not a penalty or act of fanaticism, but a normal means of healing, of saving one's life.

Few people reached old age, and those who did were necessarily afflicted in many ways by all of life's accumulated pains and losses; old age was hateful for all but very few. In the words of Dio Chrysostom (ca. A.D. 40–112), an orator contemporaneous with the writers of the Gospels:

> As for humanity, being very fond of life and devising so many things to postpone death, most of them do not even reach old age, but live infested by a host of diseases—which it is no easy task even to name—

and the earth does not supply them with sufficient drugs, but they require the knife and cautery as well. Nor [are physicians], with all their healing power, of any use to them because of their excesses and wickedness, nor are prophetic seers and purifying priests. (*Oratio* 6.23–24)

Dio blames the inability of physicians to heal the many diseases of his contemporaries on their sinfulness, but righteousness only goes so far. Arnobius (d. ca. 330) upbraids the profession, asking, "Why cannot more kinds of disease and sickness be restored to health and soundness? Why in fact do they become worse under the very hands of the physicians?" (*Adversus Nationes* 3.23). Thus the ancients understood death in a way we do not and cultivated the virtue of facing death with courage out of necessity. They taught each other about facing death in the midst of life through the stories of the heroes.

THE PRIZE OF IMMORTALITY

Not until after the time of Homer, under the influence of Orphic and Pythagorean philosophy, did the idea that the soul would live on after death in a substantial existence begin to take hold in Greece. Roughly similar ideas were beginning to gain influence among Jews at approximately the same time as a result of contact with Persian Zoroastrianism after the Exile. Plato in the fourth century B.C. became the most widely respected philosopher to promulgate this idea, but still in his time the majority believed otherwise. In Plato's *Phaedo*, set in the prison house of Socrates on the very day he is to take the poison and die, he and his friends begin, appropriately, to discuss life after death. After hearing Socrates give his reasons for his belief in this doctrine, his friend Cebes complains that the average person would not accept such a claim, believing that at death the soul dissipates "like breath or smoke" and vanishes away (70a). For the average person there was only the expectation that one's shadowy image, a mere ghost, would descend to the house of Hades, as we have seen. Skepticism concerning the afterlife held sway long after popular philosophy and religion, especially mystery religions, began to teach its existence, and their influence never was great enough to change majority opinion. From what we can judge by the vast number of tomb inscriptions that have come down to us from the Greco-Roman world, belief in immortality or a blessed afterlife of any sort for the average individual was held by only a small minority of people. A large number of grave inscriptions reflect sentiments like "Farewell forever, Maximus my brother, and forever good-bye" or, in a common and cynically humorous vein, "I was not, I was, I am not, I don't care."

But long before Plato the Greeks had a place for the blessed dead, who were the heroes. Hesiod, as we saw above, describes the heroes as a righteous group much like the Golden race. For them, Zeus made a special afterlife: they live "at the ends of the earth, and they live having hearts without sorrow in the Islands of the Blessed beside deep-swirling ocean, blessed heroes for whom the grain-giving field bears honey-sweet fruit . . ." (*Works and Days* 169–73, GJR). Homer too knew of this place; Menelaos, the husband of Helen of Troy, recounts a conversation he had with the Old Man of the Sea, who told him that he would not die at home:

> . . . but the immortals will convey you to the Elysian Field, and the limits of the earth . . . where there is made the easiest life for mortals, for there is no snow, not much winter there, nor is there ever rain, but always the stream of Ocean sends up breezes of the West wind blowing briskly for the refreshment of mortals. This because Helen is yours and you are son-in-law to Zeus. (*Odyssey* 4.563–70)

But Elysium had few inhabitants: only a small number were related to Zeus or offspring of some other deity. Heroes were technically the offspring of gods and mortals, sons and daughters of the gods, who shared in both divine greatness and human suffering. Their ancestry and talents set them apart from mere mortals: they were traditionally kings, queens, princes, and military leaders; they began their careers wealthy, famous, wise, and beautiful. These were the rightful heirs of Elysium.

The philosophers tried to make Elysium and the Isles of the Blessed the common inheritance of all who would devote themselves to philosophy and justice, but had little success in convincing more than a few followers. One of their most effective examples was Heracles, who was worshiped as both hero and god all over the Mediterranean world. He had, one may recall, performed the famous twelve labors. The Greek word for "labor" is *athlos*, which is a "contest for a prize," and *athlon* is the "prize" for which one competes. From the same root is the word *athletes*, English "athlete." The prize for which Heracles had labored was immortality, and when he threw himself on the pyre in agony, the fire was said to have burned away his mortal nature and rendered him immortal. One may see here the concept that among the ancient heroes suffering led to a prize. The prize for Heracles was immortality, but for the rest of us, in spite of the assurances of the philosophers, the prize was an uncertain remembrance of bravery among our friends and family, or perhaps nothing at all.

THE DEAD HERO AS PROTECTOR OF THE LIVING

The death of the hero was an ironic victory. The hero fought the good fight and died, yet in some way won the battle with fate and the ambiguity of the gods. What remained after death was the right of the hero to stand on behalf of his or her worshipers who themselves passed the test. This was true because through death the hero became a transformed being. Not only was the inimical relationship with the gods reversed, but the power of the gods energized the hero. Especially in popular piety, the dead hero became a remarkably dangerous entity, extremely destructive to unrighteous opponents. This viewpoint is significantly different from that of most of us in the modern era and warrants some explanation. Ancients always had a healthy respect for and fear of the dead, since the dead were still alive in a ghostly sense and always present. They were alive for help or hurt, and it was best to cultivate their good will by offerings and prayers.

Even a remarkably stupid hero could become a terrifying power after death. When Odysseus visits the underworld during his wanderings to find out from Teiresias the prophet how to get home, he meets the ghost of Elpenor, a sailor on one of his ships, "the youngest man, not terribly powerful nor sound in his thoughts" (*Odyssey* 10.552–53). Odysseus did not even know Elpenor had died. The ghost declares that he had been drunk and had gone to sleep on the roof in the cool of the night; when he heard the clamor of the departing ships, he woke up and fell off, breaking his neck. Yet he warns Odysseus to return and give him proper burial rites, "for fear I might become the god's curse upon you" (*Odyssey* 11.73). The curse would be the avenging ghost that had been wronged by being denied proper burial. But far more common than "the god's curse" was the blessing of protection of the dead hero.

Heroes offered protection and help in dire circumstances, since they themselves had overcome in their own similar difficulties. The gods in a way belonged to a different dimension from humans, far too exalted and ambiguous to offer consistent help. Who could know? They might have planned this very mess themselves. They could not die; they were never hungry or ill; they never suffered anything substantial, except occasionally at the hands of Zeus. If they were arrogant or abusive or capricious to humans, nothing untoward happened to them. If any retribution did occur, it fell on their human partisans. The gods, in their conflicts with one another, punished the worshipers of their rivals, not each other. In the competition, for example, between Aphrodite and Artemis, Aphrodite destroys Hippolytus, the single outstanding devotee of Artemis; Artemis tells the dying youth that she can offer him no help, but as compensation she will destroy one of Aphrodite's favorites. Recall the case of Job in the Bible—how he is all but destroyed in the conflict between God and Satan. People suffered for the conflicting wills of the gods, but particularly the heroes, those who were especially close to the gods. If one needed real help, one turned to those who knew and understood by experience, those who had fought the battle with fate and the gods and lost, but won. Thus the cult of heroes was the single most common and important religious aspect of the world of the early Christians. Every home had its *lares*, the heroes of the household, the founding ancestors. Every town had its protecting hero, every district and tribe, every crossroads, point of land, grove, and mountain pass.

Heroes as Examples

Heroes not only offered help—their stories also provided understanding of the proper modes of action. They were models, examples, and ideals. They had overcome, and imitation of their actions offered people some hope that they too might overcome. How could one imitate the gods? They were forever happy, deathless, without toil or pain or frustration. They never faced a real problem. They offered almost no behavior capable of imitation, and imitation of their immoral antics or capriciousness would only get a human into trouble with them. Eventually the philosophers created a new concept of the divine nature and banished the anthropomorphic gods of Homer and the poetic tradition. But the philosophers' God was a far worse model for imitation, that invisible and unknowable One, the source and ground of all being—it did nothing at all; it didn't even have a body. All it did was think, in complete bliss and silence. So it was the company of heroes who set the models for behavior, teaching by example courage, endurance, and ethical behavior. Ancients learned to be fathers and mothers, servants and rulers, soldiers and swineherds from the stories told of the heroes.

Chapter 4

THE STORY OF JESUS

If one is not a New Testament scholar, one may see with little diffi-culty from the preceding chapters that stories of the life of Jesus were very much set in the mold of the stories of the ancient heroes. Some-time around the year 400, Nonnus of Panopolis in Egypt wrote a para-phrase of the Gospel of John in the poetic style of the Homeric epics. In it, the disciples of Jesus are seen as the companions of a classic hero figure, "godlike" exactly as in Homer, and Jesus himself is a battling Achilles. Again, sometime not long after the year 800, an unknown au-thor, at the order of Louis the Pious, son of Charlemagne and Holy Roman Emperor by 814, translated the gospel into the language of the tribes of the Saxons. The story, known as the *Heliand,* or "Savior," is an epic poem recast for the times and the audience of the ninth century; it was designed to be sung or chanted at gatherings especially of the war-rior nobility. But it also expresses the old ideals of the wider Greco-Roman tradition out of which it grew—it is again a tale of heroes. For example, in the epic just prior to the crucifixion, we find that Pilate's Roman commanders

> ordered the warrior-heroes to use the edges of their battle-axes to make a mighty cross out of a hardwood tree with their hands. . . . They com-manded our Chieftain to carry it to the place where He was to die, cov-ered with blood, though He had done nothing wrong. (65)

These works are not mere aberrations. Nonnus wrote fully within the traditions of the classical world which at the time was becoming Christian, and the *Heliand* was the gospel for the Saxons, delivered to them by the order of the Catholic ruler of the Holy Roman Empire. These were interpretations of the gospel story in the style of epic according to the pattern inherent in the story itself. The gospel could be successfully recast as an epic poem of the hero because it clearly already was such a story in biographical prose.

In the minds of the ancients it had always been such a story, but this understanding has been lost to us. Because of the great respect accorded the Old Testament by orthodox Christians in the fourth century and later, the Bible became a book that wedded in one volume two quite different collections of writings, the Old Testament and the New Testament. The Old Testament preceded the New in history and time of composition and was therefore placed before it as a kind of introduction explaining the history of the world and the people who eventually gave birth to Jesus. In the modern world especially, the inference is that if one wishes to understand Jesus and the Christian tradition, one must read the Bible front to back because the true explanation and introduction to Jesus is the Old Testament. That is only partially true, a fact that has been seldom noticed because of the many often erroneous systems created by modern Christian interpreters of the New Testament to meld these two disparate collections.

The term "Old Testament" is an ancient one, coined in the first Christian century, and indicates quite obviously that for Christians the old religion of Israel was superseded by the revelation of Jesus. This fact set a serious problem for the church in its use of the Old Testament as a Christian text. Jesus had time and again deepened, changed, even contradicted the Old Testament in his teachings. For example, he tells his disciples in the Sermon on the Mount, "You have heard that it was said, 'An eye for an eye. . . .' But I say to you, Do not resist an evildoer . . ." (Matt. 5:38–39). Or again, in a controversy in Mark with some Pharisees over ritual washing of hands before eating, he states that "there is nothing outside a person [i.e., food] that by going in can defile. . . ." Mark observes that "Thus he declared all foods clean" (Mark 7:15, 19) and eliminated the kosher food restrictions of text and tradition. The apostle Paul declares in an argument over the Law that as Christians we are "ministers of a new covenant, not of letter [of the Law] but of spirit; for the letter kills, but the Spirit gives life" (2 Cor. 3:6). The words here translated "new covenant" are in Greek *kainê diathêkê*, the standard phrase for "New Testament." So Christians understood that the Old Testament could *not* be used merely as it was; it was not in fact a sufficient background in and of itself to understand the gospel.

Although interpreters saw the Old Testament as no longer valid or binding literally, they did see it as predicting and prefiguring the coming of Jesus, using typology and prophecy to support their claims. John was so bold as to have Jesus declare to Jews, "You search the scriptures because you think that in them you have eternal life; and it is they that testify on my behalf" (John 5:39). Christians saw Jesus prefigured in the Old Testament as the "Lamb of God" and as Jacob's ladder (John 1:36, 51), as the mercy seat in the temple (Rom. 3:25) and the seed of Abraham (Gal. 3:16), as the rock in the desert (1 Cor. 10:4) and the high priest (Heb. 3:1). Eventually the list became endless as Christian interpreters found Christ symbolized nearly everywhere in the Old Testament. They saw him as fulfilling the many forward-looking prophecies about the messiah, such as the prophet promised by Moses (Deut. 18:15–19), as the suffering servant of Isaiah (Isa. 53), as the Branch of Jeremiah (Jer. 23:5), and the son of man of Daniel (Dan. 7:13).

They used allegory and metaphor to bring into the understanding of the Old Testament the many fundamental changes and improvements, from their point of view, that the Greco-Roman world had supplied and on which the teaching of Jesus was based. This was not, surprisingly, a merely Christian methodology; it had been used among Jews for at least two centuries for similar reasons, to relate the old Israelite religion to the spiritual and philosophical views of the Roman world. The Old Testament contained any number of difficulties when considered from the sophisticated philosophical viewpoint of the wider culture. It was embarrassing to have a God who was jealous of other gods and had ordered the slaughter of all the people of Amalek and others. So, concerned Jews too resorted to allegory and metaphor to claim that Amalek was really representative of the passions in the soul that should be rooted out and that this Yahweh was really, despite appearances, the one God of all the universe.

More recently, a great deal of effort has been expended by some scholars to demonstrate the "Jewishness" of Jesus and to show the Jewish roots and background of Christianity. But this worthy effort should not go without explanation, since the Jewishness of Jesus was a very different thing from the Jewishness of Moses or David or the prophets of Israel. Jesus was heir, as were his disciples, to centuries of pervasive and influential new ideas and cultures. Their worldview was very different from that of the Israelite tribal religion of the Old Testament.

To illustrate the differences, one may compare the blessings and curses that Moses in Deuteronomy promises to the children of Israel: the righteous and faithful follower of Yahweh will live long and happy, see his children's children to the fourth generation, live in peace and prosperity on his own farm, resting under vine and fig tree, and be laid to rest in peace among his forefathers. Joshua reiterates these promises in the context of the entrance into the land—if the children of Israel are faithful, the Lord will grant them good success. The curses for the unfaithful and unrighteous include homelessness, persecution by enemies, capture, enslavement, and early death. Yet if anything, in the New Testament and the real world of antiquity in general, exactly the opposite seemed true: it was the innocent righteous who suffered Moses' curses and the arrogant fools who succeeded.

This reversing of the old covenant structure of Israelite religion in early Christianity can hardly be more complete, yet it goes unnoticed or even denied by many today because of the long tradition of attempts to meld the two systems. For the purpose of this argument, the differences must be emphasized to bring out a fundamental aspect of the gospel story: the most righteous person of the New Testament suffers innocently and horribly. He was crucified in the face of the Old Testament curse on anyone hanged on a tree (Deut. 21:23; Gal. 3:13). In addition, he tells all his followers to do the same: "Take up [your] cross and follow me" (Mark 8:34). This is not the pattern of the life of Abraham or David, but of a hero of the wider culture where such stories were the very substance of its construction of reality.

THE EDUCATIONAL SYSTEM OF ANTIQUITY

The Gospels are books written in Greek. Viewed from a scholar's perspective, they are literary products of a certain merit, though not of the first rank. St. Jerome was embarrassed by some of the poor writing found in various parts of the New Testament. The professional scribes of the church who copied these manuscripts generation after generation regularly corrected infelicities of grammar and syntax, eventually producing a nearly flawless Greek text. Nevertheless, the grammar and modes of expression of the New Testament Gospel writers are in the main acceptable according to the literary standards of the common language, the *koinê* Greek, as it is called, of their day. The point of these observations is that the authors are educated people, not experts or professional writers, but educated, and that fact has rather profound implications.

Very few people in antiquity could read or write. Writing as we know it was first used in the ancient Near East about 3000 B.C., and people had been living without it in Egypt and Mesopotamia for hundreds of thousands of years. All of the basic structures and duties of civilization, even empires, were wholly in place and had been functioning completely without writing from time immemorial. Writing began, presumably, as an aid to trade and business, and then was later applied to government and taxation and religious establishments. If one were not in some complex business that required it, or a professional scribe, there was no reason to learn to write. An analogy might be something like being a professional electrician today. Most people need to know very little about installing or repairing electrical equipment or services, because they rely on professional electricians to perform this specialized function in society. The vast majority of people in the Mediterranean area and Europe functioned perfectly normally as farmers or bakers or homemakers without the ability to read or write right up to the modern era.

Writing was expensive. The list of surviving materials upon which people wrote is not long: papyrus sheets, animal skins, wooden tablets covered with wax, copper and lead sheets, stone slabs, and ostraca (pieces of broken pottery). Only the ostraca were free, but one could write only a few words on them. All the others were expensive and beyond the reach of most people. Papyrus was the paper of the ancient world—we even get our modern word "paper" from the name. The papyrus plant was grown and sheets manufactured from its pith in Egypt; from there it was exported to other areas. In Egypt, at the time the apostle Paul was writing (A.D. 50s), a single sheet of papyrus cost about two-thirds the daily wage of an unskilled laborer and about one-third that of a skilled workman. Only the relatively wealthy could afford it.

Education was also expensive, especially at levels beyond the basic skills of reading and writing. There was no system of state-supported education for basic literacy; parents had to pay for their own children's schooling. The theory of universal education had been voiced only a handful of times by a few philosophers and never put into practice. Schools themselves were not to be found everywhere: cities had them, but most villages did not. The majority of people lived in villages, and *rusticus* meant "uneducated" as well as "villager." A popular saying for such people was "can't read, can't swim" (Plato *Laws* 3.689d). In villages, people often lived by barter, without money, and at a subsistence level. If they did send their sons to school for some perceived economic advantage, it would often be only to the *litterator*, the teacher of "letters," that is, an instructor of basic reading and writing. Very few but the wealthy and those who served the rich could afford to send their children to the *grammaticus* and then the *rhetor*, the instructors of the next levels of schooling, who taught literature and composition, and then declamation worthy of the courts, public speaking, and high office.

The texts for all three levels, however, were the great epics and poets, almost always Homer and the tragedians in Greek; in Latin, similar heroic tales were used, especially Virgil's epic of the founding of Rome, the *Aeneid*. There were no children's primers of easy stories, no books of the "See Spot run!" variety. Children were taught the alphabet, how to say and sound the letters and then how to write them. Then they were sent directly to the texts, to learn by reciting, memorizing, and copying the works of Homer, Hesiod, and the great tragic poets (Aeschylus, Sophocles, Euripides). So Protagoras, arguing with Socrates that virtue may be taught, tells us:

> Whenever [children] have learned their letters and are ready to understand the written word . . . [their teachers] set the works of good poets before them on their desks to read and make them learn them by heart. (Plato *Protagoras* 325e)

A third-century B.C. collection of school texts in Egypt shows that students were taught the individual letters, then the writing of single words, and then Homer; there were no intermediate "easy" texts, in fact no other texts at all. And Cicero, writing the *Tusculan Disputations* about 45 B.C. in Italy, in a discussion of the works of the poets, tells us that

"We indeed, taught obviously by Greece, both read and learn by heart these (poets) from boyhood, and consider this to be liberal education and doctrine" (2.41, GJR). On the walls of Pompeii, buried and therefore preserved by the volcanic eruption of Mount Vesuvius in A.D. 79, one finds a large collection of graffiti, some scurrilous, some announcing this or that event of sale. But among them are many examples of *Arma virumque cano* ("Of arms and men I sing") and *Conticuere* ("They were silent"), the first line of Book I and the first word of Book II, respectively, of the *Aeneid*. This is clearly evidence of schoolchildren scrawling what they were learning to write. Education in the Greco-Roman world was based in the classics of Greek heroic literature and their offspring in Latin. If one was educated at all, no matter what the level of competence, one was educated on Homer and the heroes.

This educational philosophy was deeply embedded in the ancient mentality, that such literature formed one's character according to the revered models of the past. The quotation of Protagoras above continues by describing the moral purpose of such "poems, in which are many admonitions, and many tales, praises, and panegyrics of ancient good men, so that the child may imitate them eagerly and desire to be such a person" (Plato *Protagoras* 326a, GJR). Again, at a symposium, Socrates and others are asked to declare what useful knowledge each possesses. Niceratus, one of the banqueters, replies when it is his turn, "My father was anxious to see me develop into a good man, and as a means to this end he compelled me to memorize all of Homer" (Xenophon *Symposium* 3.6). The purpose of such an education was that one should "develop into a good man." Lucian in the second century A.D. tells us that schoolmasters gave a student "books that openly or by allegory teach him who was a great hero, who was a lover of justice and purity" (Lucian *Amores* 45). Schools enforced the worldview, the morals, and ethical ideals admired and imitated by the ancients essentially by requiring every student to learn from the same narrow selection of revered heroic texts.

There was no "popular" literature—no cheap novels, no magazines, no newspapers, no gothic romances. No works were written specifically for the mass audience—there was no publishing industry and most people were illiterate. Texts were hand copied, usually by slaves, and while sold occasionally for profit in the marketplace, the normal means of dissemination was by gift to friends. The world of necessary information was kept running by heralds, town criers who announced to all who could hear the dictates of magistrates. For judges, government officials, and political officeholders, the number of heralds employed far exceeded the number of scribes: most business was conducted and messages sent orally. Most towns had a nucleus of literate men who served as intermediaries when it was necessary, but the norm was the herald and the culture at large was based on oral communication and oral literature.

Among the very rich, among those who could afford to use writing materials extensively, there was a culture of letter exchange, poetry, and speeches on philosophy and ethics. But even this literature draws its inspiration from Homer and the classics. Pliny, for example, Roman governor of northern Turkey about A.D. 110–12, although writing in Latin, seasons his formal letters with quotations in Greek from Homer as one might today use quotations from the Bible, to offer inspired comfort, base a piece of advice on higher authority, or illustrate a truth. He clearly assumes the recipient will understand and recognize their authority.

Readings and performances by professional reciters of epic, the rhapsodes, were common. The illiterate masses heard and learned the heroic epics by this means. Competitions for skill in such recitations were held in many cities, even at the major athletic games. In his conversation with such a rhapsode, Ion by name, Socrates demonstrates that this great skill is really a result of divine inspiration. He describes the typical scene of a rhapsode giving a public recitation:

> There he is, at a sacrifice or festival, got up in his holiday attire, adorned with golden chaplets, and he weeps, though he has lost nothing of his finery. Or he recoils with fear, standing in the presence of more than twenty thousand friendly people, though nobody is stripping him or doing him damage. (Plato *Ion* 535d)

Here the audience is twenty thousand people. Theaters held from five to thirty thousand people depending on the wealth of the city; Socrates is using a typical number to describe a common situation. Strabo, a Greek geographer (d. ca. A.D. 21), compares philosophy and heroic poetry, stating that "Philosophy is for the few, but poetry is more useful for the common people and is able to fill the theaters, but indeed especially that of Homer" (1.2.8, GJR). Public recitation of such stories seems to have been immensely popular. Public reading was a sign of high culture and a common form of entertainment at the symposia of the rich. Cicero even mentions with approval an old custom according to which dinner guests themselves "used to compose songs of the praises of famous men" (*Brutus* 19.75).

Education in Greek was based on Homer and the tragic poets from before the time of Socrates (d. 399 B.C.) to long after the reign of Constantine (d. A.D. 337) and into the Christian era of the Roman Empire. Even near the end of this period, Christians still did not develop their own curriculum or texts, but continued to use the same methods and system that had been in place for nearly a thousand years. Highly educated bishops and churchmen defended Greek literature as valuable and necessary preparation for service to the church; Basil (St. Basil "the Great," ca. 330–379) calls all of Homer's poetry a "high tribute to virtue" (*To Young Men, or How They Might Profit from Greek Literature* 5.6). There is no question that those who wrote the Gospels of the New Testament received the same education as other learned men of their culture. If one could read or write at all in Greek or Latin, one had learned to do so by reading and memorizing and copying the heroic literature. Thus both the writers of the Gospels and their readers knew what proper literature was supposed to be, what its ideals were, what its main characters were supposed to teach, and how its story line was to run— they expected a work like the story of Jesus to be the story of a hero.

THE STORY OF JESUS AND THE STORY OF THE HERO

One of the more interesting aspects of the preaching and teaching of the gospel was that the story of the life of Jesus was compressed into a bare outline containing very few elements at some time quite soon after the founding of the Church. The earliest writer in the New Testament is the apostle Paul, and the story apparently was already in outline form before he became a Christian within a decade of the death of Jesus (ca. A.D. 30); at least he says that he himself was taught it in this form. In a Letter to the Corinthian Church he states:

> For I handed on to you as of first importance what I in turn had
>   received:
> that Christ died for our sins in accordance with the scriptures,
> and that he was buried,
> and that he was raised on the third day in accordance with the
>   scriptures,
> and that he appeared to Cephas, then to the twelve. (1 Cor. 15:3–5)

The passage goes on to relate the postresurrection appearances to many others and finally to Paul himself. The outline has a poetic structure and was probably developed as a catechism for new Christians, one of whom eventually was Paul. He in turn taught it to the Corinthians early in his ministry among them. The written Gospels are rather full statements, including accounts of Jesus' birth, baptism, the many miracles and teachings, and especially the events leading up to and including his crucifixion and resurrection. Yet in the confessional form of the outline, all of this material is absent, though much of it must have been known. In the formula in 1 Corinthians 15, only the bare statement of four events is present.

Later in the history of the Church we find a venerable baptismal creed of the church at Rome, known as the Old Roman Creed, that contains a similar type of outline. It was used at least as early as the second half of the second century and shows a similar but not identical listing of bare events, this time numbering six. It has a triadic structure declaring faith in Father, Son, and Holy Spirit, as do all such baptismal creeds, taking their form from the command of the risen Christ in Matthew 28:19, "baptizing them in the name of the Father and of the Son and of the Holy Spirit." Only the first two parts are given here:

> I believe in God the Father the almighty
> and in Christ Jesus his only son, our Lord,
>   who was born of the Holy Spirit and Mary the virgin,
>   who was crucified under Pontius Pilate and buried;
>   he rose on the third day from [among] the dead;
>   he ascended into the heavens;
>   he sits at the right hand of the Father,
>   from where he will come to judge the living and the dead.

Much later in the history of the Church, in the time of Constantine, we find a similar simple outline as a central part of the Creed of Nicaea, drafted in 325, and the Creed of Constantinople of 381, although in these later creeds the outline is expanded with material that arose in the controversies over the nature of Christ. The point to observe is that this simple outline, the earliest catechism that we know of and the core of the great creeds of the Church, is the outline of the career of a hero.

Justin Martyr, in the middle of the second century, as noted in an earlier chapter, states just that in his defense of the faith (his *First Apology*, or "Speech for the Defense") written to emperor Antoninus Pius and his adoptive sons Marcus Aurelius and Lucius Verus. Justin was born a pagan (ca. A.D. 100) in Samaria and had studied all the major philosophies of his day. He wore the distinctive mantle of the professional philosopher to the day he was martyred (ca. 165). He was highly educated and, like many educated Christians, knew thoroughly and valued the poets and philosophers of Greek literature. Look again at the passage and see the outline of the life of Jesus:

> In saying that the Word, who is the first offspring of God,
>> was born for us without sexual union as Jesus Christ our teacher,
>> and that he was crucified and died,
>> and after rising again
>> ascended into heaven,
> we introduce nothing new beyond those whom you call sons of
> Zeus. (*1 Apologia* 21)

Here is the same basic type of outline, not identical with either of the others, but clearly descriptive of the career of Jesus. Justin is writing to the pagan emperor and knows that the emperor will quite easily recognize it as the kind of story he had heard since childhood. That would also have been true if the emperor had read Paul's catechism from 1 Corinthians 15, although he might have wondered to what "according to the scriptures" referred. He would have had no difficulty at all with the Old Roman Creed except for the final reference to the return "to judge the living and the dead"; he may have wondered why Jesus was replacing the older Greek heroes who already held the position of judges of the dead. Justin knew quite well of the apocalyptic return of Christ, as he makes clear elsewhere in the treatise, and knows that it is here that the stories of the heroes and that of Jesus begin to part company, so he leaves it out. At this point he wants to show the similarity of the Christian story to those of the "sons of Zeus."

Justin goes on to list a series of gods, heroes, and humans with differing relationships to the outline and to Zeus, all similar in ways to Jesus:

> Hermes, the interpreting Word and teacher of all; Asclepius, who was also a healer and after being struck by lightning ascended into heaven, as did Dionysus, who was torn in pieces; Heracles, who to escape his torment threw himself into the fire; the Dioscuri, born of Leda, and Perseus of Danaë, and Bellerophon, who, though of human origin, rode on the horse Pegasus. Need I mention Ariadne and those who like her are said to have been placed among the stars? And what of your deceased emperors, whom you regularly think worthy of being raised to immortality, introducing a witness who swears that he saw the cremated Caesar ascending into heaven from the funeral pyre?
> (1 Apologia 21)

We learn from his list how people of the time heard the aspects of the life of Jesus as similar to and in accord with those of the heroes and gods of their culture. Justin calls Hermes the "interpreting Word" and later the "announcing Word from God" (1 Apologia 22), because Hermes as the messenger of Zeus was by allegorical interpretation the Word of the invisible and unknown God of the universe, who makes him known to humans. This accords with the Christian claim that Jesus is the Word of God who makes God known: "No one has ever seen God; the only begotten God [Jesus]. . . has explained him" (John 1:18, GJR). So Jesus stands in the same relationship to God as did Hermes for pagans.

Asclepius, actually a grandson of Zeus, was the hero who became the patron god of healing. A bit later in his discussion Justin writes, "When we say that [Jesus] healed the lame, the paralytic, and those born blind, and raised the dead, we seem to be talking about things like those said to have been done by Asclepius" (1 Apologia 22). Dionysus, son of Zeus by Semele, also ascended to heaven "after being torn in pieces" by the Titans in the Orphic version of his story; he was a hero elevated to the status of Olympian god, the god of inspiration. Heracles, son of Zeus by Alcmena, at the end of his life put on a poisoned robe and was burned with unendurable pain. He ordered a huge funeral pyre to be lit and "to escape his torments he threw himself into the fire." He was worshiped everywhere in the Mediterranean as both hero and god; the mortal part of him was burned away in the fire and he ascended to heaven. Asclepius, Dionysus, and Heracles, prior to their ascents to heaven, all died rather violently. Justin says later, "If someone objects that [Jesus] was crucified, this is in common with the sons of Zeus, as you call them, who suffered as previously listed" (1 *Apologia* 22).

The Dioscuri were the twin brothers Castor and Pollux, who were great adventurers and went on the voyage of the Argonauts; at death they were placed in heaven among the stars as the constellation Gemini. Justin lists Perseus because he, like many others, was born of a virgin mother, Danaë. Bellerophon makes Justin's list because he "rode on the horse Pegasus," which brought him (almost) to heaven. Bellerophon in his stories did prove himself a hero in exploits and suffering; in his final ride on Pegasus he attempted to fly into heaven, but was thrown off and fell back to earth for this act of *hubris*. Justin says that Ariadne was "placed among the stars," but in fact it was the wreath given to the bride Ariadne by Dionysus, her husband, that was placed among the stars as the constellation Corona. Others like her who actually made it themselves were the Seven Sisters, who are the constellation Pleiades, and Orion, their would-be lover.

The issue that Justin is arguing with the emperor is that Rome should stop persecuting the Christians because they are saying nothing essentially different about Jesus the "Son of God" from what the Greek and Roman poets had said about their "sons of the gods." He writes, "Though we say the same as do the Greeks, we only are hated because of the name of Christ" (1 *Apologia* 24). The outline of the career of Jesus was not the point of the controversy between Rome and the Christians; that, as Justin shows, was essentially the same for all heroes. It was the Christian refusal to worship the same gods as did the Romans or to acknowledge their legitimacy—both Paul and Justin call them demons. In fact Justin says that although he and most other Christians had once been pagans and worshiped those gods, they now despised them. The Romans for their part accused Christians of gross immoralities, incest, and cannibalism. The differences were not minor, nor were the stakes low. Roman officials at the trials of the Christians often set up statues of the gods and emperors and required those accused to make a symbolic sacrifice to the images or die; Justin and many others like him went to their deaths willingly.

THE GENETICS OF THE HERO AND VIRGIN BIRTH

Like many, but not all, of the heroes, Jesus was reputed to have been a son of God born of a virgin mother. The title "son of god" did not necessarily imply divine genealogy in either the Jewish or Greek worlds. In Psalm 2:7, Yahweh declares of the king of Israel, "You are my son; today I have begotten you," at the enthronement ceremony. Justin repeats, in his defense of Jesus, what had long been Greek tradition: "Now if God's Son, who is called Jesus, were only an ordinary man, he would be worthy because of his wisdom to be called Son of God, for all authors call God father of humans and gods" (1 Apologia 22). In effect, all people, especially those of remarkable achievement, were "sons (and daughters) of God." Jesus is reported to have said much the same thing to the Jewish authorities in the Gospel of John:

> Is it not written in your law, "I said, you are gods"? If those to whom the word of God came were called 'gods'—and the scripture cannot be annulled—can you say that the one whom the Father has sanctified and sent into the world is blaspheming because I said, "I am God's Son"? (10:34–36)

Among Jews there was debate as to the genealogy of the messiah. Those who followed Christ saw in the text of Isaiah a prophecy of the virgin birth of Jesus: "Behold, a virgin shall conceive and bear a son . . ." (Isa. 7:14, RSV). Yet the proper interpretation of the text in Isaiah was disputed by those who did not believe, and a virgin birth was denied. A messiah for Jews did not have to have been virgin born: Simon Bar Cochbah, leader of the second great rebellion against Rome in A.D. 132–35, was declared to be the messiah by the most influential rabbi of his day, Rabbi Akiba, but no claim for a virgin birth was made; everyone knew who his father and mother were. In the New Testament itself, two versions of the virgin birth are to be found, in the Gospels of Matthew and Luke, and have become central features of the Christian understanding of the human and divine nature of Jesus. The other two

Gospels, Mark and John, have no such story, and John even includes the saying of a group of detractors, "Is not this Jesus, the son of Joseph, whose father and mother we know?" (John 6:42). We are told by several church writers who later wrote of heresies that certain Jewish-Christian groups thought that Jesus was a "mere man" whose father was Joseph and that he had been chosen to be the Messiah because of his piety. So the virgin birth of Jesus was a matter of some controversy.

But there was no denial of virgin birth in the wider culture: heroes of every description were born of virgin humans as the partners of divine fathers and mothers. But these stories were notorious for their (apparent) ascription of sexual passion and immoral behavior to the gods. Ethically minded philosophers had long banished such ideas as inventions of the poets not worthy of the divine nature: God was without passion, in fact without a body, resting in silence and joy for eternity. Christians sided with the philosophers: Justin, in rejecting the old gods of the poets that he had once worshiped, tells the emperor that he has dedicated himself to the "unbegotten and impassable God" (1 *Apologia* 25). But so had the emperor in his own way, as had his successor, Marcus Aurelius (r. 161–80), to whom Justin dedicated his *Second Apology*. Marcus became one of the most influential Stoic philosophers of his day; his book *Meditations* is still read with profit today. Both sides of the argument, in less heated moments, would have agreed that a true understanding of divinity required the conclusion that God did not have physical sex with anyone.

So what happens in the case of the virgin birth of Jesus? By the time the birth stories of the Gospels of Matthew and Luke were composed, the conception of the deity as a wholly spiritual being was well in place among the philosophically minded. The old ideas of gods with bodies who looked like large and beautiful humans, made of heavenly but nevertheless material "stuff," were no longer defended seriously, though such ideas lived on in festivals, pageantry, and dramatic performances. Now there was but one God, sometimes seen as including all other divine expressions and sometimes excluding them as enemies. Zeus and Hera and Apollo could be positive manifestations of the one God, as in the writings of the Greek philosophers, or they could be demons, as in Zoroastrian and later Christian polemic. But in either case, God did not have passion: God was righteous and at peace, spiritual, self-sufficient, and eternal. The astronomers had discovered that the universe was enormous—God must be larger still, even infinitely large. Some called God "the Place," a name that pointed to the fact that God contained everything; God was the place in which everything existed, but who was not contained by anything. And God lived in complete silence, unknown and unknowable by us in our dark ignorance, weighed down as we are by bodies and material desires. Without God reaching out to us to communicate, we would never know of its existence. "It" is the proper pronoun here, since the divine nature had no gender, but contained all within itself as the source of all things. The ancient philosophical problem was conceived of as "the many and the One," the multiplicity of things in the world arising from the one God as source.

These changes and progress in ideas about God had some rather interesting consequences for understanding the birth of Jesus. Mary was a virgin, but she could in no way engender the Messiah in the manner of the poetic tradition. The poets told of Zeus and other gods lusting after beautiful virgins and having sexual relations with them. The new ideas conceived of a God who had neither a body nor the passion to go with it. Either Joseph would father the child or the one God would send the Spirit, but the old poetic methods of engendering a child were out of the question. Matthew does not explain how Mary came to be pregnant, saying only that she "was found to be with child from the Holy Spirit" (Matt. 1:18). Luke relates that the angel Gabriel tells Mary: "The Holy Spirit will come upon you, and the power of the Most High will overshadow you" (Luke 1:35). This is clearly a spiritual, nonphysical occurrence, and the authors are quite circumspect in their treatment of it. In time, a great deal of energy was expended by Christian writers and scribes to safeguard the virginity of Mary even after the birth of Jesus. They produced a doctrine of the perpetual virginity of Mary even in the face of such New Testament passages as "he [Joseph] . . . had no marital relations with her [Mary] until she had borne a son" (Matt. 1:25), and "Is this not [Jesus] the carpenter, the son of Mary and brother of James and Joses and Judas and Simon, and are not his sisters here with us?" (Mark 6:3).

Not all Christians believed in the virgin birth or thought it a necessary element in the story of Jesus. Recall that the early catechism of Paul makes no mention of Jesus' birth, though the later creeds composed for Roman readers do. Christianity spread among many people of the East who did not have access to Greek heroic tradition to the same extent as did those around the Mediterranean. They did not speak Greek, but Syriac or Aramaic or some other Semitic language. In Greek, the word for "spirit" is *pneuma*, of neuter grammatical gender. The Holy Spirit is properly an "it," which works perfectly for Luke's purpose in showing the nonphysical nature of the conception of Jesus. In Latin, *spiritus* is grammatically masculine and less precise for Luke's purpose, more in concert with the poetic tradition. But in Semitic languages, the word for "spirit" is grammatically feminine, and for a female Spirit to engender a child seems logically impossible:

> Some say, "Mary conceived by the Holy Spirit." They are in error. They do not know what they are saying. When did a woman ever conceive by a woman? Mary is the virgin whom no power defiled. [. . .] The powers defile themselves. The Lord would not have said, "My Father who is in heaven" unless he had had another father. (*Gospel of Philip* 55.23–36)

The passage is from the *Gospel of Philip*, a Syrian Christian writing of the second century. It is not a Gospel like those in the New Testament and does not compete with them for a place in the Bible, though it happens to carry the title "Gospel." It is instead a series of wise sayings representative of one branch of Christian thought in the Eastern empire in the second century. Note the way this group of Semitic-speaking Christians understood Jesus: the passage as a whole is arguing against the virgin birth, but the author knows full well that other Christians affirm it. Two proofs are brought up as countermeasures. First, the word "spirit" is feminine, and therefore the Holy Spirit is feminine and could not have caused a woman (Mary) to conceive a child. A large number of texts from Semitic areas of the Eastern empire speak of the Holy Spirit as the mother of Jesus and present a holy family of Father, Spirit/Mother, and Son in contrast to the holy family so common in Western Christian art and Christmas displays of Joseph, Mary, and baby Jesus. In these Semitic areas, as in our passage, the natural father of the physical body of Jesus is Joseph, while the "mother" of the divine nature in him is the Spirit. So Jesus has a "heavenly Father" (God) of his divine nature and "another father" (Joseph) of his physical body.

It is the second issue in the passage, however, that concerns us much more: the author is at pains to conserve the virgin purity of Mary against the defilement of the "powers." In Eastern tradition derived from Persia, the gods of the pagans were the demonic "powers" who ruled the world of darkness. Recall that many Christians had demonized the Greco-Roman gods who mated with humans; for them the gods of the pagans were servants of the Devil and the only possibility for sexual relations between gods and humans was demonic. So here the author declares that there was no virgin birth because the "powers," the demonic rulers of the world, did not "defile" Mary. There is a break in the papyrus that leaves us in doubt as to the remainder of one of the sentences (symbolized by the "[. . .]" in the translation above), but the general tenor of the passage is clear: a virgin birth by a "god" must mean physical sexual union between a demonic power and Mary and therefore is impossible—she cannot have been defiled. This author is willing to deny the virgin birth before allowing a deity, that is, for him is a demon, to impregnate Mary. Here, and emphatically, the old stories of the poets about the lusts of the gods meet their match.

But for most Christians, the circumspect spiritual accounts of Matthew and Luke sufficed. Gabriel told Mary that because the Spirit of God would engender the child, he would "be called Son of God" (Luke 1:35). There was another consequence of divine genealogy: Jesus called God *Abba*, "Daddy." He seems to have had a relationship with God as personal Father quite unlike what was customary in his own Jewish tradition, a much closer relationship than was common among the teachers and rabbis of his day. Later Jewish tradition had certainly taught that God was the "father" of Israel and that therefore God was the father of the individual Jew. And from much earlier, Greeks, as we saw in the text of Justin, often spoke of God as "father of gods and humans." This was, in fact, one of the most common epithets of Zeus in Homer. But Jesus seems to have had an especially close relationship with God, and this fact brought him into conflict with Jewish tradition and the Jewish authorities. For example, he contravenes the Law of Moses that permitted divorce by appealing to the (real and) original will of God: "from the beginning it was not so" (Matt. 19:8). And he contradicts the Mosaic Law "eye for eye" (Exod. 21:24) by commanding followers not to resist an evildoer (Matt. 5:39). Of the tradition to "hate your enemy," he says "Love your enemies . . . that you may be children of your Father in heaven" (Matt. 5:44–45), implying clearly that to do otherwise is to be something else.

Consider the controversy over the point in the Gospel of John. Jesus has just healed a paralyzed man at the pool of Bethesda on the Sabbath by commanding him, "Stand up, take up your mat and walk" (John 5:8). Certain Jewish authorities see the man carrying his bed and accost him for breaking the Sabbath. He replies that the one who had healed him told him to do so and eventually reports Jesus to them. They therefore go to Jesus and accuse him for "working" his miracles on the Sabbath. Jesus replies to the effect that his Father is in the business of doing good, Sabbath or no Sabbath, and therefore so is he; he is not going to stop because of some tradition. John the Gospel writer adds:

> For this reason the Jews were seeking all the more to kill him, because he was not only breaking the sabbath, but was also calling God his own Father, thereby making himself equal to God. (John 5:18)

The Jewish authorities also believe that God is their Father, as is made clear later in the same Gospel (8:41). But here the level of intimacy and degree of relationship is different. They persecute Jesus because he is saying that God is his "own private Father"—the Greek text is quite clear that this is the point—setting him apart from the tradition and "making himself equal to God": he is God's son in a way no regular Jew could ever claim.

But this radical new sense of the close bond between God and Son of God does not stop with Jesus. It is basic to Jesus' religious mission to give to all his followers what he himself is and has, in effect to democratize his special status. This is the argument of this book and the basis of the appeal of the message about Jesus—everyone who followed him would become children of God in the special way that he was, not merely in the traditional way in which they already were considered so or that everybody was considered so. So Jesus taught his followers to pray "Our Father," and Paul taught that God had sent his Spirit into them to adopt them as children, that they too could call out to God, *Abba*—"Daddy."

REMARKABLE TALENTS

Such a lineage had consequences—children of the gods had talents beyond their mere mortal contemporaries. Jesus, according to our sources, was a healer and miracle worker and teacher. People hearing and seeing him were amazed and said, "Where did this man get all this? What is this wisdom that has been given to him? What deeds of power are being done by his hands!" (Mark 6:2). He stilled the storm, walked on water, multiplied the loaves and the fish, turned water into wine, healed the sick, and even raised the dead. These were amazing deeds, but the same or similar deeds had been claimed for others of divine lineage before. Tablets giving accounts of the healings of Asclepius could be found within his main sanctuary at Epidauros.

In the late fourth and third centuries B.C. there arose a type of literature known as "aretalogy," an account (*logos*) of the wonderful earthly deeds (*aretai*) of a god or hero. Scholars have long suspected that there existed such an account of the miracles of Jesus, written before the composition of the canonical Gospels and used by the authors of Mark and John. In John there is a series of miracles, the first of which are numbered. Changing water to wine is called "the first of his [Jesus'] signs" (John 2:11), and the healing of the nobleman's son is called "the second sign" (John 4:54). There may have been a numbered list of signs from which John worked, not all of which were used in the composition of the Gospel, for he concludes: "Jesus did many other signs . . . which are not written in this book" (John 20:30).

Jesus could have done anything, apparently: "Who then is this, that even the wind and sea obey him?" (Mark 4:41). If the early Christians had thought it necessary, he would have been able to fly or, if he had wished, to turn the Pharisees into green frogs. This last is not just humor—like so many heroes before, he was a kind of soldier or military captain locked in a deadly battle. He "frees the captives," those enslaved by dark forces, by casting out demons and healing diseases; he "binds the enemy" and sacks his belongings. But his kingdom and weapons are spiritual ones, and he does not choose to fight by other means. John tells us that just before the crucifixion, when asked by Pilate what he had done wrong, he replies (as so often, without answering the question):

My kingdom is not from this world. If my kingdom were from this world, my followers would be fighting to keep me from being handed over to the Jews. But as it is, my kingdom is not from here. (John 18:36)

All the power there is is in his hands, yet he chooses not to defend himself. And perhaps most significantly for later Christian history and the rise of the Church, he commands his followers not to defend themselves either: "Turn the other cheek." Follow the leader. Take up your cross also. Fight with spiritual weapons only. And if necessary, go to your death as well.

INTERWOVEN DESTINIES

Recall that the *Iliad* is part of an epic story that involved the whole of the Greek world; essentially everyone was included. The gods and fate had designed the plan and had placed at its center Achilles. He was not only "the best of the Achaians," the best soldier, but in one version of his possible lineage he had been destined to become the heir to the throne of Zeus himself. He is the central pivotal point around which the progress of the war and the plan of the gods revolve, yet the plan is larger than he is and involves all lands and peoples important to Greeks.

Jesus too is part of a story that involves the whole of the Greco-Roman world, but his is on an even larger scale because it eventually includes the cosmos itself and all of history. The difference in scale stems from the deep influence of Persian apocalyptic conception in postexilic Judaism that had expanded the scene to involve the whole universe and expanded the enemies to include cosmic forces of evil. We saw a related phenomenon in the story of the Four Ages in Hesiod, where the cycle of ages comprised all of humanity and history. The Persians had added to this the coming of a captain of the forces of righteousness who would defeat the Devil and his dark powers. When melded together as they were in Palestine, the two story lines result in what we find in the stories of Jesus, a hero from among the Jews with cosmic destiny. Nevertheless, the role played by the central human figure remains that of the classic hero.

The destinies of the world are woven together in the story of Jesus. Luke tells us that when the week-old child is dedicated at the temple, the aged Simeon recognizes the promised Messiah, whom he had been waiting to see before he died; he takes the child into his arms and proclaims, "This child is destined for the falling and the rising of many in Israel" (Luke 2:34). But not for Israel alone. Luke slowly develops his story into one that expands beyond the small nation of Israel to encompass the whole world; the risen Jesus instructs his disciples, "you will be my witnesses in Jerusalem, in all Judea and Samaria, and to the ends of the earth" (Acts 1:8). So in Paul's speech at Athens, "God . . . now . . . commands all people everywhere to repent, because he has fixed a day on which he will have the world judged in righteousness by a man whom he has appointed" (Acts 17:30–31).

The Trap of Fate and Free Will

One of the most endearing aspects of Greek heroic literature is that the individual heroes are often forced by an aspect of personal character into the tragedy that defines their lives. Achilles is a man of passionate anger when wronged, and while in a sense justified, it is his anger that eventually brings his fate upon him. For Helen of Troy, her very beauty is her qualification for tragic circumstance. For Antigone, it is her piety in insisting on the burial of her brother against the command of the king that brings her death. A similar connection between character and fate may be found in the stories of Hippolytus, Oedipus, and many others. Much the same could be said for Jesus. It is his very character, it seems, that caused him to be caught in his own web of fate—he can do no other than declare what is true, and that truth brings his fate upon him.

For each of the Gospel writers, but especially in Luke's story, Jesus' life is seen as having been predestined by God's plan. Although he had been crucified by Romans, he was "handed over to you according to the definite plan and foreknowledge of God" (Acts 2:23). Later the apostles give God praise that the authorities in executing Jesus did "whatever your hand and your plan had predestined to take place" (Acts 4:28). In fact, Jesus in the book of Revelation is called "the Lamb that was slaughtered from the foundation of the world" (Rev. 13:8). But he is not trapped or taken against his will. He knows, as did Achilles, that if he continues on the course set for him, he will be killed. The Gospel of Mark turns on this very point. Jesus' miracles and teaching bring him fame and a large following, but also offense and anger on the part of the authorities. In the midst of the story he tells his disciples that he will be killed, and Peter rebukes him, which elicits the angry retort, "Get behind me, Satan!" (Mark 8:33). From here on he sets his course toward Jerusalem and the cross.

He is at last forced, or directed by the will of God, into a situation intriguingly like that of Achilles, choosing death with honor over life. Jesus faces his fate and prays in Gethsemane that "the hour might pass from him" (Mark 14:35), but it does not. Like Achilles and many others, he chooses to go to his death. We never learn what the alternative might have been, if it existed at all. It is the defining moment in his life, the most important decision he ever makes, and he makes it entirely alone.

Consider this last issue from the point of view of the story as opposed to some theory of the historical memory of the events of Jesus' life. According to Mark, Jesus is alone in Gethsemane at the critical moment. He leaves most of the disciples at some place in the garden and goes farther on, taking with him only Peter, James, and John. He then leaves even these three and goes somewhat farther to pray concerning his choice: "Father, for you all things are possible; remove this cup from me; yet, not what I want, but what you want" (Mark 14:36). He returns to find the three asleep. He awakens them to tell them to lend him some support; he retreats to pray and returns two times more to find them again asleep. He has been left to make the choice entirely alone. From the point of view of history, who would have known what he was praying about or that he was making the choice at all? But from the point of view of story, Mark knows that Jesus must face his fate and choose: he is a hero.

DIVINE ENEMIES

Heroes had divine enemies. Without such enemies they would never have faced the tragic circumstances that showed forth their character, for heroes were superior to mere mortals and would have overcome and won in any contest with lesser foes. It is the fact of divine power set against them that intrigues us as readers. We all live in an ambiguous world, perhaps a random world, but one that at times seems to be set against us. With it we must struggle by our best efforts, yet we know that one day it will overwhelm us also. Homer tells us that Zeus has two urns from which he dispenses the fate of each individual, "an urn of evils, an urn of blessings" (*Iliad* 24.528). He mixes evil and good for the (semi)fortunate, and only trouble for the unfortunate. No one, apparently, receives only blessing, for "such is the way the gods spun life for unfortunate mortals, that we live in unhappiness, but the gods themselves have no sorrows" (24.525–26).

The heroes fight against the gods most like themselves or against those with whom they compete most directly, which is at times the same deity. Jesus fights throughout his public life with the divine enemy most (un)like him and against whom he competes directly, the Devil, the other claimant to the title Lord. In Mark, the battle is engaged immediately after his commissioning as Son of God at the baptism administered by John the Baptist. The Spirit impels him into the desert to begin his fight with the Devil. He then casts out demonic powers from many oppressed and ill people. In Luke's story, this activity brings to Jesus a vision, and he stands watching "Satan fall from heaven like a flash of lightning" (Luke 10:18). The point is that he is the captain of the forces of the kingdom of God that have invaded the realm of the enemy; the preaching of the gospel is designed to cause people to "turn from darkness to light and from the power of Satan to God" (Acts 26:18). For the Greeks the divine enemies were inimical fate and the ambiguous jealousies of the gods, who as often fought against worshipers as heard their prayers. For the Persians, these forces were personified as the Devil and his minions, who sought to control the fortunes of all of creation. This is the form of the story as it was inherited by segments of Judaism after the exile, and this is the form of the enemy that stands behind the Gospels. Again, the scale is greater and the divine enemies are different from the ones in the stories of Homer, but the role is the same.

Rulers as Human Enemies

Both God and the inimical gods, understood to be the Devil and his demons, use the agency first of the Jerusalem authorities and then the

Roman government to persecute and finally crucify Jesus. His life is seen to be lived out on two levels, in two dimensions, the earthly and human, on the one hand, and the invisible and divine, on the other. In the book of Acts, we find that the Jerusalemites were part of this life in two dimensions. They are told by Peter about Jesus, that "this man, handed over to you according to the definite plan and foreknowledge of God, you crucified and killed by the hands of those outside the law" (Acts 2:23). And later, in a prayer to God, Peter again claims that "both Herod and Pontius Pilate, with the Gentiles and the peoples of Israel, gathered together against your holy servant Jesus, whom you anointed, to do whatever your hand and your plan had predestined to take place" (Acts 4:27–28). Jesus' life and career are determined by higher powers, but played out on the human level among the various authorities and rulers who unconsciously follow dictates they do not understand.

Between the unknowable counsel of the highest God and the unwitting human rulers are the spiritual enemies, the inimical gods, who motivate the evil human agents into the persecution and destruction of the righteous ones. This produces a cosmic drama of four elements: God and the Devil unseen, their agents on earth, the human rulers who persecute the righteous, and the righteous themselves. The basic idea is old in the culture, stemming from Zoroastrianism but finding its own type of expression in Greece. The persecutors of the righteous are unwitting agents of the inimical gods, who themselves are unwitting agents in the plan of God. Only God knows the whole story, yet to some small extent the righteous on earth are allowed to see into the mystery. Paul expresses this well in his discussion of the mystery of the wisdom of God, that "None of the rulers of this age understood this; for if they had, they would not have crucified" Jesus (1 Cor. 2:8). They were unwitting agents of the divine plan.

The old idea that the human agents of evil would suffer the consequences for their acts, even though they are, without knowing it themselves, fulfilling a divine plan, is found in the Christian understanding of the fall of Jerusalem in A.D. 70 to the Roman legions. The Gospels predict the destruction as a consequence of the murder of Jesus. In the parable of the vineyard (Mark 12:1–9), when the tenants (Israel) refuse to pay the owner (God) his proper share of the crops, the owner sends first several servants (prophets) and then his son (Jesus) to collect.

When the son of the owner is killed, Jesus asks: "What then will the owner of the vineyard do? He will come and destroy the tenants and give the vineyard to others" (Mark 12:9). In Luke, Jesus weeps over the city of Jerusalem, and predicts that it will be destroyed, "because you did not recognize the time of your visitation from God" (Luke 19:44). In Matthew, in the parable of the marriage feast, when the invited guests refuse to come to the feast and then kill the servants sent to them, "The king was enraged. He sent his troops, destroyed those murderers, and burned their city" (Matt. 22:7). This is the basis for the Christian understanding of the eventual murder of thousands of Christians as martyrs. Eventually the Roman government was seen, especially in the book of Revelation, as the agent of the Devil in its persecution of Christians. They, like Jesus, were part of a cosmic drama far beyond their individual lives, playing a real part in a real, but unseen, divine plan.

The Test of Character

Jesus experienced several critical tests of character and resolve in his story that often go unnoticed as tests, given our inheritance of the doctrine of Jesus as the Second Person of the Trinity. How could a test of character be a real one, if Jesus is God—"God cannot be tempted by evil" things (James 1:13). The point is not a small one, for during the theological controversies of later centuries it was discovered that if Christ were not fully human, then he could not stand in human stead for the salvation of the world; he could not die in the place of what he was not. But we at this point are not at the time of the Christological controversies of the fourth and fifth centuries, but much earlier, when not only the leader but all of the followers were required to show the quality of their souls through testing and suffering.

Recall that the first thing Jesus is required to do by God is to go out into the desert alone and be tempted by the Devil. More than once the offended "scribes and the Pharisees . . . cross-examine[d] him about many things, lying in wait for him, to catch him in something he might say" (Luke 11:53–54). His own closest disciple rebukes him for announcing that he is to go to his death, for the Messiah could not possibly be one to die; Jesus must stand against Peter as a representative of Satan. And later the chief priests send emissaries "to trap him in what he said"

(Mark 12:13). He faces his most critical moment in the garden of Geth-semane, where he "offered up prayers and supplications, with loud cries and tears, to the one who was able to save him from death, and he was heard because of his reverent submission" (Heb. 5:7). His prayers were heard, we assume, and he submitted, but he was not saved from death. Finally he goes literally to trial, caught for something that he probably did say about the temple, but that was garbled and turned into an accusation by false witnesses. Mark has the witnesses testify, "We heard him say, 'I will destroy this temple that is made with hands, and in three days I will build another, not made with hands'" (14:58). He is condemned and after that repeatedly beaten and finally crucified.

His trials teach him and test his character. In a passage clearly draw-ing on the heroic model and one seldom used in the later Christian world, the writer of the Letter to the Hebrews tells us that Jesus "learned obedience through what he suffered" (Heb. 5:8). What could this mean in the world of the creeds? The text continues that God "per-fected" him through sufferings (Heb. 2:10; 5:9). The idea of a messiah who is killed was found in the Scriptures in Isaiah 53, the famous pas-sage about the suffering servant. But that was not the general expecta-tion in the culture for the messiah; he should have been a victorious military leader like David (recall the title "son of David"). We see the same expectation in Peter's rebuke of Jesus: he cannot be allowed to be killed. That he should learn through and be perfected through suffering and then be killed is the heroic model. For the hero, *pathei mathos*, "learning comes through suffering."

BAIT IN A TRAP

Jesus was very definitely seen to be a test of the character of others, as a kind of bait in a trap that went unrecognized. Simeon in Luke's Gospel declares that the child Jesus "is destined for the falling and the rising of many" (Luke 2:34), but that fact was hidden even from his own disci-ples. The Gospel writers tell us that not until after his resurrection did the disciples understand who he was. For example, when Jesus taught of the gate of the fold of sheep, the gatekeeper, and the good shepherd, the disciples "did not understand what he was saying to them" (John 10:6). And after Jesus entered Jerusalem riding on a donkey, thus

fulfilling an Old Testament prophecy, the disciples were uncompre-
hending. Something was going on that they did not get: "His disciples
did not understand these things at first; but when Jesus was glorified,
then they remembered ..." (John 12:16). Mark makes their stupidity a
central feature of his Gospel. In a classic passage, Jesus is warning them:

> "Beware of the yeast of the Pharisees and the yeast of Herod." They said
> to one another, "It is because we have no bread." And becoming aware
> of it, Jesus said to them, "Why are you talking about having no bread?
> Do you still not perceive or understand? Are your hearts hardened? Do
> you have eyes, and fail to see? Do you have ears, and fail to hear?"
> (Mark 8:15–18)

Mark paints the disciples as the twelve stooges. The motif is known
among scholars as the "incomprehension of the disciples" and is part of
the "messianic secret." This is a literary device of Mark the author and a
central feature of his Gospel. Jesus is unknown to all, even to his disciples, who should know him. All the demons, of course, recognize him
immediately—he is like a light on a dark night to them—but Jesus commands them to be silent. Occasionally an enlightened human does recognize him, and even Peter finally declares, "You are the Christ," but Jesus
each time "ordered them not to tell anyone about him" (Mark 8:30).

The motif may be found to some extent in each of the Gospels, reflecting both literary design and historical reality. Most people, in fact,
especially those in authority, didn't recognize Jesus as Christ during
his lifetime. He did not seem to fit the mold of a classic prophet or a
messiah or a new king of Israel—he did not fit their expectations. When
Jesus begins teaching in the temple in John, the authorities are amazed:
"How has this man become learned, never having been educated?"
(John 7:15, GJR). The crowd is divided: some side with him because of
the miracles he performs; others including the authorities turn against
him because he arose in Galilee. When Nicodemus attempts to defend
him, he is rebuked: "Search [the Scriptures] and you will see that no
prophet is to arise from Galilee" (John 7:52).

One of the most difficult issues raised by Jesus was his willfulness in
breaking traditional rules connected with observance of Mosaic Law—
he is perceived as a breaker of the Sabbath and other traditions. He as-
sociates not with rulers and the upper classes, but with prostitutes, tax

collectors, and society's rejects. He does not seem to care about what he should—he recommends paying taxes to Caesar and seems not to want an independent political kingdom. In John, he predicts his death on a cross, and the crowd disbelieves again over the issue of a Christ who can be killed: "We have heard from the law that the Messiah remains forever. How can you say that the Son of Man must be lifted up [i.e., crucified]?" (John 12:34).

This was the final proof that he was not the fulfillment of Jewish expectation—he was not the messiah because the messiah could never be crucified, and he was not a prophet or the king of the Jews. The law had pronounced a curse on the crucified; therefore, or so it seemed, this man was not the promised one. So in the accounts of the trial he is beaten, humiliated, and mocked. He had told them to live righteously and exposed their hypocrisies; he seemed to be claiming some status, and that offended them. So they blindfold him and hit him and say "Prophesy!" He is made to wear a royal robe and crown of thorns, and they bow before him saying, "Hail, king of the Jews!" They crucify him and say, "Let the Messiah, the King of Israel, come down from the cross now, so that we may see and believe!" (Mark 15:32).

These were bad ideas. The bait in the trap comes in deceiving forms. It is meant to trick. It is designed in such a way that one is not supposed to be able to recognize it for what it really is, only to react to it according to one's own inner character and be exposed. In words from John's Gospel: "This is the judgment, that the light has come into the world, and people loved darkness rather than light because their deeds were evil" (John 3:19). The proof that these were bad ideas, that Jesus was something not to be mocked or left unrecognized, comes immediately—darkness at noon for three hours during the crucifixion and the rending of the curtain of the temple from top to bottom at the point of death (Mark 15:33, 38); Matthew adds an earthquake (27:51).

Recall that Odysseus returned home as a wrinkled and dirty beggar. How he was received determined life or death for those he met in his house. He did not look like the real Odysseus, the real lord of the island, but he was. He did not appear to have the power of the gods in his hands for retribution, but he did.

Herodotus tells us the story of Onesilus, who began a Cypriot revolt against the Persian Empire but was killed by traitors. The people of

Amathus, at whose town the war had begun, severed his head and hung it up above the gates. Eventually it became hollow and bees used it for a hive, filling it with honeycomb. The people understood the threat: their act of *hubris* had made them liable to suffer the wrath of the dead but righteous man, and the skull filled with honey was the enigma. They were instructed by an oracle to take the head down and bury it and thereafter to honor Onesilus as a hero with an annual sacrifice (*Histories* 5.114).

In another story Herodotus tells of a wicked Persian governor who stole the treasures out of the shrine of the dead hero Protesilaus. Eventually he was besieged and captured, and when one of the guards began roasting a salt fish, it began to jump on the coals as though alive. The governor said, "This prodigy . . . applies to me: Protesilaus is telling me that though he is as dead as a dried fish, he yet has power from the gods to punish the one who wrongs him" (9.120). The governor and his son were both killed. That signs and portents should accompany the dead hero who has been mocked and unjustly treated was an old motif; they were signals from God that the hero had been wronged and that injustice would have its consequences.

Early Death in the Midst of Life

Jesus was killed in his thirties, as far as we can determine. Luke tells us that he was about thirty years old when he began his ministry (Luke 3:23), and an investigation of the Greek phrasing tells us that "thirty" does not mean exactly thirty. So Jesus was either twenty-eight or twenty-nine, or thirty-one or thirty-two, approximately, if Luke is correct. The length of his ministry is in question. Mark seems to have Jesus complete everything in one year, though this is not so stated; nor is it an issue in Mark—he never addresses the problem directly. John's account requires at least three years because of the number of major festivals mentioned and the large amount of travel he relates. Luke includes a unique parable of the barren fig tree that did not bear fruit for three years (Luke 13:6–9). The owner instructs the keeper to cut it down, but the keeper asks that it be left one more year that he might fertilize it and tend it; if it should not bear fruit after that, then let it be cut down. There is no interpretation of this parable in the text, and we do not know with certainty to what it refers, but it seems that Jesus himself is the keeper and God is the owner. If so, Luke may be telling us that the ministry of Jesus lasted four years, after which the ministry to Israel was "cut down" with the crucifixion of Jesus and the gospel was sent to the Gentiles, as we learn from the book of Acts. Jesus, by this reckoning, was between thirty-three and thirty-five years old when he was killed.

Jesus died a death that defined his life. If one returns for a moment to the outlines of his life, the catechisms and baptismal creeds cited earlier in this chapter, it is his death that is the central point of focus around which the story turns. He was killed because of what he was—his lineage, his abilities, his character. The way the world was conceived, he had to be killed—he was light shining in darkness, and the darkness would try if it could to kill him. Paul understands that the real enemies Jesus faced were the spiritual demonic "rulers of this age" (1 Cor. 2:8). God had predestined it, but the demonic forces did not understand the plan; in attacking him they destroyed themselves. The hero is the bait in the trap, and his death seals the fate of the unrighteous. This is not as common a way of constructing reality any longer, but it was the way of those in the first century. Jesus' kind of life required his early and tragic death. If he had not been killed like one of the heroes, it would only have meant that he was not worthy of that status, that he was not a son of God, that he was not valuable enough to draw down on himself the jealousies of the gods or fate or the wrath of the powers and their religious authorities. The fact of his unjust death not only proved the real value of his life, it authenticated his right to complete the creedal journey, to ascend into heaven and someday stand as judge.

THE PRIZE OF IMMORTALITY

The heroes gained immortality for themselves because of their divine ancestry and their suffering. But among lesser souls, among mere mortals, there was little optimism concerning the possibilities for life after death. Mystery religions offered initiations and promises, a subject for a later chapter, but to judge from the vast majority of tomb inscriptions, few were persuaded. To paraphrase an ancient saying, many joined in the festival processions, but few actually believed. Even among the philosophers, whose profession led them to meditate on such questions, there was no settled opinion. Socrates, at the end of Plato's *Apology*, in his speech in his own defense at his final trial, tells the minority of the jury who voted for his acquittal:

> Death is one of two things. Either it is annihilation, and the dead have no consciousness of anything, or, as we are told, it is really a change—a migration of the soul from this place to another. (40c)

Socrates is ambivalent, even agnostic, although he clearly prefers the second possibility. Plato believed strongly in the immortality of the soul, as did members of most other sophisticated schools of thought, each in its own way. Epicurus (341–270 B.C.), however, claimed that the soul was material and perished with the body. He taught his followers that "The most terrifying of evils, death, is nothing to us, since when we exist, death is not present. But when death is present, then we do not exist" (Diogenes Laertius 10.125). So the Epicureans repeated as a kind of gospel, "Death is nothing to us." Most people, apparently, agreed at least with the general conclusion that after death we do not survive in any substantial form.

But Jesus rose from the dead. It is difficult in the extreme for us to understand how this claim might have sounded in the world in which it was preached. Many uninformed Christian teachers today have claimed that the resurrection of Jesus was the one most unique feature of the gospel, that of all the other gods and heroes of antiquity Jesus alone rose from the dead. That, as Justin so clearly taught us above, is not even close to true. All the heroes, or nearly all, rose from the dead and ascended to heaven. But this was an impossibility for a mere human and a shocking claim for any real and historical man who lived in recent times. It meant that in our times one like the heroes of old had appeared among us and taught and suffered and died; because he rose from the dead, this was certain, and he had to be taken seriously. His resurrection was authentication of his status. In Paul's speech to the Athenians in the book of Acts, the listeners are to understand that Jesus is God's appointed one because God has "given assurance to all by raising him from the dead" (Acts 17:31).

In a fascinating passage that shows the interweaving of Jewish and Greco-Roman ideas, Paul wrote to the Romans, living in the very heart of the empire, that Jesus was "from the seed of David according to the

flesh, designated as Son of God ... by resurrection from the dead"
(Rom. 1:3–4, GJR). The Greek text would allow the translation "son of
God," or "a son of God," or even "a son of a god," though the last is
clearly not the intention of Paul. The language itself, however, points to
the fact that resurrection is proof that Jesus has God as father; it was
proof of his divine genealogy. Paul sets up a parallelism here of two op-
posites: son of David and Son of God. Jesus is son of David according to
the flesh, that is, a direct descendant of King David according to his
human genealogy. That genealogy was, one assumes, at least claimed
for him if not actually kept intact; the genealogies for Jesus found in
Matthew and Luke do not agree with each other. But how do we know
that he is Son of God? Recall that one does not need to be raised from
the dead or have a virgin birth to be called "son of God" among Jews.
And those who were so called, the kings, did not need to contrast the
designation to their fleshly genealogy; it was in fact because of it that
they were kings and adopted sons of God. Jesus is shown to be "son of
God" because of the proof provided by the resurrection, something that
no Jewish king needed or could possibly obtain for the title. We are so
used to thinking that there is only one Son of God and one culture in-
forming our texts (that so many try to construct from the Old Testament alone), we forget that Paul could write in all seriousness, "in fact
there are many gods and many lords" (1 Cor. 8:5). He doesn't believe in
the worth of these gods and lords—he is no pluralist—but he does not
deny their existence. And he knows the stories and so do his Roman
readers. They all know that Jesus was son of God because he rose from
the dead. That is what the stories had taught: if you rise from the dead,
you had a divinity as one of your parents. Eventually Paul himself and
some of his readers would be killed by order of one of these "lords,"
these so-called sons of god in the person of the Roman emperor.

But here Jesus and the Christians made a radical claim. Jesus had
risen from the dead and so could anyone—now eternal life was available
for all who dared to follow him to the end of their lives. The claim that a
normal individual could gain immortality was not entirely new, not
without precedent, as we shall see. But it had been reserved for the few,
the initiates in secret mysteries or the expert practitioners of philosophy.
The teachings of Jesus, on the other hand, were for everyone, but especially for those who could not afford initiations and were uneducated in

philosophy. They were for the vast majority of the people in the lowest classes: "Blessed are you poor, for yours is the kingdom of God."

The Dead Hero as Protector and Judge

And finally, the dead Jesus becomes, in early Christian preaching, perhaps the most dangerous being ever to have been born, on the one hand, a protector of those who are his own and, on the other, one who will someday return from heaven to judge the living and the dead.

We have seen that the dead hero was a protector of the living, of those who turned to him or her for help, and an avenger of wrong, both against those who had wronged the hero, alive or dead, and against those who wronged the worshipers. A classic case of this is found in the *Libation Bearers* of Aeschylus. The wife of Agamemnon and her lover, Aegisthus, had murdered him on the day of his triumphant return from Troy. Agamemnon's son was exiled and his daughter held in virtual slavery. In a chilling opening scene, the two now grown children and a chorus of assistants gather at Agamemnon's grave and call his spirit out of the ground to avenge himself and them. As they pray, the chorus observes that "powers gather under ground to give aid" (376–77), and Orestes prays, "Zeus, Zeus, force up from below ground the delayed destruction" on his mother and her lover (382–83). Subsequently, the dead hero brings destruction on those who wronged him in one of the most famous plays written in antiquity.

Socrates, at the end of Plato's *Apology*, tells those who voted for his acquittal not to grieve that he has been condemned unjustly and is about to die, for

> If on arrival in the other world, beyond the reach of our so-called justice, one will find there the true judges who are said to preside in those courts, Minos and Rhadamanthus and Aeacus and Triptolemus and all those other half-divinities who were upright in their earthly life, would that be an unrewarding journey? (41a)

These upright among the "half-divinities," heroes with one divine and one human parent, had traditionally been appointed the judges of the dead in the underworld, granting rewards and punishments after death to individuals for deeds done while alive. Minos and Rhadamanthus were brothers, sons of Zeus and the virgin Europa, and Aeacus was the son of Zeus by Aegina; all three were famous as lawgivers and for personal integrity. According to another passage in Plato, the three are appointed judges of the dead at the crossroads from which one path leads to the Isles of the Blessed and the other to Tartarus, the place of torture of the wicked (*Gorgias* 524a). Triptolemus was son of the king of Attica, born at Eleusis, where he established the cult of Demeter known as the Eleusinian mysteries. According to the myth of the cult, he taught farming and the mysteries of Demeter to humanity as a kind of culture hero and after death was made a god.

Earlier I observed that emperor Antoninus Pius, if he had ever had the chance to read the Old Roman Creed (which he did not), may have wondered why Jesus in Christian understanding replaced the older Greek heroes who already held the position of judges of the dead. It is here that the stories of the heroes and that of Jesus part company. Jesus and the Gospel writers were heirs to more than one major culture; through the other branch of Indo-European influence, specifically Persian Zoroastrianism, they had inherited apocalyptic eschatology as it was mediated by Jewish writers in the period from the Exile to the first century. Eschatology was not unknown among the Greeks, as we saw in the poem of Hesiod on the Four Ages, but it was never as developed in Greece as it was in Persia and then among some sects of the Jews. There, one major role of the quintessential hero had been projected into the future—he was the captain of the forces of righteousness that would destroy the forces of the Devil and his minions in a cataclysmic last battle, to be followed by a new and clean heaven and earth. Among the Jews this role was assimilated to old ideals of the Israelite kingdom of David and Canaanite mythology, and the coming one became the future "son of David," the anointed one ("messiah") of God. Yet neither the Zoroastrian captain nor the Jewish messiah was supposed to suffer horribly and die on a cross. These were never thought to have to endure death, resurrection, and ascension, but instead were supposed to march on to a divinely directed military victory on a cosmic scale and remain forever. This was not yet the career of Jesus. Christians used these apocalyptic ideas to understand how Jesus would someday return from heaven a second time to fulfill this role. As for his first appearance, Justin was right—the story of Jesus, so far, was the story of a hero.

Chapter 5

MANY CHRISTS

That Jesus was a Jewish man in Palestine whose life story was under-stood against the background of the stories of the Greek heroes of the wider Greco-Roman world had rather important consequences. He was a miracle worker, a teacher of divine wisdom much like a philoso-pher, and an innocent victim of the violence of the rulers, insofar as one who opposed the religious and political power structures of his day could be called innocent; he then rose from the dead and ascended to heaven. All that was simple and familiar enough from the stories of the heroes. To become a Christian one had only to follow the leader and then be faithful to the end to inherit the promise of eternal life.

But how are we to understand Jesus himself? What kind of being was he? This is not a question of personal assessment, whether he was kind or truthful or something else. For that we have ample evidence from his sayings, although those teachings have led to rather differing interpretations of him. Yet consider one of his most famous sayings:

> Come to me, all you that are weary and are carrying heavy burdens, and
> I will give you rest. Take my yoke upon you, and learn from me; for I
> am gentle and humble in heart, and you will find rest for your souls.
> For my yoke is easy, and my burden is light." (Matt. 11:28–30)

It is a beautiful saying and typical of the sort of thing that has drawn so many people to Christianity over the centuries. But what kind of per-son could say such a thing? What kind of being can give all who are weary—and that is nearly all of us—rest for the soul? Or look at another saying, one that many scholars put in the earliest layers of the tradition of Jesus: "Foxes have holes, and birds of the air have nests; but the Son of Man has nowhere to lay his head" (Matt. 8:20). Normal living things have somewhere to live: normal people have houses; even lowly birds and foxes have nests and holes. But one as exalted as the Son of Man is sleeping in the bushes. What kind of person says that?

The question is about what class of being Jesus belongs in, if one recalls the discussion in Chapter 3 of Hesiod's Four Classes of Beings: gods, *daimones*, heroes, and humans. The classes of being by the time of Jesus had been under discussion by some of the most intelligent minds in history for several centuries, and the "theology" of the classes had become far more sophisticated than it was in Hesiod's day. Deity itself had become something quite different from the simple gods of Homer and Hesiod's time. Now there were not only the gods, but the One God of the various types of monotheism to be found nearly everywhere, and several layers of lesser and lesser divine beings stretching all the way from the Infinite One to the earth and below—the Great Chain of Being as it came to be known. Now there were even more possibilities for understanding "being," and the melding of the cultures of Palestine and the Greco-Roman world had produced a rather bewildering array of additional mixtures and new types altogether. And this array of choices stood as the multifaceted conceptual framework available to the early Christians as they began the long process of trying to answer the question, what kind of being was he?

It seems that there never was unanimity of opinion concerning Jesus, and that he himself did little to clear things up. Recall the famous question he asks his disciples in the middle of the Gospel of Mark:

> "Who do people say that I am?" And they answered him, "John the Baptist; and others, Elijah; and still others, one of the prophets." He asked them, "But who do you say that I am?" Peter answered him, "You are the Messiah." (Mark 8:27–29)

Four different answers are given, and one of the points of the Gospel of Mark is to redefine the correct one, to claim that Jesus is the messiah but not the type of messiah Peter was looking for. Mark, therefore, gives a fifth answer. The confession that Jesus was Messiah, of course, is what made a Jew into a Christian Jew, but immediately there was fundamental diversity of opinion about what that might mean.

There were different opinions in the culture of Palestine as to what kind of being the messiah would be, and where the gospel was preached to Gentiles, there was no concept of a messiah at all. A clear message gained from reading the New Testament is that early Christian teachers and apostles argued rather strongly for different interpretations, different ways of understanding Christ. There was at the core one Jesus, but as soon as the people who followed him as leader began to try to understand what he was, they created a bewildering array of answers—they produced many Christs.

We have been kept from appreciating this diversity of opinion in the early history of the Church by the original and most influential Church historian, Eusebius of Caesarea (ca. 260–340), the "Father of Church History," and by some of his predecessors. Eusebius lived through one of the most dangerous and exciting periods of the Church: he was forty-three when the Great Persecution broke out in 303 under the emperor Diocletian (r. 284–305), which lasted until the edict of toleration, in the Eastern empire by the dying pagan Galerius in 311, and in the West by Constantine in 312. Eusebius spent time in jail as a Christian confessor during the persecution and became bishop of Caesarea on the coast of Palestine about 315. He then found himself an important player in the single greatest debate over the nature of Christ the Church ever encountered, the Arian controversy, which led to the Council of Nicaea and the Nicene Creed, the basic orthodox Christian creed still employed today. The rooting out of heresy and the defense of the true doctrine of the Church were substantial parts of Eusebius's life and work. His *History of the Church* is the earliest such account to come down to us; the last part of the work was finished in 323. In it he traces the story of the Church from its beginning to his own day. Eusebius inherited his theories of the church and the rise of heresy from a second-century Jewish Christian, Hegesippus. Eusebius writes that Hegesippus claimed that until the reign of Trajan,

> the church remained a virgin, pure and uncorrupted, while those who were trying to corrupt the healthy standard of the savior's preaching, if any even existed, were still until then in some unclear darkness as though lurking in a hole. But when the holy chorus of the apostles had in different ways come to the end of life, and that generation of those counted worthy to listen with their own ears to their divine wisdom also

passed away, then the conspiracy of godless error took its beginning through the deceit of heterodox teachers, who, inasmuch as none of the apostles still remained, with bared heads tried to preach the falsely named "knowledge" against the preaching of the truth. (*Histeria Ecclesiastica* 3.32.7–8, GJR)

For Eusebius and his source Hegesippus, heresy began with Gnosticism, the "falsely named knowledge" that took its name from the Greek word for "knowledge," *gnôsis*. Up until that time, according to Eusebius, the apostles and their direct disciples had been alive and kept the doctrine of the Church true and "orthodox," befitting the purity of the virgin Church. We still suffer under this false account of the origins of the Church—the Reformation, in part based on this misconception, with its cry "*Sola Scriptura*" ("Scripture only") attempted to jump back in time over the history of Catholicism to the pure origins that the New Testament apparently represented. But at the time of the New Testament, the Church was not "pure" in its doctrine: its doctrine had not yet been systematized and established into a theological whole; there was as yet no "pure" doctrine, no orthodoxy.

During the period between Hegesippus and Eusebius, there developed a rather winsome legend about the composition of the Apostles' Creed that may have been known to Eusebius; it certainly supported his position. We find the term "Apostles' Creed" used for the first time in a letter from about 390 of St. Ambrose (ca. 339–397), bishop of Milan, but by his time the legend of its composition was already fully in place. Earlier, just after the year 200, we find in the opening lines of the apocryphal *Acts of Thomas* another interesting legend, that the twelve apostles while still in Jerusalem divided up the regions of the world into twelve parts and drew lots for the part to which each was to go as a missionary. Yet there is no mention of the legend of the Apostles' Creed. Sometime between those dates there arose the story that these apostles, about to leave on their journeys, discussed what they should preach and came to the decision that they should frame a message on which all would agree so that they would all be preaching the same gospel and teaching the same things. So, as the legend explains, each apostle contributed a phrase until the whole of the creed was composed, and then each carried that identical message throughout the world. The preaching of each original apostle, the legend would have us believe, was identical to that of every other apostle and very much in form and substance like the creeds so familiar in later times. This idea served the needs of Eusebius and the Church in the fourth century well in its battle against heresy and allowed it to claim that the great creeds of the Church were in fact based on the very message of the original apostles.

But the legend was not true. The picture of the Church it calls to mind is that of a tree with straight trunk that gradually branches out in many directions, symbolizing the single beginning of the true faith eventuating in the many and various "heresies" of later times. The actual historical picture is much more like an hourglass or barbell, with wide bottom, narrow middle, and wide top, symbolizing rather wide differences of opinion at the beginning of the history of the Church, opinions that were then narrowed by the age of the creeds beginning with Constantine in 325 into a single orthodoxy lasting until the time of the Reformation, and then bulging again into the rather spectacular diversity of Christianity in the modern world. The Church did not begin as a pure virgin and then later suffer attacks from heretics. There were no "orthodox" or "heretics" in the beginning—the first Christians did not originally know quite what to think of Jesus beyond the fact that he was their hero and leader and that they should follow him as best they could to the death. They started with a wide variety of ideas in their attempts to explain his career and person, often quite contradictory, drawn from the various possibilities already present in their culture and experience. These they combined and interpreted in new ways to produce the various views of Jesus and the Christian gospel we see so clearly in their writings. One glaring example we often miss today has been pointed out earlier—the combination of the idea of the Jewish messiah with that of the Greek hero, which answered the question brilliantly, How could the messiah be killed? He was the Son of God, and the sons of the gods were always getting killed, and then ascending to heaven; but someday, according to the traditional function of the messiah, he would return from there to "judge the living and the dead."

Another of the grave difficulties facing the modern interpreter of early Christianity is the fact that the early Christians necessarily, because of their own Jewish origins, used the Old Testament to try to explain the life history of Jesus. They had something new and wonderful, even spiritually intoxicating, in the message of Jesus and his living spiritual presence among them. Yet they naturally tried to show that this new way of being, this spirituality of the Christian way of life, was somehow foreshadowed and prophesied in the Old Testament. And they were brilliant at seeing Jesus and his life story there, at finding new ways of understanding old passages, at grasping the true, that is, Christian, interpretation of the prophecies of the Hebrew prophets. No matter that such interpretations had not been found there before; the era had changed. Had not the risen Jesus, in his resurrection appearance to the gathered disciples in Jerusalem, "opened their minds to understand the scriptures" (Luke 24:45)? Paul tells us that the stories of the Old Testament, in this case the desert wanderings of the children of Israel, "were written down to instruct us, on whom the ends of the ages have come" (1 Cor. 10:11). The old age of the Law had passed, and the new age of the Spirit was dawning; few people understood that fact as well as did Paul, who had been deeply involved in both. For Paul, the Law of Israel, the Old Testament, was a tutor that led one to Christ (Gal. 3:24), but it was no longer the way to live one's spiritual life.

A number of Jewish and pagan detractors objected that the Christians were using the Scriptures in ways not intended by their original authors, but such criticisms had little effect on Christians, for whom the resurrected presence of Christ as spirit in the Church was proof beyond refutation. And the critique cut both ways; the objection contained its own refutation, according to the theories of divine inspiration long honored in ancient society. The prophet did not control the prophecy; that was of divine origin and its meaning was of divine, not human content. Whatever the individual prophet might think the prophecy meant or what the audience addressed might think was immaterial or even missed the point entirely. That fact can be demonstrated a number of times from ancient stories. The prophecy had originated with God and meant what God intended, not what the prophet or the audience thought was intended. In fact, the intention of the prophet and the understanding of the audience could often be a guide to what the prophecy did not mean.

Nearly four hundred years earlier, Plato had defined the problem and its solution in such a way as to leave no reasonable refutation: the prophecy was larger than and even hidden from the prophet; the poem was greater than the poet; the song was more substantial than the singer. In an encounter with the rhapsode Ion, Socrates has the following discussion. Rhapsodes were professional reciters of poetry, especially Homeric and tragic poetry, who performed in competitions in the theaters and amphitheaters all over the Greco-Roman world. We have had occasion earlier to mention the vast audiences they could draw. Competitions between rhapsodes at the Olympic and other games, in addition to competitions devoted exclusively to recitations, were held throughout the Greco-Roman world with prizes of enormous worth awarded to the winners. They performed a basic function of inculcating the heroic ideals into the population at large; they were a large part of the entertainment industry of antiquity. In his conversation, Socrates examines the seemingly unexplainable ability of Ion to hold his audiences spellbound, weeping and horrified, laughing and joyful, while he himself personally knows almost nothing about the actual skills and actions he describes in the Homeric poems. Ion cannot drive a chariot or fight a battle and has no ability at wise counsel. Socrates, in offering a solution, describes Ion as a kind of inspired interpreter of the poet, as though Homer, like a magnet, has magnetized another piece of iron, Ion, whom Homer has touched by his art. Socrates says of the inspiration of the poet (and finally prophet):

> The poet is a light thing, and winged and holy, and not able to be a poet before he becomes inspired and out of his senses and his mind is not in him. As long as he has this [mind] in his possession, no one is able to chant poetry or prophesy. (Plato *Ion* 534b, GJR)

As long as they are in a normal state of mind, poets cannot sing and prophets cannot chant prophecy. Prophecy in all ancient cultures, that of the Hebrews included, was most often poetic chant and song, a sign of inspiration.

That the Christians could claim against their Jewish and pagan detractors that the prophets had prophesied about Jesus could not in fact be met with a denial based on the reason that the prophet or the original audience would not have understood the prophecy in such a way. If these were genuine prophecies at all, the prophets were by definition under the inspiration of God and not in their normal minds when they prophesied; likely they did not understand what they had said at all. Otherwise it was not prophecy from God, but merely the statements of angry human beings denouncing the failings of their contemporaries. No other possibilities existed: either the prophets were possessed and out of their normal minds, or what was said was not prophecy from God. So the prophets, from the Christian perspective, could prophecy to their own time and about Jesus in the future, no matter what their opponents claimed, and given the ancient understanding about prophecy, they carried the argument. No one, neither the prophets nor the self-proclaimed descendants of the prophets, were greater than the prophecies themselves, for the prophecies were directly from God about what God wanted them to be about and were not under the control of anyone on earth, let alone those descendants of the children of Israel whom the very prophecies condemned over and over again.

☙━━◆━━❧

THE FACT THAT THE EARLY CHRISTIANS made extensive use of both Old Testament and Greco-Roman images in their attempts to understand Jesus produced a number of difficulties and ambiguities both for themselves and for us in the modern world, one of which is visible in our earliest account of a Christian worship service preserved in a pagan source, the letter from Pliny the Younger, governor of Bithynia, to emperor Trajan, written about 110, that we had occasion to refer to earlier. Pliny had begun a persecution of the many Christians in his area because of a series of anonymous accusations, and in a letter to Trajan he describes what he had discovered in his investigation about the manner in which Christians conducted their services:

> They affirmed, moreover, that this had been the whole of either their crime or error, that they were accustomed on a specific day to convene before dawn, and to sing a hymn to Christ as to a god antiphonally among themselves, and to bind themselves under an oath not for any crime, but that they not commit any thefts or robberies or adulteries, nor violate a trust, nor deny a deposit when called upon to return it. When these things were completed, it had been customary to go away, and to come together again for the taking of food, common, however, and harmless. (*Epistulae* 10.96, GJR)

The "certain day" was of course Sunday, the first day of the week, when these Christians in northern Asia Minor met twice, once before the workday began and again in the evening for the Eucharist. Sunday did not become an official holiday until it was so designated by Constantine in 321. In the predawn service two elements are singled out, the singing of an antiphonal hymn "to Christ as to a god" and a mutually binding oath to uphold certain basic moral precepts.

What Pliny refers to in his report of the binding oath to avoid immoral practices is unclear. The moral strictures against theft, robbery, adultery, and the rest are common enough in Greco-Roman ethics; there were laws everywhere against those sorts of things. The common misconception among Jews that Gentiles were sinners unlike themselves was, of course, false. One can see the prejudice, however, even in a passage from Paul's Letter to the Galatians. There Paul rebukes Peter for refusing to eat with gentile Christians, as he had been doing previously, because a group of Jewish-Christian rigorists had come up from Jerusalem and somehow influenced him to withdraw from meals with the Gentiles. In the midst of the argument, Paul states that "We are Jews by nature and not sinners from the Gentiles" (Gal. 2:15, GJR). But the "sinning" the Gentiles were doing here had to do with eating things forbidden by Old Testament and Pharisaic rules. They were "eating cheeseburgers," which Jews like Peter and the Jerusalem contingent refused to eat. The Gentiles' other great "sins" had mostly to do with "idolatry," the worship of the gods of Greece and Rome and the eating of food sacrificed to them, things that were sins only for those who thought so. Otherwise, basic ethics were quite similar throughout the Mediterranean world; it was nowhere permitted to murder or steal or commit adultery.

The early Christians were pledging themselves to obey some list of ethical standards. Mystery religions often required ethical standards of quite admirable quality from their adherents. Yet the Christians are reciting and swearing to uphold some list, and the fact of reciting a list is the point, for this was not a normal Greek practice so far as we know. Some have thought that they may have been reciting the Ten Commandments. Pliny, we assume, knew little or nothing about Old Testament law and would not have recognized the elements of the oath as having come from the Ten Commandments if such had been the case. His list includes things found in the Ten Commandments, but they are not in the same order, nor are all the elements Pliny lists among the Ten

Commandments. This is not the Ten Commandments. Their swearing not to commit a list of sins and crimes had a far more sinister origin, as we shall see.

The fact that the song is antiphonal is of no small interest. We do not know whether there was more to the meeting, but it likely also included some sermon or instruction from the leaders. The leaders are mentioned, if tangentially, by the fact of the antiphonal nature of the song. Also, later in the letter, Pliny describes his torture of "two female slaves who were said to be deaconesses." So there was some authority structure in place. It was common in other early Christian worship settings for the leaders to speak out something and the others present to respond with a simple but heartfelt word or phrase at the proper time. Such responses included "Amen," "Maranatha," "Come, Lord Jesus," or "Jesus is Lord," words and phrases we find in liturgical responses in several of our early texts. We do not know what the song was or what the words and responses were in Pliny's example, but by comparing other liturgies it seems likely that some of the responses included the declaration of Jesus as "Lord." Pliny tells us that the hymn is addressed to Christ "as to a god." This portion of the text of Pliny's letter is preserved for us in both in his own Latin and in a Greek translation (of a Latin excerpt in Tertullian) by Eusebius, but neither of these two languages has an indefinite article; we cannot tell from the language whether we should translate "to Christ as to a god" or "to Christ as to God." And here is the problem—he is probably Lord and some kind of god in the minds of these simple Christians, but what kind?

Doubting Thomas in the Gospel of John, after encountering the risen Christ, exclaims to him, "My Lord and my God?" (20:28). This phrase is more complicated than it appears on the surface. It was the required mode of address to the emperor Domitian (r. 81–96), who ruled while Pliny was working his way up in government and at the same time that the Gospel of John was being written. The Roman historian Suetonius, a friend of Pliny's and for a time present with him in Bithynia, tells us of a number of Domitian's pretentious acts, but among them was this:

> With equal arrogance, when he would dictate a formal letter in the name of his own administrators, it began thus: "Our Lord and God

order this to be done." From that time it became customary afterwards that neither in writing even nor speech he be addressed otherwise. (*Domitian* 13, GJR)

Domitian required that people address him as "Our Lord and God." Recall that the line between divinity and humanity could be easily crossed, and the sons of the gods, such as Heracles and Dionysus, became gods themselves. The Christians of Pliny's persecution sang a hymn to Christ as to some order of divine being, something quite natural in the Roman world. Doubting Thomas, however, is telling us that the proper person to whom such a title should be addressed is not the Roman emperor, but, in the Christian perspective, to the real Lord and God, the risen Christ.

That Jesus should have been understood as a divine being in human form was one of the more natural inferences from his abilities and career. We today are almost unable to appreciate how easily an ancient audience could jump to the conclusion that they were in the presence of a god on earth. We no longer have their frame of reference. It has been (wrongly) said at times by scholars that the "high view" of Jesus of the Gospel of John, in which he is called the Word of God and God, must have taken considerable time to develop and that lesser views describing Jesus as a prophet or teacher or some type of messiah came first. But consider the example given above about the mode of address demanded by Domitian. The book of Acts tells us of three additional instances that are even more remarkable.

In the first, Herod Agrippa I, ruler of Palestine from 37 to 44, decides to reconcile himself to the cities of Tyre and Sidon, with whom he had been at odds. The people invite him to address them, and

On an appointed day Herod put on his royal robes, took his seat on the platform, and delivered a public address to them. The people kept shouting, "The voice of a god, and not of a mortal!" (Acts 12:21–22)

The acclamation may have been mere sycophancy, which was common enough; fawning parasites fairly flocked around Domitian, referred to above. The writer of Acts goes on to say that because of his *hubris* in arrogating to himself divine prerogatives ("because he had not given the glory to God"), Agrippa was eaten by worms and died (12:23). But the people proclaim him a god, nonetheless.

Later, in the second case, as Paul and Barnabas are missionizing in south-central Asia Minor in the town of Lystra, Paul healed a lame man by commanding him, "Stand upright on your feet!"

> And the man sprang up and began to walk. When the crowds saw what Paul had done, they shouted in the Lycaonian language, "The gods have come down to us in human form!" Barnabas they called Zeus, and Paul they called Hermes, because he was the chief speaker. The priest of Zeus, whose temple was just outside the city, brought oxen and garlands to the gates; he and the crowds wanted to offer sacrifice. (Acts 14:10–13)

Paul and Barnabas are immediately classed as gods who have come down to earth because they have performed a miracle and healed a man. This apotheosis of Paul and Barnabas apparently took very little time, mere moments. It was the logical and natural inference given the frame of reference. From their youth the people had heard stories of the gods coming to earth in the guise of humans, and who but God could heal the lame? In order to stop them from sacrificing, to Barnabas and himself, Paul has to tear his clothes and shout, "We are mortals just like you." (14:15).

In the third example near the end of the book, as Paul is being taken as prisoner to Rome by ship, the ship is lost in a storm, and all aboard swim and struggle their way to land on the island of Malta. The inhabitants in their kindness make a fire to warm them, and Paul, in placing a bundle of sticks on the fire, is bitten by a viper that comes out of the bundle and hangs from his hand until he shakes it off. The onlookers decide that he must be a murderer and that the goddess Justice was bringing about his death despite his being saved from the sea.

> They were expecting him to swell up or drop dead, but after they had waited a long time and saw that nothing unusual had happened to him, they changed their minds and began to say that he was a god. (Acts 28:6)

Here Paul is declared to be a god in about an hour, more or less, because he survives a snakebite that should have killed him and would have killed an ordinary human. The onlookers conclude therefore that he could not be a mere mortal, that he must be a divine being on earth.

This is no longer our view of deity. Yet as foreign as it seems, there is continuity with our own view. The point needs some discussion if we are to understand the efforts of the early Christians to understand Jesus, the rise of Trinitarianism, and even the development of some of our own most productive modes of spirituality. From the point of view of the ancients, a human being, or better, someone who appeared to be human, could in fact be a divine being in disguise, especially if there were portents or miracles or other signs beyond the ordinary. This is not merely a "pagan" or "gentile" view. Such an understanding also existed among Jews.

In Genesis, three visitors to Abraham appeared to be human but were in fact heavenly beings. The account says that "Yahweh appeared to [Abraham] . . . and he [Abraham] lifted up his eyes and looked, and behold, three men were standing before him" (Gen. 18:1–2, GJR). These are the gods. If one looks at this passage from the standpoint of the ancient Near East in general, they are the high God of Israel and two of his ministers, lower deities here called angels, who appear as men. Later, Moses is hidden in a cleft of rock on Mount Sinai, covered with the hand of God while his glory passes by, and then is allowed to see God's back; he is prevented from seeing his face (Exod. 33:23). Here is Yahweh in his glory, and the sight of the glory of his face would have been fatal, but he has a hand and a back that somehow are seen; he is God in human form. At a much later time, this passage would be reinterpreted to mean that the Angel of the Lord and two other angels had appeared to Abraham and the Angel of the Lord had appeared to Moses, since the Lord himself came to be interpreted as the One, the monotheistic God of the universe, and could not lower himself to this anthropomorphic level. But that type of interpretation was to come much later and was apparently unknown to the author(s) of Genesis and Exodus. The Christians, of course, interpreted these anthropomorphic passages to be appearances of the heavenly Jesus before his incarnation.

We are used to monotheism today, and we are unused to this ancient view in which deity and humanity stood much closer to each other, where gods could look like humans and humans could be gods or gods and humans could mate and produce divine-human heroes. But the difference is not so foreign in fundamental conception to some of our most productive ideas about God. Consider two different (but simple-minded) models for understanding the nature of God, both monotheistic, both current in more sophisticated forms in today's world and that of the early Christians: God as something hard, and God as something fluid.

The first says that God is One and indivisible and with a nature that is absolutely bounded, "hard," if you will, like a bowling ball (without, of course, the holes). The spherical shape is an ancient concept; when early people thought about the shape of the One God, it had to be of the most perfect shape, that of the sphere. The "hardness" is the fact that the substance of God, the "stuff" God is made out of, could not be shared with anything and was reserved only for itself. All other things in the universe, all other beings, are merely creations, toys, "things," alien in essence to the one God. God is "wholly other," to use a famous phrase, different from creation and the universe in essence. This conception lay at the base of the Arian controversy that so deeply shook the theology and Christology of the fourth-century Church. Arius and his party did not allow that the essence of God could be shared; monotheism for Arius left God entirely alone in substance. Jesus had to be a creature, a creation, "Son of God" only in name, an honorific title, no matter how highly exalted above the rest of us or the rest of creation. For all the religious language of the love of God for creation, for people, in this model, it is never based on shared nature, like a parent for a child, but is at best that of an artisan for a piece of artwork; in this type of theological world, humans are "children of God" only in name, like mud dolls. It is, surprisingly, based on the old understanding of the absolute separation of gods and humans in polytheism found in the Semitic East: the gods make people out of dirt to be their slaves.

The other conception used by the ancient world, especially the Indo-European Greeks and Persians in several different ways, was the one that eventually undergirded the orthodoxy of Christianity: the divine nature was something in essence fluid, capable of being shared, of flowing into those created, or better, those engendered. It originally was expressed in the stories of the gods engendering other gods, at times lesser and occasionally greater than themselves, and further, of gods and humans engendering the semidivine heroes. These were simple stories based on the physical models of living things found in nature: the gods were quite like humans and the universe was small. But three developments changed this picture irrevocably and brought with them the most sophisticated philosophical and theological developments ever to arise. First, as science and theological understanding progressed, the universe was discovered to be huge and, necessarily, the God who created it became infinite, the One, the God who stood behind everything. Second, human beings acquired souls separable from their bodies; the soul was the "real person" clothed in the flesh of the body. Third, both the essence of God and the "stuff" of souls were understood to be composed of spirit; the divine substance and the essence of a human being were made of the same thing.

Originally, the gods had bodies, and those bodies, although made of heavenly materials, were still composed of some physical substance. The gods looked like large and beautiful humans, or if nonheavenly deities, sometimes like monsters of the sea or underworld. They acted in much the same ways as humans would under the same conditions, though if heavenly gods, in ways the ancients envied. They ate and drank (ambrosia and nectar in Greece), sat on thrones, lived in luxury, and ruled from their heavenly palaces and temples without interruption. But these old stories, especially those that seemed to attribute immoralities to the gods, were rejected for a whole new cause—they were rejected not only on moral grounds, but because they required the impossible. God had become infinitely large and did not have a physical body; union with God could only be spiritual. Humans for their part had originally been composed of clay to resemble the gods in appearance and to serve them. Into these clay pots the gods had blown the breath of life; at death the air went out and the body returned to dust. Now, however, humans were seen as composed of two essential parts, body and soul, and only the body perished at death, while the soul as a spiritual entity and as the "real" person continued to live on.

The Gospel of John declares in the first century something that was not possible to say before these developments took place: "God is spirit, and those who worship must worship in spirit" (John 4:24). Both God and humans are spiritual beings, though humans are encased in bodies. God in this conception can flow in and out of creation, can reach into and can meld with the spirits of its inhabitants. God can infuse one's spirit and engender one's soul; again from the Gospel of John, one can be "born from above" (John 3:3, usually mistranslated "born again"). And Jesus prays to the Father for his disciples that Jesus may be "in them and you in me, that they may become completely one" (John 17:23). There is a unity of essence in this understanding impossible with the "God as bowling ball" model. Human beings can in actual reality be sons and daughters of God by shared essence, much like the physical models of nature, but in the realm of the spirit. Among the most influential Greek and Roman philosophers, the Platonists and Stoics, the soul had actually come from God and, if it lived a just life, was destined to return to its original and proper home.

The mechanism by which the One shared its essence was emanation, by which means the "stuff" that God was made of could proceed out and form another being, and this process was a very old idea. It made its appearance in Zoroastrianism in the second millennium B.C. in the form of the Holy Spirit, the archangels, and the angels, on the one hand, and the Devil, the archdemons, and the demons, on the other. The archangels were originally aspects of the nature of God that were emanated out of the divine essence and became established as beings in their own right, "hypostasized" qualities of God, to use the technical term. So the wisdom of God could become the divine person Wisdom, considered to be Athena by philosophical Greeks, whom we meet in a different form in Proverbs 8, or in a similar idea using a different term, the Logos of God, God's reasoning power, often translated as the "Word" of God, whom we meet in Stoicism as the agent of creation and in the Gospel of John as Jesus.

The idea that God as a spiritual being whose essence had emanated out to create not only such exalted beings as these, but also human souls was an idea old already in the background of the Christian message. Consider Paul's sermon in the book of Acts to the Athenians. He says of God, "'In him we live and move and have our being'; as even some of your own poets have said, 'For we too are his offspring'" (Acts 17:28). The soul, according to ideas among some philosophers and mystery religion initiates at least five hundred years old in Greek culture, had come from the divine nature and become incarnated in human bodies here in the material world, but had as its proper destiny a return to the divine; the "home" of the soul was heaven and God. The soul was considered immortal and divine; Cicero in the first century B.C. goes so far, in one of his most famous passages concerning the soul, to write: "Know that you are a god" (*De Re Publica* 6.26). A person separated from the body is divine because the soul had proceeded out of the essence of God, and for Cicero and many other philosophers of his time, its goal was to make its return. These ideas had powerful influence when they were encountered and appreciated, but recall that no such ideas existed in the old Semitic world, for God was not a spiritual essence in this sense, nor did people have separable souls; and similarly in the Greek world, the vast majority of people continued to believe that the gods were like Zeus and Hera and that after death everyone went to the house of Hades.

And then came Jesus. After his life and teachings, which his followers barely understood at the time, and then his heroic death and resurrection, the choices and possibilities the early Christians faced when they began to try to understand what kind of person he was, their "Christologies," to use the theological term, were remarkable in their variety. Scholars have tried to classify their solutions on a continuum running between the poles of "Low Christology" to "High Christology." Low Christology held that Jesus was at base a human being, born of human parents, who because of his wisdom, righteousness, and obedience, was chosen by God to be the Messiah; or since in the providence of God it was foreknown that he would be so righteous, he was predestined and appointed to such a position. Such a view was common among the so-called Jewish-Christian sects in the East and lay at the base of Adoptionist Christology, which we will explore. The opposite view, High Christology, was that Jesus was in reality God or a god, a divine being who descended to earth from heaven and took on some form of humanity and then reascended to where he originally belonged. This view was especially common among Gnostic groups of the second century and lies at the base of the Christology of the Gospel of John. Later orthodoxy made a valiant effort at melding these two views, developing in the fifth century the doctrine of the Hypostatic Union (the "union of persons"), the teaching that Jesus was both God and Man in whom these two complete natures were present in one individual.

Between these poles, there were a great number of intermediary positions, especially in the first and second centuries, among the many Christian groups in various geographical areas of the Mediterranean world. In general scholars have tended to place the higher Christologies later in time than the lower ones, for which there is some warrant in the fact that the doctrine of the Trinity as it was to be found in the creeds was not articulated until the creeds were framed in the fourth century. The doctrine was not invented then, but many of its aspects were conceived and its intricacies worked out during the theological arguments that began in the middle of the second century and came to full flower during the reign of Constantine and later. "High" and "low" had much more to do with culture, education, and geography than with time.

CHRISTOLOGIES AND THE FOUR CLASSES OF BEING

Aside from modern scholars, we have seen that the ancients themselves had a classification system for understanding what sort of being one was, the Four Classes of Being of Hesiod and Plutarch. That system, moreover, had become quite sophisticated by the time early Christians were attempting to understand the "being" of Jesus, especially in the category of deity: deity now had become spiritual and could now enter into a normal human body. As we did with Hesiod in Chapter 3, let us begin at the end of their list.

Humans

The lowest estimation of Jesus was of course that of the disbelievers, the Romans who crucified him as some type of political troublemaker and the Jewish authorities who rejected him and agreed with the Romans. The Romans were not looking for a new world ruler. And Jewish tradition had in general either rejected the idea of a messiah entirely, understood it purely in human political terms, or defined it as inherited from the Persians—the messiah was to be sent to defeat the enemies of God; he was not supposed to get himself killed, no matter how heroically he lived. As the stories about Jesus circulated, the level of calumny sank to a remarkable low among those who found it to their pleasure or advantage to disparage him, both Jewish and pagan.

We find in later texts the claim that Mary, his mother, was really impregnated by a Roman soldier (a name is actually invented for the soldier) and that she claimed a virgin birth to hide her shame. His miracles could not be real miracles, for that would have put him on the side of God. They must have been magic he had learned in Egypt. Even in the Gospels he is accused of casting out demons by the prince of demons,

Beelzebul, which elicits from Jesus the sane response that "If Satan also is divided against himself, how will his kingdom stand?" (Luke 11:18). He didn't really even worship God, it was said, but set up a brick and worshiped that like an idolater. And his resurrection? His disciples came and stole the body by night and then claimed that it had been raised. Their experiences of the postresurrection appearances were hallucinations or, worse, were fabricated so the disciples could become the center of attention and astound others with their tales. Religious arguments have seldom brought the best of human qualities to light.

The crucifixion was a problem. In fact, the earthly life of Jesus itself was a problem. That Jesus was falsely accused of any number of errors and considered a threat to ruling authorities, that he was arrested, tortured, and judicially murdered, was not an insurmountable problem for most believers, as shameful and humiliating as it was. They knew the stories; these and similar sufferings were part of the normal course of life (and death) for many of the heroes. In fact the persecution and sufferings authenticated Jesus' place in the scheme of things as God had planned them. Christians lived in an inimical world, ruled by the Devil and his own, both human and divine, and the Captain of the faith had gone through every test, even death, and come off victorious. They were involved in the same story, the same struggle against spiritual darkness, and they too would come off victorious one day, when their turn came to face the same representatives of darkness. But other Christians sought to understand the earthly life of Jesus differently and circumvent the shame of the cross. Depending on the level of Christology, on what kind of divine being the individual interpreter thought Jesus was, the life story and crucifixion could be dealt with in a number of other ways, as we shall see.

At the low end of the scale among Christian groups, conceptions of Jesus could be quite "human." One view, reflected in (and rejected by) the noncanonical *Gospel of Thomas* and much in vogue among a small group of scholars, was that Jesus was a kind of philosopher. The *Gospel of Thomas* is a document that preserves over a hundred sayings of Jesus, many with roots in the earliest traditions of Gospel literature. In one saying similar to the famous "Who do people say that I am?" of Mark 8:27, Jesus asks his disciples to describe what he is like. The second answer (of three) is, "You are like a wise philosopher" (*Gospel of Thomas*

13, GJR). The Coptic text even contains the transliterated Greek word *philosophos*. The point of the passage is clearly that this was one of the ways certain Christians understood Jesus, but that from the point of view of the community of Thomas, their view was inadequate. In defense of the "small group of scholars" mentioned above and the Christians represented by the reply to Jesus' question in *Gospel of Thomas* 13, it is certainly correct to say that Jesus was a kind of philosopher: he taught a way of life and a new way of understanding the world; he made disciples; he founded a "school" of thought; he even directed his twelve disciples to dress in some way different from but with similarities to itinerant philosophers (cf. Luke 10:4). But the *Gospel of Thomas* and the rest of the early Church would say that he was also much more; this conception was too "low."

Another view, reflected in the New Testament, was that Jesus was the "Son of David," a political ruler of the lineage of David. The expectations for the Son of David were that he would revive the Davidic kingdom, throw off the yoke of Roman rule, and restore political independence. This was, apparently, the usual expectation among Jews who were looking for a messiah at the time of Jesus, and the one that both the crowds and the disciples expected. Jesus was asked on more than one occasion "when the kingdom of God was coming" (Luke 17:20). Even after his resurrection, the disciples ask, "Lord, is this the time when you will restore the kingdom to Israel?" (Acts 1:6). The descendant of David who would recover his kingdom did not need to be divinely born in any way or be born of a virgin; he merely had to be a successful military leader. Cyrus, king of Persia, who defeated the Babylonians while Israel was in Babylon in exile, was called the messiah (Isa. 45:1). Later Simon Bar Cochbah, who led the Jewish uprising against Rome and revived independence from 132 to 135, was proclaimed to be the messiah, until he was killed. So Jesus, insofar as he fulfilled the role of this type of messiah, did not have to be anything more than human, the son of Joseph and Mary.

The most important (and notorious) Christian group who saw Jesus in this light were the Ebionites. In the early period while the apostles and their disciples were still alive, the issue of whether Mosaic Law and its traditions were still binding, especially on Gentiles, was very much in contention. This point is quite visible in the Letters of Paul and the book of Acts. One of the purposes of the book of Acts is to emphasize the unity between the Jewish Christians of Jerusalem and the gentile mission of Paul, but the dissension between the groups over the Law is still present. In Acts, when Paul visits Jerusalem for the last time, he is told by James, the leader of the Jerusalem Church,

> You see, brother, how many thousands of believers there are among the Jews, and they are all zealous for the law. They have been told about you that you teach all the Jews living among the Gentiles to forsake Moses, and that you tell them not to circumcise their children or observe the customs. (Acts 21:20–21)

This is not in fact what Paul was teaching, but what was being said about him in the East. These Eastern Jewish Christians held to the Law and circumcision and the customs that had grown up around the Law over time. Paul and the Western Church understood that the age of the Law was over, but that was not so among many Jewish Christians in the East.

These Christians whom we see in Acts are the forebears of the Ebionites. The Ebionites gained their name from the Hebrew term for "poor" (*ebion*), one of the original names of the Jerusalem Christians, perhaps reflecting the saying of Jesus, "Blessed are you who are poor" (Luke 6:20). Christian groups going by this name lived in Palestine and eastern Syria at least until the fourth century. Eusebius of Caesarea in Palestine, writing in the early fourth century, describes their doctrine:

> They thought that [Jesus] was a plain and common man justified only because of his progress in ethics, and that he had been born out of the intercourse of a man and Mary; and that the religious observance of the law was necessary for them on the grounds that they would not be saved through faith in Christ and a life in accordance with [faith]. . . . They refused to confess that he preexisted as God, being Word and Wisdom . . . (*Historia Ecclesiastica* 3.27.2–3, GJR)

Among one branch of these Jewish Christians of the East, Jesus was thought to have been born naturally from his parents as a normal human, as a "mere man" as the writers are fond of explaining. Some of them rejected the claim that Jesus had been born of a virgin and followed an interpretation that the proper understanding of Isaiah 7:14,

"The virgin is with child," was that a "young woman" would conceive, a view also championed by non-Christian Jews in the argument with Christians over the proper use of the Old Testament. They held to a traditional Jewish way of life, keeping the Law and the Sabbath and practicing circumcision. They used the Gospel of Matthew exclusively, without the birth narrative, and rejected the apostle Paul as an apostate from the Law. Hippolytus (ca. 170–236), writing from Rome, tells us they believed that

> Jesus was justified because he accomplished the law. Therefore he was named both the Christ of God and Jesus, since no one else fulfilled the law. For if some other person had accomplished the things commanded in the law, that one would have been the Christ. And they themselves, if they had done likewise, would have become Christs, for in fact, they say that he was just like everyone else. (*Refutatio* 7.34.1–2, GJR)

We are told that they thought that Jesus had become the Messiah because of his high level of personal righteousness—he had been the only one to have kept the Law perfectly and so had been named to be the Christ. But there was nothing, apparently, special about Jesus—if some other person had kept the Law perfectly, then he would have been named the Messiah. He had been a "mere man," no different from one of the prophets.

Apparently there were others among the Ebionites who did accept the virgin birth. Origen (ca. 185–254) lived in Palestine and writes of two groups:

> They boasted that they were Christians, but still wanted to live according to the law of the Jews like the majority of Jews. And these are the two kinds of Ebionites, some confessing as we do that Jesus is from a virgin, and others that he was not born in such a way but as the rest of people are. (*Contra Celsum* 5.61, GJR)

This acceptance of virgin birth had important consequences, because with it, though not only by its means, Jesus begins to ascend the scale from "mere man" to some higher level of divinity: God is his father in some way beyond others. By the time of the Arab conquests in the seventh century, we find that Christians living in the area of Medina and Mecca on the southwest coast of Arabia hold doctrines that are similar to this type of Ebionite, but with the addition of a crucifixion only in appearance.

Heroes

The factors of a virgin birth and a crucifixion only in appearance bring us to the next category of Hesiod's Classes of Being, that of the heroes. Because of the increased sophistication of views of divinity and the importance of the idea that the soul had come from God, the category of hero in the Christian period as applied to Jesus becomes vastly more complicated. The human story of Jesus, his suffering, death, resurrection, and ascension, matched that of many of the heroes, as we are told by Justin Martyr and Tertullian and others—the story of Jesus is like the stories of the sons of Zeus. The early believers in Jesus were certainly not proclaiming the similarity of Jesus to the Greek heroes, but his superiority over them and every other deity. Nevertheless, the stories of heroes included many aspects and actions similar to those of Jesus. It is among the heroes that one finds virgin births, heavenly portents, so many healings, miracles, battling of unjust authorities, divine enemies, innocent suffering or suffering only in appearance, resurrection, and ascension. These similarities had quite significant effects on the Christologies of some Christian groups in the early centuries of the Church. Stories of the heroes provided more than one possibility that influenced the ideas of early Christians in their theories of the nature of Jesus.

Heroes, as the sons and daughters of the gods, came in several varieties, and these differing types of divine-human beings provided models for the different Christs of more than one community. Four may serve as illustrations. Sarpedon, son of Zeus and Europa, is the "normal" divinized hero who never makes it to Olympus at all. Heracles, the son of Zeus and Alcmene, is a representative of the suffering hero "adopted" into the divine sphere. Asclepius, son of Apollo and Coronis, represents the god-man, savior, miraculous healer, and lover of humanity, who becomes the human expression of the invisible God on earth. And Dionysus, the son of Zeus and Semele, is the fully divine human.

Sarpedon was the "lowest" example and represents the most common type. Almost all of the usual characteristics of the story of the hero are present in his human life. His father was God (of the Greeks), Zeus, and he was born of the virgin Europa. His divine parentage notwithstanding, his relationship to the divine world was like that of a mere mortal. He fought in the Trojan War (on the wrong side), died, and went under the earth to the house of Hades. He could never have been divine while alive, and he achieved nothing more than "normal" hero cult status after death, as did numerous others of those who fought at Troy. He and they came to be honored on earth as protecting "saints" of their local areas. Outside of his genesis and death, however, he could not serve well as a model to understand Jesus because there was no legend of his ascension to heaven and divinity; he was too low on the scale.

Heracles, an example of the next stage, became the most widely worshiped hero in antiquity. He had to struggle through a real human life as a quintessential hero, with all the qualities of strength and destiny we examined in Chapter 3. He had been born of Zeus and, like Jesus, as an infant faced and survived an attack designed to kill him, here designed by his divine enemy, Hera. As a man he was set a series of impossible tasks by his jealous uncle, but ultimately again behind the scenes, by Hera. To accomplish these he had divine, and even "miraculous," help and his own intrinsic qualities, but eventually he was overcome by his fate and died horribly. Yet he ascended to heaven and was assumed into the company of the gods. He was not a god while alive, but was "adopted" after death by Hera, his one-time enemy, and raised to the level of divinity and inclusion among the Olympians. As such he made numerous postmortem appearances as a god to help his petitioners and became widely admired as an example of suffering and as deliverer and protector. This adoption of an earthly son of god into heaven to become one of the gods himself was one of the possibilities for Christology, and "adoptionism," as it came to be called, was one of the ways that certain Christians understood Jesus. Heracles became a god and Sarpedon did not—the difference between Sarpedon and Heracles was the ascension and "adoption" of Heracles.

Such a model clearly stands in the context of the kind of language used by Paul to the Romans that Jesus "was declared to be Son of God with power . . . by resurrection from the dead" (Rom. 1:4). And similarly, in the speech of Paul to the Greek Athenians in Acts, the writer states that God will judge the world "by a man whom he has appointed, and of this he has given assurance to all by raising him from the dead" (Acts 17:31). Neither of these authors held to a "low" Christology, and they would have been horrified by a suggestion that Jesus was merely another kind of Heracles, but that is not the point. Resurrection from the dead did at least prove that one was a son of god in the minds of the people whom these writers addressed, the Romans and Greeks. It was a kind of authentication that one was a son of the gods, a sign learned from the stories of the heroes. For Paul and Luke, of course, Jesus was uniquely the Son of God, far superior to anyone's Heracles, but they were willing to use the language and symbols of their own wider culture to communicate their message.

Yet note the language of the passage just quoted from Acts: "a man whom [God] has appointed" (Acts 17:31). Common among the Ebionites was a position that would have found support in this language: that Jesus became God, was appointed or adopted to be Son of God. Irenaeus, in a refutation of their position, asks, "How shall a man pass over into God, if God did not pass over into man?" (*Adversus Haereses* 4.33.4, GJR). The Ebionites were claiming that Jesus had become God, but rejected the preexistence of the Son and his incarnation as Jesus; they would not allow that God had first "passed over into man." In the words of Hilary of Poitiers (writing around 356–59), the Ebionites claimed that Jesus was "not man from God but God from man" (*De Trinitate* 2.4, GJR). That is, Jesus had been a man born not from God but from Joseph, and then was "adopted" to become God.

The descriptions of the Ebionites and their Christologies come from their opponents, the Church writers who opposed the "heresies," among whom the Ebionites were classed. We do not have the Ebionites' own writings, and therefore do not know what they would have meant by Jesus becoming "God." What kind of God? What level of God?

The Ebionites were Jewish Christians who used the Gospel of Matthew in Hebrew (or Aramaic). They lived in Semitic-speaking areas and, unlike the Greeks and Romans, did not inherit a tradition of people becoming gods, except as they might have acquired through contact with Greek culture. They did have a tradition of divine beings appearing occasionally on earth in the form of humans, but that is not at issue in these texts about Jesus. They also knew of the examples of Enoch and Elijah, who had been taken into heaven while alive and became, especially in the traditions surrounding Enoch, more than mere humans. They heard the story of Jesus, of his resurrection and ascension, and, one assumes, accepted this as his "adoption" into heaven to be among the divinities, who for them would have been God and the angels, called in the Old Testament and Canaanite culture God and the sons of God (cf. Job 38:7). So the "adoption" into heaven among the Ebionites in the East, in Semitic cultures, places Jesus among the angels. We find in these areas from the first century to the later controversies over the nature of Christ of the third and fourth centuries, Jesus as an angel, "angel Christology." But more on that after the categories of the heroes.

A hero similar to Heracles, but at a higher stage and much more likely to have been in the minds of the simple Christians persecuted by Pliny, was Asclepius. Asclepius was the kindly god of healing and as such could evoke some of the warmest emotions among his worshipers of any of the Greco-Roman deities. He was one of the most popular gods of the Greco-Roman world from the fourth century B.C. through the fourth century A.D. One of his epithets is "most renowned," and over the course of those eight hundred years his cult grew in wealth and theological sophistication to extraordinary levels. By the second century A.D., there were hundreds of cult centers devoted to Asclepius all over the Roman world. Some of the most important centers were at Epidauros, Pergamum, Kos, Athens, and Rome, but every town of consequence had, and apparently felt the need for, a healing center of Asclepius. Emperor Julian tells us in the middle of the fourth century A.D. that the cult centers of Asclepius "are found everywhere on earth" (*Contra Galilaeos* 235C).

But Asclepius had a checkered career. Pindar (*Pythian* 3) tells us that his mother, Coronis, had been executed by Artemis under her brother Apollo's command because Coronis, although Apollo's consort and pregnant by him with Asclepius, lay with a stranger and defiled herself in the eyes of the gods. She was killed by the arrows of Artemis and consigned to the pyre, while Apollo rescued Asclepius from her womb. He was then brought up by the centaur Chiron to become the world's greatest practitioner of the art of medicine. Yet he too was subverted, and after being bribed with gold, consented to break the law of Zeus and bring a man back from the dead. For this impiety, Zeus incinerated both him and his patient with a thunderbolt (Pindar *Pythian* 3.1–60). Yet this very penalty secured his apotheosis, his rise to the status of deity: Sophocles, himself a devoted follower of Asclepius, tells us that Zeus's lightning is the first choice of means for the divine world to make off with a mortal (*Oedipus at Colonus* 1657–63).

All but the Christian apologists were willing to forgive Asclepius this transgression, and his skill as a healer brought him the reputation for being "of all the gods the most loving of humans." He earned a number of other similar epithets: "gentle and kind," the one who "gives ear" or "listens" to prayer, "lover of the people," "most loving of humanity." His most common epithet, found scores of times on dedications, reads, "Asclepius the Savior." So we find the prayer, "You, in your gentleness and love of humanity, grant me health." Note the similarity of titles for and concepts about Jesus. The reputation of Asclepius was such that Christians faced a serious problem. Justin Martyr tells us in the second century that

> when we say that [Jesus] healed the lame and the paralytics and those ill from birth and raised the dead. we seem to be saying the same things said to have been done by Asclepius. (*1 Apologia* 22.6, GJR)

Justin notes later that the claim by Christians that Jesus could "heal every disease and raise the dead" was the same as what was said of Asclepius (54.10).

In Pergamum, the center of the Asclepius cult in Asia Minor, we find a dedication to "God the Highest" as a thank offering for a healing miracle received. In the Greek and Roman world, this title is properly and normally a reference to Zeus. Yet the Asclepieion, the main cult building, is dedicated to Zeus Asclepius, to the syncretized "One God in many expressions" that philosophical monotheism had produced over the previous six hundred years. Thus here we have evidence of a prayer to and answered by Zeus Asclepius, the god-man of healing who is an expression of the highest God. By the fourth century, Asclepius became the pagan answer to the doctrine of Christ. Julian the Apostate (or "the Great," depending on one's point of view; emperor from 361 to 363) tells us in his argument against the Christians that

Zeus engendered Asclepius from himself. . . . Asclepius, having made
his visitation to earth from the sky, appeared at Epidauros singly in the
shape of a man, but afterwards multiplied himself, and by his visita-
tions, stretched out over the whole earth his saving right hand. . . . [H]e
raises up souls that are sinful and bodies that are sick. (*Contra Galilaeos*
200 A–B, GJR)

One of the reasons why Asclepius could have been the model for the
God worshiped by the humble Christians encountered by Pliny was that
they were singing a "hymn to Christ as to a god antiphonally." One of
the epithets of Asclepius was "Paian Asclepius." In the *Iliad*, Paian is the
physician of the gods, and eventually that name and function was transferred to Apollo as god of healing, and then to Apollo's son, Asclepius,
who took over Apollo's healing functions. The name *paian*, however,
had a second meaning: a *paian* was a hymn or chant, often a choral
hymn, allowing the method of antiphonal singing. Hymns were normal
aspects of the worship of the gods, but the vast number of hymns dedicated to Asclepius show that hymn singing was especially characteristic
of his worship. A number of hymns to Asclepius have been preserved;
one especially famous was used in Athens for over five hundred years
and is found in Macedonia and as far away as Egypt. A number of them
included the response "Hail Paian" interspersed throughout the hymn
as a shout of praise. For example, a hymn from the cult center of
Epidaurus from about 300 B.C. concludes:

> Asclepius, . . . the one who makes diseases cease, the one who gives
> health, the great gift to mortals, Hail Paian! Hail Paian! Welcome
> Asclepius, may you send shining health to our minds and bodies.
> Hail Paian! Hail Paian! (Edelstein T594, GJR)

As all ancients would from time to time find it necessary to pray for
health and healing, the god to whom such prayers would be addressed
was Asclepius, accompanied by the hymn.

Asclepius was the kindly god-man who heard prayers and healed
and became the human expression of God on earth and the direct competitor of Jesus. If we ask why Asclepius should have been succeeded by
Christ, another healing god so similar, the answer may be found in the
issue of death. Asclepius was the healing Savior, but he could not over-

come death; he himself was killed for raising a dead man. Death was a defilement to him; no one was allowed to die in a healing center of Asclepius. He forced those who were not healed but dying to go outside the walls of his precincts, to face their last and greatest trial alone. In contrast, we see the opposite effect of Jesus on his followers in the sarcasm of Lucian, the second-century satirist, as he describes the foolish and ignorant sect of the Christians that Peregrinus Proteus dupes in his wanderings. Lucian tells us that "The poor devils have convinced themselves first off that they will be completely immortal and will live forever, on which account they despise death and the majority hand themselves over (into custody) willingly" (*Peregrinus* 13, GJR). In the end, Asclepius was banished from the empire and eventually from living memory by the new healing god of the Christians. Christians in their turn, as Julian had done to Christ, plundered his resources, building churches and hospitals on the very sites of his temples and centers of healing. Yet it is clear that early on they owed much to Asclepius, the kindly hero who became the healing god, in constructing their understanding of Jesus the Savior.

The final example of a hero, Dionysus, was the most divine of all the god-men and stood behind more than one important Christology of the first-century Christians. One of the most interesting problems faced by early Christians of the first and second centuries and completely lost to the modern Church was the argument over whether or not Jesus had a normal human body. This was the first "heresy," as opposed to a doctrinal controversy, known as Docetism. Paul had argued vehemently against those who preached "another Jesus" and a "different gospel" (2 Cor. 11:4), but he was dealing with people who thought that the Law of Moses was still in force, that Jesus had not fulfilled the Law, and that it was still binding on Gentiles. This was an argument over the function of Jesus and the efficacy of his sacrifice, an argument that is still being waged today. Docetism, however, claimed that Jesus was a different class of being. Both Paul and his opponents apparently agreed that at some level Jesus was a man, but disagreed on what he had accomplished for humanity. Docetists did not care particularly about such mundane matters, for Jesus in their opinion, was above the human sphere.

Clement of Alexandria, in a statement preserved from the beginning of the third century, tells us: "It is reported in the traditions that John, when he touched [Jesus'] outward body, put his hand deeply in, and that the solidarity of the flesh did not resist him, but made room for the hand of the disciple" (*Hypotyposes* Frag. 24.3 Stählin, *In 1 Joh.*). This is, for us, a rather surprising report. We are far more used to hearing of Jesus as the wise teacher, critic of hypocrisy and pretense, gently receiving into his embrace children especially. Imagine the reaction of the crowd if these children, scurrying in their eagerness to greet and hug him, had run straight through his body clasping only themselves. Clement here relates a tradition that he had received concerning John the Beloved Disciple, who is said to have leaned on Jesus' breast at the Last Supper. John was also the spiritual father of an enduring community that produced varied literature in his name, divided, among other ways, on the issue of the nature of Jesus' body.

In this story of Clement, John reaches out apparently to lean on Jesus, and his hand passes right into his body. This illustrates two properties that are defining characteristics of "Docetism": Jesus had the appearance of a normal human, but was somehow different in substance. "Docetism" refers to the doctrine found among certain Christian groups that Jesus was a divine being with a nonfleshly, spiritual body, that he merely "appeared" to be human. The word itself derives from the Greek verb *dokeô*, which means among other things "to seem to be" or "to appear to be." Thus, Jesus "seemed to be" a normal human, but in their view was something else. Related to this is an adverbial use that may be translated as "in appearance only." It is this form that is used by Ignatius, bishop of Antioch, at the beginning of the second century to describe Christians of docetic bent who thought that Jesus existed and suffered on the cross "in appearance only." He writes to the church at Smyrna (*Smyrnaeans* 2): "He truly suffered . . . , not as some unbelievers say that he suffered in appearance only." The "unbelievers," of course, are real Christians who think that Jesus was some order of being other than a mere human in a fleshly body. The model for this understanding of the body of Jesus comes in no small part from Dionysus.

Dionysus was born of Semele, the virgin daughter of Cadmus, king of Thebes, when Zeus mated with her as a flash of lightning. She was, of course, instantly annihilated, but the just-conceived baby, Dionysus, was snatched from her body and sown into Zeus's own thigh as surrogate womb. From his birth Dionysus was a deity in human form, the highest of all heroes on the scale of divinity, impervious to attack, able to appear and disappear at will, to suffer without suffering, and to effect miracles. He belonged at all times among the gods of Olympus. Olympians were, of course, free to appear to humans in whatever form was convenient for their purposes. So in Euripides' play *Bacchae*, Dionysus comes to Thebes to establish his worship there and counter the calumny against his mother that Zeus had killed her for falsely claiming to have had him as mate. He says, "I, Dionysus, the son of Zeus, have come to the land of the Thebans. . . . And here I stand, having changed from god to mortal form. . . . I have changed into mortal image and exchanged my form into the nature of a man" (1, 4, 53–54, GJR). Here is one who is technically a hero, that is, born of a god and a mortal, but who in fact is a deity to be worshiped, disguised for a time as a mere man on earth.

Dionysus explains that he has changed his likeness from that of a god into that of a mortal man and then come to the city of Thebes. A very early Christian hymn, found in Paul's Letter to the Philippians says much the same thing about Jesus, "who, though he was in the form of God, . . . emptied himself, taking the form of a slave, being born in human likeness" (Phil. 2:6–7). Jesus is here depicted as a god from heaven who has laid aside his deity and come to earth as a man. But this is the point where docetic Christians and the rest of the Church part company. The hymn continues, "he humbled himself and became obedient to the point of death—even death on a cross" (Phil. 2:8). Dionysus in *Bacchae* does not die. He suffers humiliation and rejection; he is persecuted and imprisoned, chained and threatened with beheading. But he had warned his captors as he was led away: "I will go, for whatever it is that is not fated, it is not fated that I suffer" (*Bacchae* 515, GJR). The palace in which he is guarded is destroyed by earthquake and lightning, and he escapes completely unharmed and master of the situation. He performs miracles, as do his followers, and eventually it is those who persecute him who suffer.

Two signature aspects of Dionysus are found in the Gospel of John, the community in which Docetism is first visible in the first century. In John 2 Jesus is at a wedding in Cana of Galilee and the wine gives out; apparently the guests have already drunk deeply. Almost secretly, without fanfare or announcement, he turns 120 gallons of water into wine of excellent vintage; the wine steward compliments its quality. The sheer quantity of wine produced, after the host's own supply has already run out, is significant: it can only have been for the purpose of rendering the guests quite drunk, quite possessed by the spirit of wine. This is said expressly to be Jesus' first miracle, and we must not be so ignorant as to fail to recognize its import—this is the signature miracle of Dionysus. Dionysus was well known in Galilee in the first century; during the ritual year Dionysus regularly turned water into wine at his temples throughout the Roman world.

Again, in John 6, Jesus feeds the five thousand and then begins a discourse on manna, claiming that he himself is the bread from heaven. Finally he claims, "Those who eat my flesh and drink my blood have eternal life. . . . Those who eat my flesh and drink my blood abide in me, and I in them" (6:54–56). This shocking claim offends his listeners, and all but his closest disciples withdraw. But he is again drawing on the imagery of one of the aspects of Greco-Roman culture: a central feature of the mysteries of Dionysiac religion was the ritual and symbolic consumption of the flesh and blood of the god. The raw flesh of a young animal was touched to the lips as a reenactment of part of the myth of Dionysus, the eating of the young deity by the Titans. The Titans, enemies of Zeus and righteousness, had murdered and eaten the divine infant Dionysus. For this heinous crime Zeus struck them down with his lightning and created humanity from their ashes. Humans were thus a mixture of the divine and earthly: they bore the "Titanic nature" (Plato Laws 701c) in their bodies, but derived their souls from the ingested Dionysus. Thus he was celebrated as one who had survived death and granted immortality, as Lord of Souls. This symbolic act brought union with Dionysus, Dionysus within the celebrant, who granted eternal life. So Jesus in the Gospel of John accomplished, in changing water to wine, and claimed what no ancient world person would have missed or misunderstood—he was a new, but superior, Dionysus.

Daimones *and Angel Christology*

The heroes in the scheme of Hesiod were a step down from the *daimones* in his ranking of the Classes of Being. Yet because of the development of the idea of the soul and emanation of the divine essence, the heroes provided an essential part of the answer to the nearly intractable problem, from the point of view of the first Christians, of what kind of being Jesus might be. The eventual answer was still three to four hundred years in the future for the churches of the first century, who were faced with trying to understand him by drawing on the models already present in their own culture. These models were all they had to work with at the outset, and the various churches and theologians seem, at one time or another, to have tried them all.

The *daimones* were originally for Hesiod the souls of the race of the Golden Age, who, when they finally died, became guardian spirits who watched invisibly over humanity and administered the justice of Zeus on earth. The function these spirits performed was that of the angels in Jewish and Christian belief. Canaanite religion had provided Israel with the sons of God as ministers and messengers. So Yahweh had the Angel of the Lord and numerous other "angels" as lesser spirits to do his bidding. Greek religion had supplied Zeus with numerous lesser divine sons and daughters to do his will. Zoroastrianism had provided for ranks of angels of various powers and duties and had demonized everyone else's gods. For them, the gods of the nations were evil beings, "demons" in league with the Devil, and for those who fell heir to Zoroastrian tradition, namely a minority section of Judaism after the Exile and from them Jesus and therefore the Christians, the category of *daimones* was divided into angels and demons. The universe was full of spiritual beings stretching from the highest gods to the lowest tree and water sprites in every culture of the ancient Near East, known as the Great Chain of Being, as previously noted. There were no cultures that were strictly monotheistic, that is, ones that had only a single ("bowling ball") God and humans without intermediary beings. Those few that did eventually develop still had angels, but now the claim was that they were mere creations. The starkness of the "god and his little mud dolls" model did not appeal especially to the ancients, though they certainly understood the concept.

The original angels were not creations *ex nihilo* ("out of nothing"), but offspring of the high gods either by generation (that is, sex between gods and goddesses) or emanation of the substance of the One God into personified divine aspects in an entirely spiritual, sexless, and bodiless divine world. Both of these concepts preceded the nation of Israel and were inherited and assimilated into Israelite and Jewish tradition and the Bible. One finds there both the "sons of God" (e.g., Gen. 6:2) and the archangels who bear the names of personified qualities of God (e.g., Gabriel, Raphael). It was inevitable, as one may guess, that one or more Christian groups would try to understand Jesus as an angel. The obvious first attempts were made by Jewish Christians who had inherited stories of the Angel of the Lord and applied the category to Jesus, but later attempts were made by quite sophisticated Greek theologians to relegate Jesus to the level of an angel in order to safeguard ("bowling ball") monotheism.

That Jesus should have been understood as the highest angel arose quite naturally among Jews and Semitic groups. The Angel of the Lord received worship in the Old Testament (e.g., Exod. 3:2ff.) and was in appearance a man, the "man of God" who is called God (Judg. 13:6, 22). The worship of lesser angels in the context of Jewish rules and regulations is mentioned (and condemned) in the New Testament (e.g., Col. 2:18; cf. 1 Tim. 1:4–7). Jesus was clearly to be differentiated from the highest God, but was his main servant. So many church interpreters saw in the figure of the Angel of the Lord a prefiguring of the God-man Jesus. That type of figure was also to be found in the book of Daniel, where "one like a son of man" is presented to the Ancient of Days in the midst of tens of thousands of angels (Dan. 7:13). These concepts in Daniel were derived, but considerably upgraded, from very old Canaanite images of God and his chief son who is granted the rule of the land. For most Christians, of course, the Son of Man becomes a title for Jesus and the figure is considered a divine-human, not an angel. But sometime in the first century there arose among some Jewish Christians an angel Christology. If we return to the passage in the *Gospel of Thomas* quoted above (*Gospel of Thomas* 13), the first answer given to the request of Jesus that his disciples tell him what he is like is "You are a righteous angel." Epiphanius, a native of Palestine and bishop of Salamis writing in the late fourth century, claims that Ebionites say that Jesus "was created as one of the archangels, and that he rules over the angels" (*Panarion* 30.16.4).

Greek philosophy complicated the picture considerably, and in the Christological controversies of the fourth and fifth centuries the old angel Christology was melded with the idea, found most easily in the *Timaeus* of Plato and the Logos doctrine of the Stoics, that the Logos of God (the "Word of God") stood as an intermediary between God and creation. God was entirely immaterial and too exalted to contact the material world directly, so God's Logos had actually accomplished the acts of creation as agent. The Arian controversy of the fourth century centered on the issue of whether or not this agent, the Logos, was an emanation or a creation, a true God or an angelic being. Arianism was the last flowering of the early idea of Christ as angel and it was in this controversy that the formulation and understanding of the person of Christ for the subsequent Church took shape.

Gods and the God Christ

The simple people whom Pliny had caught and killed sang hymns to Christ as to a god, but we are unable to determine from the meager evidence of Pliny's report what that might have meant, what kind of God they thought Christ was. But the language of hymn and worship traditionally made much of the deity to whom it was addressed, granting titles and praise beyond what one from the outside might suppose was the proper sphere of the individual deity. Some of our best examples of syncretism, the melding of one god with another, especially gods of different levels of power and influence, come from the language of worship. We saw earlier the melding of Asclepius with Zeus, granting Zeus the ability to heal and Asclepius the status of Highest God. In Israel, it is especially in the Psalms where Yahweh takes on the attributes of the greater gods of the Canaanite pantheon. Isis, the Egyptian deity spread throughout the empire, is called "the single expression of gods and goddesses" (Apuleius *Metamorphoses* 11.4).

In several early Christian hymns and praises, Jesus is called God with very high Christological titles. Christians are looking forward to the appearance of "our great God and Savior, Jesus Christ" (Titus 2:13). Paul, in a rather shocking passage for one usually so clear in his language differentiating Father and Son, inserts into a discussion of Israel what appears to be a piece of liturgy concerning "Christ according to the flesh, the God who is over all things, blessed forever. Amen" (Rom. 9:5, GJR). Ignatius, writing at the beginning of the second century, is able to speak several times of "Jesus Christ our God" (*Ephesians* prol. 18.2).

And the second epistle of Clement, written approximately at the same time, opens with the line, "We ought to think of Jesus Christ as of God" (*2 Clement* 1.1, GJR).

In concert with this Christocentric language of worship, there arose a theological position, known as Modalism, that melded the persons of Father, Son, and Spirit into one deity with three different phases or duties. According to this position, God is found in three successive modes of activity: the Father became the Son at the incarnation, and then the Father-Son (such a Greek word is actually used, *huiopatôr*) becomes the Spirit at the resurrection. The advantages of such a position were that it preserved the unity of God, the "Monarchy" as it was called, and essentially any language could be used of Christ in worship and praise without scruple. Modalists believed in both monotheism and the deity of Christ. The difficulties, of course, were manifold, and many Church writers were quick to point them out. To whom did the earthly Christ pray if he was in fact the Father in another, earthly form? More offensive to opponents like Tertullian was the logical consequence that if Christ was the Father, then the Father had died on the cross and undergone the Passion. So those who held such a view were branded with the label "Patripassionists." But Tertullian admits that the majority of believers sided with the Modalists. Writing just after 200, he states that

> The simple people, indeed (lest I should call them imprudent and ignorant), who are always the majority of believers, since the rule of faith itself transfers them from the many gods of the world to the one and true God, not understanding the One indeed, that it must be believed in according to its own arrangement, are startled at the *oikonomia* (of the Trinity). They presume that the number and disposition of the Trinity is a division of its unity, when the unity, deriving the Trinity from itself, is not destroyed but administered by it. And so they boast that two or three (gods) are preached by us, but presume that they are worshipers of one God, as if both unity considered irrationally does not produce heresy, and the Trinity rationally explained does not constitute truth. (*Adversus Praxean* 3.1, GJR)

The simple believers do not accept the doctrine of the Trinity, but worship the One in three modes. These Christians in the majority laugh at Tertullian and others for preaching two or three gods, since, according to Tertullian, they do not understand the *oikonomia* (a Greek word from which we get "economy"), the way of arranging the Divine Persons that the church eventually articulated as Trinitarianism.

Behind Tertullian's formulation stood the emanation doctrine of the Logos, familiar to every reader of the Gospel of John. It was an old philosophical position, held by the most important philosophical schools of the empire, Platonism and Stoicism, and articulated in the myths of more than one widely spread cult, sections of Judaism included. But philosophical doctrine and theology is not for the illiterate and uneducated, and so the idea took centuries to spread into the wider Christian population, and it may be fairly said that it still is widely unknown or misunderstood.

Ignatius explains the relationship of the Logos to the one God quite well: "There is one God, who revealed himself through Jesus Christ his son, who is his Logos coming forth from him in silence" (*Magnesians* 13.8). The infinite and unknowable God dwells in complete silence (and self-sufficient bliss, one must add). The Logos is God's mind, God's reasoning power, which is emanated out into a Divine Person. This person creates the world and later, when things become a big mess here below, descends from heaven and, in Christian belief, undergoes the career of the earthly Jesus, and then returns to heaven and God. But just how that career worked, how a wholly divine being could undergo a human life, presented grave difficulties for many, and produced several creative solutions.

We have touched on the doctrine of Docetism in connection with the almost wholly divine hero Dionysus. But the Docetism of Dionysus derived from the fact that the gods were docetic, and he was but one small step from the full gods. The Logos, however, is always wholly divine, since it derives from the very substance of God, "consubstantial" ("of the same substance") and coeternal with God, for there never could be a time when God did not have the power of Reason. So what happens when the Logos descends? What kind of human life could it have? In a passage from the *Acts of John*, written at the end of the second century by one wing of the community that looked to the apostle John as its founder, we read of the recent female convert Drusiana reporting an appearance of Jesus to her while she had been imprisoned in a tomb for refusing to relinquish her new vow of chastity. She tells John and her amazed audience of fellow believers: "The Lord appeared to me in the

tomb in the form of John and in that of a young man" (*Acts of John* 87).
All are perplexed. The apostle in turn attempts to explain this remarkable phenomenon from his own experiences with Jesus. He tells them
that when Jesus first called him and his brother James to discipleship,
James saw Jesus as a child, while John saw him as a full-grown man.
Later, as they came to shore and began to follow Jesus, he seemed to
John to be a bald-headed man with a full beard, but to James to be a
young man with the mere start of a beard. Sometimes he was small and
without good looks, and at other times the opposite. And, he tells us,
when he reclined on Jesus' breast, "sometimes his breast was smooth
and soft, and sometimes hard like a rock" (*Acts of John* 89). Later in the
account we find a description similar to that related by Clement. John
tells us that

> Sometimes when I meant to touch him I encountered a material, solid
> body; but at other times again when I felt him, his substance was im-
> material and incorporeal, as if it did not exist at all. . . . And I often
> wished, as I walked with him, to see his footprint in the earth, whether
> it appeared—for I saw him raising himself above the earth—and I
> never saw it. (93)

Jesus is polymorphic, of many forms, able to appear young or old,
however and as whomever he wishes. The substance of his body is
something other than human flesh: it is soft or rock hard, material or
seemingly immaterial. These are signature characteristics of the gods.
In fact, John tells us that "it is not a man that I exhort you to worship,
but God unchangeable, God invincible, God who is higher than all authority and all power and elder and stronger than all angels" (*Acts of
John* 104). Somehow, in a way unexplained, it is not the heavenly Christ
who suffers on the cross, for he speaks to John in a cave on the Mount
of Olives while the crucifixion is going on below, withdrawing to heaven
and "discarding the man" (*Acts of John* 101).

More than one Christian group thought that something other than
the heavenly Christ had suffered on the cross—who could crucify God?
We are told that Basilides of Alexandria, Egypt, in the early second century taught that Jesus exchanged places with Simon of Cyrene; he had
Simon, who had carried Jesus' cross, be crucified in his place after being

transformed into his likeness. Others taught that the spiritual Christ had descended on the mere man Jesus in the form of a dove at his baptism and then departed from him at the crucifixion. The idea had been developed among the disciples of the Gnostic teacher Valentinus in Rome, who taught that the cry from the cross, "My God, my God, why have you forsaken me?" was evidence of the departure of the heavenly Christ from the crucified man Jesus. The idea was still the subject of contention more than a century later when Paul of Samosata, bishop of Antioch (the third largest city in the empire and the center of Christianity after the fall of Jerusalem), was condemned in 268 for teaching such a combination of low and high Christology. For him, the Christ had descended on the man Jesus in the form of a dove at his baptism and rested on the (mere) human Jesus as one person on another.

Both of these positions considered the man Jesus and the heavenly Christ to be two separate beings, an issue that was to figure centrally in the Christological controversies of the later fourth and fifth centuries. Was Jesus Christ one person or two separate beings, human and divine, combined somehow in one body? Did he have one nature or two? Was he only partially human, with only body and animal soul like a cow, while the Logos replaced his human spirit, the part that differentiated humans from mere animals? Did he have one will or two, both a human and divine will?

The questions were seemingly endless, but had by the time of these great Christological controversies gone far beyond the cultures out of which Christianity had originally emerged. No one ever asked whether Achilles had one will or two, or a divine spirit but human body and soul, or if he had not died at Troy but had made for himself a body-double to suffer while he reascended to heaven whence he came. These were Christological speculations that depended entirely on the long and sophisticated development of the argument that had asked questions about human-divine nature never before possible and had developed terminology and concepts brand-new and entirely dependent on Christian theologizing. They were not "right" or "wrong," but new and impossible in the early centuries; the questions were not asked because no one was yet viewed in that light and the theological terminology had not been developed.

An example may be drawn from the Gospel of John, without whose concepts the entire development of the doctrine of the Trinity would have been impossible, but within which such a doctrine is not articulated and can be found only in embryo, if at all. For John, the divine Logos is incarnated, that is, it clothes itself in a body as one might dwell in a tent. That is, as a matter fact, the very image used: in John 1:14 the Logos "became flesh and dwelt (in a tent) among us." The verb *skênoô*, most often translated here as "dwelt," means literally "to pitch a tent, to live in a tent" (*skênê*, "tent"). The Logos takes up living in a body as though moving into a tent or putting on clothing. The apostle Paul says much the same thing about himself. In 2 Corinthians 5:1, he says, "we know that if the earthly tent we live in is destroyed, we have a building from God, a house not made with hands, eternal in the heavens." He is speaking of his body as a tent in which he, that is, his real person of the soul, dwells until death. After death he will inherit a new and eternal "dwelling" for his soul, a resurrection body of glorious and incorruptible material, for "flesh and blood cannot inherit the kingdom of God" (1 Cor. 15:50). This is the old and venerable doctrine of the descent of the soul from God into a material body and its eventual reascension to its heavenly home. Jesus in the Gospel of John is the Man from Heaven incarnated in a physical body.

But how did he get there? There is no account of the virgin birth in John; Mary is rebuked (in 2:4) and Joseph is declared to be his father (in 6:42), which fact is apparently accepted as true (in 7:28). The motivation for such a change from the virgin birth stories of Matthew and Luke may be because of the problem we saw earlier in the community of John: one faction thought that Jesus was a god and docetic (like Dionysus), and virgin birth was exactly what was necessary to produce docetic individuals. If Joseph was his father, on the other hand, then his body must have been normal human flesh (what else could it be?), while his spiritual part could be the Logos, dwelling in a normal body like in a tent.

In a closely related community that arose around the apostle Thomas, the Thomas Christians held a quite similar view: no mention in their literature is made of the virgin birth, and therefore Jesus had a fleshly body that really died, while his real person was God and eternal, preexistent, and raised spiritually again to heaven. This idea that the Logos could inhabit a fleshly body as though in a tent was quite grossly expressed in a late-second-century document found in the Nag Hammadi library, the *Second Treatise of the Great Seth*. In this work, the Son was able to descend from heaven and take over the body of some earthly person by ejecting the original owner's soul from it: "I visited a bodily dwelling; I cast out the one who was in it previously" (51, 21–23). Recall that the body and soul are separable entities and that the body is only a temporary dwelling for the soul. In this book, the heavenly Son uses the body of an already grown man, just as though he had descended as a dove on the man Jesus at his baptism, but kicked out the soul of the man and took over his body instead of resting on him, as in the teaching of Paul of Samosata. No mention, by the way, is made of what happened to the soul of the poor original owner of the body.

Eventually the Church built on such ideas the doctrine that the Logos of God, who was in fact truly of the substance of God, had been incarnated and lived a human life. The model for the incarnation had come from the old philosophical doctrine of the descent of the soul from the divine realm into a human body, the "journey of the soul" as it was called. The model for the career of the human life had come from the stories of the heroes. But the new problems surrounding the relationship of the human and divine natures of Christ were never solved satisfactorily. The problem did not exist for the heroes, who were in fact both human and divine; they were hybrids, completely one person. The Church, however, began asking questions about two distinct natures in one envelope that the model of the hero was never designed to handle. The Creed of Chalcedon (451), which articulated the doctrine of the Hypostatic Union, the union of the two persons, Logos and Jesus, for all its confidence, cannot be said to have solved anything. It merely declared as fact what needed to be explained:

> one and the same Christ, Son, Lord, only-begotten, made known in two natures unmixed, unchanged, undivided, unseparated, the difference of the natures in no way removed on account of the union, but rather the property of each nature being preserved and mingling into one person and one substance, not parted into two persons or divided, but one and the same Son and only-begotten God, Logos, Lord Jesus Christ. . . .

So there was Jesus Christ with two complete natures "unmixed" and "preserved," but "mingled into one person and substance." Such a contradictory formulation would never have occurred to Hesiod; it would have been unnecessary and likely would have seemed ridiculous.

We began this chapter on the immense diversity of conceptions about Jesus by recalling the Four Classes of Being of Hesiod from about 700 B.C. and traveled through more than a thousand years of theological speculation and creativity in several cultures until the fifth century and the age of the creeds in Christianity. The Four Classes had developed and become more complex and sophisticated, while other ideas of the spirituality of the divine nature complicated the picture, adding even further possibilities. One aspect of the genius of Christianity, in its solution to the seemingly intractable problem of understanding the nature of Jesus, was that it found a way, in its traditions and stories and liturgy and creeds, to meld what was important, the two categories of heroes and gods, and allow them to serve as means to understand Jesus, the God who had descended from heaven and lived as hero and savior.

Chapter 6

CHRISTIANS AS HEROES AND
THE PATTERN OF EARLY CHRISTIAN LIFE

The disciples of Jesus, according to tradition, took the gospel to all the known world. In the beginning Jesus himself had preached and was their model, example, and forerunner. After his death the disciples expanded his message to include preaching the story of the leader himself, which led to the diversity we examined in the previous chapter. But the message had a center that was rarely compromised. What was it like to hear that message in the Greco-Roman world? What did those who heard the gospel think the Christians were, and what did they think they were being asked to do? This is no idle question, nor had it been addressed adequately by scholars.

The story that the disciples proclaimed was one of a man of remarkable talents and accomplishments who had suffered horribly and unjustly and then been vindicated after death by God through resurrection and ascension to heaven. That is the quintessential story of the hero, as we saw in Chapter 4. Jesus was a teacher and his words were worthy of one inspired by God, but that was true of others who had gone before. He was an example of kindness to the lowly and courageous confrontation in the face of religious hypocrisy, like Socrates and many others. And he died bravely, as had all the heroes almost without exception.

What was new, and what caught one's attention especially, was the promise of eternal life for those who would follow him. He was not merely one to learn from by example and pray to for help in time of need; for that there were Achilles and Heracles and so many others. His was not merely an inspiring and tragic story told for entertainment and encouragement. In this new message followers were required to join the drama as real participants, to follow the very life pattern of the forerunner and become heroes themselves, with the promise that, as he had been vindicated after death, so would they.

In the main the ancients were pessimistic about death and by tradition told stories of the underground kingdom of Hades to which all the dead must go. Hades was one of three brothers who had divided the cosmos among themselves. In a famous passage from the *Iliad*, another of the brothers, Poseidon, speaks:

> We are three brothers born by Rheia to Kronos, Zeus, and I, and the third is Hades, lord of the dead men. All was divided among us three ways, each given his domain. I when the lots were shaken drew the grey sea to live in forever; Hades drew the lot of the mists and the darkness, and Zeus was allotted the wide sky, in the cloud and the bright air. But earth and high Olympus are common to all three. (15.187–93)

The three have divided the cosmos into equal parts: the upper world of Zeus, the outer world of the surrounding ocean held by Poseidon, and the lower world of the dead, of which Hades was the king. Hades is the ruler of the dead and not merely the place of the dead. The Greek text of Homer makes this quite clear: it is the house of Hades the king to which all must go, always to Hades' (house, with an apostrophe), never to Hades (as a place).

His kingdom was a kind of island house or fortress surrounded by impassable rivers with terrifying names: Styx ("the Abhorrent"), Acheron ("the Woeful"), Pyriphlegethon ("the Fiery"), and Lethe ("Forgetfulness"). According to custom, those who died required burial or cremation with due ceremony, after which the ghost was led by Hermes to the shore of the border streams and given over to Charon, the ferryman. If a person was not properly buried, the ghost would not be allowed to cross. If allowed to cross, it had to pay for its passage, so the dead were buried with Charon's obol (an ancient penny) in their mouths. Upon arrival on the other shore, they were greeted by Cerberus, the terrifying multiheaded dog who stood guard outside the gates, allowing passage through the wall to the inside only, but never allowing anyone out.

This cosmology was essentially the same for many of the cultures surrounding the Mediterranean, with differing names for the main characters. The basic division of the world into three great domains was relatively common. In the Canaanite East, of which Israel was a part, the ruler of the underworld was Mot, "Death" personified. So in the New Testament world, where the two cultures are at times conflated, we find in the book of Revelation that Death (personified) of Canaan and Hades of Greece, both rulers of the underworld, are paired as representatives of the powers of death. They ride together on the fourth and most destructive horse of the Apocalypse (Rev. 6:8). But in Christian understanding they are spiritual enemies and at the end of time are thrown into hell:

> Death and Hades gave up the dead that were in them, and all were judged according to what they had done. Then Death and Hades were thrown into the lake of fire. (Rev. 20:13–14)

Hades is not the Christian Devil. He is stern and humorless, but a just ruler and in appearance like Zeus when he is angered, to determine from ancient art. He does not tempt people to sin or desire evil. In Canaan, however, the figure of Mot ("Death") is a competitor and enemy of the upperworld gods, and in appearance a great dragon. Here the Persian concept of the Devil finds a model, and Death becomes an adversary. So Paul can write that "The last enemy to be destroyed is death" (1 Cor. 15:26). This verse is usually found in modern translations with a small *d* in the word "Death," as though Paul meant to say, "The last enemy is the cessation of heartbeat and brain activity." But that is impossible—he knew nothing of brain waves, and death was not for him a random or mechanical event. Modern translations reflect a modern worldview and make it seem as though Paul is talking about death as the mere physiological absence of life. But very few people in antiquity, only the small handful of atheists, saw death this way, and Paul was definitely not among them.

The traditional view for the vast majority of people was that every occurrence was planned and motivated by some spiritual power. Length of life and time of death were determined by the Fates and there was nothing whatever that one could do to change their dictates. When the time of death arrived, the gods sent the death spirits to take one's soul to Hades' house. One did not merely die; everyone was killed by the gods according to a predetermined plan. There was no such thing in antiquity as dying of random or merely natural causes; all causes originated with the gods. If one died, it was because the gods and fate had decided that the time had come, sent some disease or directed some arrow or placed some stone on which to stumble, and caused one to die—the gods controlled everything. Even chance, Lady Luck, was a female deity to whom worship and temples were dedicated, Fortuna in the Latin world and Tyche in the Greek. Nothing happened for no reason, and nothing happened because of a merely mechanical series of events; the gods and the lesser deities who were their servants were unseen, but behind everything.

In the Gospel of Matthew, Jesus tells Peter, "You are Peter, and on this rock I will build my church, and the gates of Hades will not prevail against it" (Matt. 16:18). The gates of Hades' house were locked and permitted no release for the dead. Only a handful of heroes had ever entered and escaped alive. Odysseus had visited the shores of the underworld during his wanderings in order to consult the dead prophet Teiresias about how to find his way home. He did not enter Hades' house, but nevertheless it is this point in his life that symbolizes his conquering of death and after which he becomes the terrifying beggar who destroys his enemies when he returns home. But the more common pattern is that the hero descends to the house of Hades to save a loved one who has died. The loved one has made the journey to the underworld and been locked inside Hades' gates; the hero enters (and escapes) to gain immortality for someone else. Dionysus descends to retrieve his mother, Semele, and bring her up to heaven and immortality. Orpheus descends to recover his wife, Eurydice. Heracles descends in the most difficult of his twelve labors to bring up the dog Cerberus and succeeds in releasing his friend and fellow hero Theseus. Polydeuces trades his immortality for the sake of his mortal twin brother Castor, and the two then spend alternate days in Hades' and Olympus. Here in the Gospel of Matthew, Jesus stands in the tradition of the hero who saves his loved ones from death. He promises that Hades' gates will not be able to hold in the Church; that is, when the members of the Church die, they will be released from the kingdom of death and gain immortality. Their hero had himself died, gone into Hades' realm, and returned by resurrection and ascension. This same promise is held out to his followers. He had made a way through the wall, opening the gates. His disciples were but to follow him, through death into life. This is the message composed in and for the Greco-Roman world.

THE GOSPEL AND PHILOSOPHY

We asked what the culture at large thought the Christians were. Essentially two means were available in the larger culture for overcoming the apparent finality of death and gaining immortality: the pursuit of philosophy and initiation into one or more of the mystery religions.

Philosophy had based its claim for life after death on the existence of the soul as an entity separable from the body. Recall that in the earlier monistic conception, the only two means to overcome the finality of death were one's progeny and lasting reputation. The Orphics, a religious tradition that predates Plato in Greece (sixth century B.C.), had both a sacred story and a saying on which Plato builds. The saying was *soma sema*, "The body is a tomb." The life of the soul in the body was understood as a person buried in a tomb. Death is a release and resurrection; death is really life. Plato used this dualistic tradition in his understanding of the human condition: the body is a weight, an encumbrance, and a deceiver of the soul. It is made of earthly elements and belongs in the earth. The soul is made of divine elements and belongs in the heavenly world. So a kind of physics lay at the base of the ethical and philosophical life. The "scientific" truth that the soul belonged to the heavenly realm and the body belonged to the earth led to the conclusion that the two were only provisionally compatible. If the soul was controlled by the dictates of the body, "weighted down" by its desires, at death it would not be able to rise to its natural home, but would remain in the earth and (for Plato, but not all others) be condemned to reincarnate into another body. Only a life of abstinence and ethical behavior by which the soul ruled the body and its excesses could purify the soul. We are told:

> Unless one has practiced philosophy and is completely pure when [the soul] leaves [the body], it is ordained that it not attain to the race of gods,

but rather [that is] for the one who loves learning. And on this account
. . . those who practice philosophy correctly abstain from all bodily desires and bear with them and do not yield themselves to them. (Plato
Phaedo 82b–c, GJR)

"Unless one has practiced philosophy and is completely pure . . ."
The great mass of people have no chance. Philosophy is a literate study
with a master in a school, most often with a series of masters in a series
of schools. The cost could be considerable and education took years.
The pursuit of philosophy was not for the poor or for the illiterate, nor
was it for those of average or below average intelligence.

But the gospel was quite like a philosophy, and Jesus looked to the
world of the first centuries A.D. like a philosopher of sorts. Christian de-
fenders even enjoyed describing him as such. He had taught and his
sayings were remembered and repeated as wise sayings of the master.
He had followers, much as had Socrates, Plato, Aristotle, Zeno, and
many others who founded or participated in schools of thought that
lasted for centuries. What Jesus taught was based fundamentally on the
dualism of body and soul so important to philosophy: "What does it
profit one to gain the world and lose one's soul?" That is fundamental
to his message in the Gospels and a classic restatement of the teaching of many of the philosophers. Christians presented themselves consciously as adherents of a new philosophical school. Their name for
themselves was "the Way," and they were called a *hairesis* in Greek
(from which we get our word "heresy") and *secta* in Latin, the standard
designations for a school or branch of philosophy. Tertullian (ca. 200)
declares that unbelievers "think that our business is surely no divine af-
fair, but rather a kind of philosophy" (*Apoloceticus* 46.2, GJR). Eventually
it attracted some of the most influential and highly educated philosophical minds in antiquity. But unlike the other philosophies for the highly
trained and intelligent, it was a philosophy for everyone and its promises were for everyone.

THE GOSPEL AND THE MYSTERY RELIGIONS

The other means for overcoming the finality of death to be found in the
culture at large was by initiation into one of the mystery religions. Mys-

tery religions get their name from the Greek word *mystêrion*, which commonly designates a "secret," but in this context it refers to the secret divine teachings that lay at the core of these old and closed societies. They were properly cults within a larger religious milieu, not separate religions, for they shared a relatively common pantheon and worldview. The goal of these cults was to secure a better life and afterlife by means of obtaining the favor of the otherworldly powers, both above and below ground, through secret rites and doctrines and knowledge of magic and astrology. They taught a new religious and philosophical orientation when compared with the "official" view of the Homeric world of the Olympian gods, leading the subjects to view the cosmos, the gods, and themselves in a fresh way. The means was enlightenment, achieved by a powerful but stressful initiation experience that granted entrance into a bounded community of the elect.

The actual doctrines at the core of the mystery cults were kept hidden from all but the initiated, and the concealment was so successful that we today know little of what was taught. In general, however, they maintained that the human soul has share in the divine world; that people are caught in the material world of the senses, of chaos, fate, and death, and are in need of deliverance; that salvation cannot take place in this world; but that after suitable ritual, ascetic, and ethical practices in this life, one may gain immortality. The similarity in worldview to that of the philosophers is not superficial. Socrates tells his friends in his final conversation that in fact the two are quite close in objective, but that the mysteries used symbol and myth to reach the same ends:

> It is likely that those who established the initiations are not just commoners, but in fact long ago told a riddle that whoever arrives in Hades uninitiated and uncompleted in the mysteries will lie down in mire, but the one who arrives there cleansed and completed will dwell with the gods. (Plato *Phaedo* 69c, GJR)

And Cicero, a Roman statesman and philosopher and one of the most highly educated men of his day (106–43 B.C.), tells us that the mysteries gave "a reason not only for living with happiness, but also for dying with better hope" (*Laws* 2.36).

Quite effective use of symbols brought home to the individuals their new way of understanding themselves. We are told in a sarcastic denunciation of the Demeter cult by a Church writer that at the height of the initiation process, the initiate was shown an ear of grain, as though that were somehow foolish and meaningless. But for one who has eyes to see and ears to hear, the grain becomes the symbol of the life and death of the individual, and as Demeter controls the never-ending cycle of life of grain, so she would exercise control over the life of her worshiper. The symbol became a profound image of the victory of life over death, an image that was basic to the Christian message also. Paul says to one who denied resurrection, "Fool! What you sow does not come to life unless it dies" (1 Cor. 15:36). And in the words of Jesus, "unless a grain of wheat falls into the earth and dies, it remains just a single grain; but if it dies, it bears much fruit" (John 12:24). The mysteries of Demeter predated Christianity by many centuries, and any possible influence to explain the obvious similarities in these images and their meanings can only have gone in one direction.

In addition, some mystery cults apparently used a sacred story or myth that was symbolic of the doctrine that the god or subject of the cult was the prototype of the initiate, suffering, dying, and rising to a new life. At the core of the story was often a hero who had lived out exactly the type of story we have been examining; in fact many of the heroes we have met were the subjects of such cult stories. Just as they had suffered and died, but lived again, so would the initiate.

Mystery cults were old in the culture and became quite influential by the time of the Roman Empire. Originally they had to do mainly with Demeter, the grain goddess, and Dionysus, the god of wine and inspiration, though a number of other smaller cults existed. They were so successful in providing hope and meaning to their adherents that eventually all cults borrowed at least some of their characteristics. They were not exclusive cults; members were often initiated into more than one. They were syncretistic; that is, they melded and borrowed ideas and rituals from one another, identifying their gods with those of other cults. Adherents formed associations, often headed by professional priests, who presided over magical rites, purifications, baptisms, and sacraments. Membership was determined by initiation, and all were subject to a hierarchical organization. There were regular meetings, including sacramental meals according to rites held in the presence of the deity, and often an admirable moral code including more or less ascetic commitment. By Roman times even cults of the old Olympian gods instituted "mysteries" and initiations, set up private organizations with leaders and priests, and fixed memberships and regular meetings, intending to provide new meaning for the old cults. A number of Roman emperors were counted among the initiates of various mysteries, and even the cults of the emperor, in which he played the role of hero/deity, acquired mysteries.

To the normal inhabitant of the first-century Greco-Roman world, the new group called Christians looked most like a new mystery cult. It did bear some resemblance to a school of philosophy, and Christian writers often tried to present it as such, but it was immediately classed by nearly all as a mystery religion. One remarkable testimony comes from the Greek writer Lucian (ca. 120–after 180). Lucian was born in Palestine and probably spoke Aramaic originally, but he studied Greek and became a lawyer and later a traveling lecturer. He practiced sophistic rhetoric until moving to Athens (ca. 160), where he became a philosopher. He wrote eighty satiric dialogues in which he demonstrates his cynicism of nearly everything. One is *The Death of Peregrinus*, a bitingly humorous denigration of Cynic philosophers, represented by Peregrinus Proteus. Peregrinus, a Greek from the Hellespont, burned himself alive as an old man during the Olympic games of 165; according to Lucian this was an attention-getting stunt that well fit the character of this clever pseudo-Cynic philosopher. But the satire also recounts, among earlier misadventures of this resourceful charlatan, his easy entrance into the Christian community. He began his adult life, according to Lucian's story, as an adulterer and pederast who finally strangled his sixty-year-old father to get his inheritance. Because of suspicion in his hometown, he left and began traveling in the East. Lucian writes sarcastically:

> That was when he learned the marvelous wisdom of the Christians, associating in Palestine with their priests and scribes. And what else? In a moment he showed them up as children, on the grounds that he by himself was prophet and sect-leader and synagogue head and everything, even exegeting and clarifying some of their books, and writing many himself; and they thought of him as a god and used him as lawgiver and enrolled him as leader, after, to be sure, that one whom they still worship, the man who was impaled in Palestine because he introduced this new mystery cult as a way of life. (11, GJR)

Note that Lucian has little but scorn for the simpleminded and gullible Christians; he is a pagan philosopher. But what he sees when he observes the Christian movement is a "new mystery cult."

There has been a great reluctance among modern writers and schol-ars to acknowledge the early identification of Christianity as a mystery cult and take the significance of that fact into sufficient account. Such a classification, it seems, calls into question for many the uniqueness of Christianity and its divine provenance. They find it proper to compare the new religion favorably to Judaism, but comparison to Greek mys-tery religion is assimilation to "paganism," which is for some reason undesirable. But mystery religions existed and expanded their influence because they were positive forces in the lives of their adherents. They worked for people, and worked well enough that nearly all cults of the first century, Judaism included, borrowed from them and made use of their basic ideas. Christians themselves at some level clearly saw that their new faith was a kind of mystery cult. Mark preserves the saying of Jesus concerning the parable of the sower: when the disciples ask him about it, he replies, "To you has been given the mystery of the kingdom of God, but for those outside, everything comes in parables" (Mark 4:11, GJR). What Jesus is teaching is termed a "mystery" for his insider disci-ples, and the outsiders get hard-to-understand parables. "In order that," Mark continues (v. 12), "they may indeed look, but not perceive"—they are purposely excluded. Paul tells us much the same thing. He writes to the Corinthians that "We speak the wisdom of God in a mystery, the hidden [wisdom]" (1 Cor. 2:7, GJR).

Christianity had as its entrance requirement an initiation similar to that of many such cults. A period of instruction was followed by a bap-tism, held at night after vigils and prayers, in which the initiate wore white clothing over the naked body. The rite brought the initiate into a new state of being and membership in the community of the elect. The writer of the Letter to the Hebrews refers to this individual as one who has been "enlightened" (Heb. 6:4). Justin describes the process as it was done in the next century (ca. 155):

All those who have been convinced, and who believe that our instruc-tion and our message are true, and promise that they are able to live according to them, are admonished to pray and with fasting to beseech God for pardon for their past sins; and we pray and fast with them. Then they are conducted by us to a place where there is water, and are reborn with a form of rebirth such as we ourselves have undergone. . . . We, however, after thus washing the one who has been convinced and signified assent, lead him to those who are called brethren, where they are assembled. Then they earnestly offer common prayers for themselves and the one who has been enlightened. (*1 Apologia* 61–65)

The process of baptism was the Christian initiation, understood to be an "enlightenment" in the manner of the initiation of the mystery cults. Recall that in this *First Apology*, Justin is showing an emperor who is persecuting Christians how similar Christianity is to the best of paganism and therefore that it should be considered to be above suspicion.

The Eucharist also was celebrated as a mystery that guaranteed immortality. Scholars have readily derived the celebration of the Eucharist from the Jewish Passover feast, and it is so represented in the Gospels as the Last Supper, a kind of Passover invested with new meaning. But Christianity was very much indebted to both cultures, Jewish and Greco-Roman, and from the beginning Christians called the Eucharist a mystery and invested the elements with power. Paul tells us that those who ate of them in an unworthy manner became ill or died (1 Cor. 11:29–30). Ignatius of Antioch (d. ca. 107) calls the Eucharist the "medicine of immortality, the antidote that we should not die, but live forever in Jesus Christ" (*Ephesians* 20.2). Justin tells us that "we do not receive these things as common bread or common drink; . . . we have been taught that the food . . . is the flesh and blood of that incarnate Jesus" (*1 Apologia* 66). None of this was true of the traditional Passover.

Essentially everyone in the first centuries A.D., Christians included, understood the new faith as a kind of mystery religion, revealed by Jesus to his followers alone. In one of our earliest texts, Jesus declares:

I thank you, Father, Lord of heaven and earth, because you have hidden these things from the wise and the intelligent and have revealed them to infants. . . . All things have been handed over to me by my Father; and no one knows the Son except the Father, and no one knows the Father except the Son and anyone to whom the Son chooses to reveal him. (Matt. 11:25–27)

The Christians were proud to declare that theirs was the highest form of divine mystery, that they like no others before knew the true mysteries of the Father and his kingdom; it was "the mystery that was kept secret for long ages but is now disclosed" (Rom. 16:25–26). Christian philosophers for the first three hundred years and more showed time and again how Christianity built upon and then superseded the best results of the philosophers and cults of the Jews, Greeks, and Romans.

But the fact that Christianity to some degree presented itself and was understood as a mystery cult had some terribly negative consequences as time passed. The treatise of Justin quoted above was written to the emperor to convince him to stop persecuting the Christians, which he was doing precisely because the Christians had been classed not with the traditional and acceptable mysteries, but with the cult of Bacchus, a mystery cult that had been outlawed by the Romans in 186 B.C. for its immoralities and excesses. This is one great irony of the scholarly reluctance to understand the early Christian movement as had the ancients themselves: Christians were persecuted and killed not because the Eucharist was perceived as a new Passover, but because, to the world that heard of it, it was cannibalism, the eating of the flesh and blood of Jesus. One of the horrors and glories of the early Christian movement was that because the Romans classed it as an illicit form of mystery religion, it was persecuted, and therefore it was given occasion to show its real strength.

PAUL THE FORMER PHARISEE

This chapter opened by asking the question, what did those who heard the message think the Christians were, and what did they think they were being asked to do? As a movement, Christian groups presented a kind of philosophy to the world and organized themselves as a kind of mystery cult, except, of course, that they claimed their "way" to be far superior to any wisdom of the world's philosophies and their mystery to be the one true one, hidden from all time and now in their possession. We saw in the last chapter that, although they saw their philosophy and mystery as superior, they could not decide on what exactly it was and argued rather bitterly among themselves as to its content until the fourth and fifth centuries, much to the amusement of their detractors. The power and draw of the new movement did not rest on the agreement of its adherents to a set of doctrines, but on the second part of the question: What was it that they were asking people to do and be?

Paul heard the story and encountered the risen Jesus, yet spent the rest of his life in part arguing with other Christians over what the proper meaning and interpretation of the gospel was. But he was more importantly one of the founders of the Church, so influential that he stands just after Jesus as a source of Christianity. Early in their history, when the New Testament Scriptures were new and beginning to be read in the churches, it was "the gospel and the apostle" that were read, the story of Jesus and the Letters of Paul, as though there had been only one apostle. What did Paul understand that he was supposed to do and be?

Paul was once Saul the Pharisee, with very different values from those he acquired after becoming Christian. He tells us little about his former life, but he does say a number of revealing things that show how proud he was of his heritage and achievements. Part of his psychological makeup was a quite understandable confidence in his genealogy as a Jew who was heir to the promises of Abraham.

There was in his day an idea, later articulated as the "merits of the fathers," that applied to the descendants of the patriarchs, Abraham, Isaac, and Jacob, and the rest, but especially Abraham. Because of their great worth as holy men and because of the promises granted to them and their descendants, any reasonably faithful Jew of Jesus' day would fall heir to the promises. We see this idea in the opening scenes of the story of Jesus. When John the Baptist

> saw many Pharisees and Sadducees coming for baptism, he said to them, "You brood of vipers! Who warned you to flee from the wrath to come? Bear fruit worthy of repentance. Do not presume to say to yourselves, 'We have Abraham as our ancestor'; for I tell you, God is able from these stones to raise up children to Abraham." (Matt. 3:7–9)

"Do not presume to say to yourselves, 'We have Abraham as our ancestor.'" To counter this bit of foolishness, John the Baptist here uses a rather sarcastic joke to call the behavior of the Jewish authorities into question and counter their presupposition that merely because they are descendants of Abraham they will be acceptable to God. To paraphrase,

"God can make better sons of Abraham than you from hockey pucks." Their reliance on ancestry, on the "merits of the fathers," is worthless.

Again, in one of the major controversies of the Gospel of John, Jesus and the Jewish authorities are arguing over righteous deeds as opposed to correct lineage. They claim that "Abraham is our father," and Jesus retorts, "If you were Abraham's children, you would be doing what Abraham did" (John 8:39). They do not, and although they may be confident because of the fact that they are the physical descendants of Abraham, they disqualify themselves by their behavior. Jesus retorts, "You are from your father the devil" (John 8:44).

Likewise, Paul himself takes up the question and discusses the "advantage of the Jew," saying that it is "much, in every way" (Rom. 3:1–2). But he tries to show that the advantage lay not in "Jewishness," but in that the Jews had been given the Law, "the embodiment of knowledge and truth" (Rom. 2:20). And again, as with the previous texts, Paul teaches that only those who act righteously according to the Law, Jew or Gentile, are approved by God. Yet he himself had clearly once thought otherwise and knew that his new opinion was hardly that of the majority. He tells his Jewish readers in the same passage, "If you call yourself a Jew . . . and if you are sure that you are a guide to the blind . . ." (Rom. 2:17–19). This is what he once thought of himself; he is speaking from his own personal experience.

Paul was not the only one to have become a Christian apostle from among the ranks of educated Jews, and like him there seem to have been many others outside of the Twelve who began to take the gospel to the nations. But they put great trust in their lineage, as he had once himself, and apparently used it to advertise themselves. In a very sarcastic and humorous passage, Paul says of these other missionaries, "Are they Hebrews? So am I. Are they Israelites? So am I. Are they descendants of Abraham? So am I" (2 Cor. 11:22). Part of their legitimation was to tout their lineage. He is quite conscious of their claims and his own former basis of "confidence in the flesh":

> If anyone else has reason to be confident in the flesh, I have more: circumcised on the eighth day, a member of the people of Israel, of the tribe of Benjamin, a Hebrew born of Hebrews; as to the law, a Pharisee; as to zeal, a persecutor of the church; as to righteousness under the law, blameless. (Phil. 3:4–6)

Paul's competitors were making similar claims for themselves. This pride of lineage was something he grew up with, apparently: he was a "Hebrew of Hebrews," a reference to his parents, and they had named him "Saul" after the first king of Israel and the most famous person of their tribe of Benjamin. The two texts just cited show that these claims were not isolated to a single group, for these are two different sets of competing missionaries: the first group, encountered in Corinth, does not require the Corinthians to be circumcised, while the second, found infiltrating the church of Philippi, apparently does. And if not, those whom Paul counters in the Letter to the Galatians certainly did require it.

In Paul's Galatian Letter we learn a good deal more of his attitude toward himself before he became a Christian. He tells us:

> You have heard, no doubt, of my earlier life in Judaism. I used to persecute to extremes the church of God and was destroying it, and I advanced in Judaism beyond many of those my age among my people, for I was far more zealous for the traditions of my ancestors. (Gal. 1:13–14, GJR)

What must Paul have thought in his earlier self-confidence that allowed him to persecute the "heretics," his fellow Jews who had become Christians? He had once had the confidence in the "merits of the fathers" so normal for his time and religious compatriots. And he was advancing up the ranks more quickly than others of his own age, competing in some way with them and winning the approval of those in authority in Judaism. That he was seeking the approbation of those in authority he states plainly: "Am I now seeking human approval, or God's approval? Or am I trying to please people? If I were still pleasing people, I would not be a servant of Christ" (Gal. 1:10). Here he shows that he was once motivated to gain the attention and positive commendations of those above him, as though in some spiritual corporation with a hierarchy of positions of authority. And he was succeeding, sure of himself and the just nature of his opinions and actions, convinced of his right to persecute others.

This attitude was not atypical for his day and tradition. Long before, Moses and Joshua had led the armies of Israel against the Canaanites. The prophet Samuel took a sword and "hewed Agag [king of the Amalekites] in pieces before the Lord in Gilgal" (1 Sam. 15:33). And David had said that the Lord "trains my hands for war" (Ps. 18:34). The tradition had given the righteous Israelite the right to kill others in the name of the Lord. And not only Canaanites; the enemies of the Lord could be interpreted to mean those closer to home. After the Exile up to Paul's day, religious Jews had persecuted and killed Samaritans and other Jews over religious questions and struggles for power many times, and they continued to do so for a long time after Paul's death. Saul the Pharisee, the persecutor, was acting solidly within the norms of his culture and times.

And then came the experience on the road to Damascus, where, according to the Book of Acts, Saul met the risen Christ. What an unimaginable conflict of ideas and conceptions and values! "Saul, Saul, why do you persecute me? It's a hard thing for you to kick against spikes" (Acts 26:14, GJR). Jesus, the crucified "criminal" Saul so hates and whose followers he is seeking to destroy, the one who for him was a deceiver and an impostor and a breaker of the law, appears to him and his entourage in an overwhelmingly brilliant light that physically blinds Paul and knocks the whole group to the ground. Yet Jesus doesn't kill him as he should, or upbraid him, or even blame him; he tells him a joke based on an old Greek proverb of warning to the one who would fight against God (cf. Euripides *Bacchae* 795). He tells Paul that what he is doing is futile: he is not hurting Jesus but himself. Paul is wearing open-toed sandals, and in persecuting Jesus he's kicking a cactus: "It's hard to kick a cactus." The joke is on Paul, that in trying to stop the rise of Christianity, he is trying to stop the rising of the sun, or the coming tide, or the advent of spring, and he is only bloodying his own feet, damaging himself.

The tradition of stories of dead heroes coming back from the grave to bring vengeance on those who wronged either them or their followers would have dictated that the risen Jesus here kill Paul in some way worthy of his crimes against the young church. When, for example, the Persian army of Xerxes attacked the shrine of the Delphic oracle, the local heroes Phylacus and Autonous rose from their cultic grave sites and fought them off, killing many and routing the army (Herodotus *Histories* 8.37–39). Yet Jesus does not kill Paul and his fellow persecutors. Instead of punishment, Jesus shows him a level of mercy that transforms him. He invites him to become a follower himself and take on the role that Jesus himself once had. Nevertheless, he is not released so easily. Paul is led into the city blinded, and Jesus appears to Ananias, a disciple inside the city, and instructs him to heal Paul's sight: "I myself will show him how much he must suffer for the sake of my name" (Acts 9:16). The time for vengeance against the enemies in the Christian story would come soon enough, at the apocalyptic end of the age, soon to come, they thought, at the time of the return of Jesus as judge. Now was the time to invite those who would to follow, and themselves to become as Jesus had been. That was in no small part the genius of the gospel, the "good news" if that is what it was, for it was not a lighthearted invitation: "Take up your cross and follow me."

Paul was met by a crucified messiah. What a contradiction in terms! What an impossibility! We can hardly imagine the shock it must have been to face what for Paul was now incontrovertible fact: this Jesus who had been crucified by legitimate authorities and whose followers he was persecuting was in reality the Messiah. Ideas surrounding the role and function of the messiah differed among different groups in Palestine, but none of them included a messiah who would be killed, and especially not one executed with common criminals in such a publicly humiliating manner. And among Jews, one who would die such a death seems to have been purposely excluded: was it not written, "anyone hung on a tree is under God's curse" (Deut. 21:23). In perhaps the most famous example in the Gospels, after Jesus states clearly for the first time that he will be killed, Peter takes him aside and harshly reproaches him (Mark 8:32). When the time of his crucifixion came, even his own disciples fled and abandoned him to face his fate alone. The whole idea was impossible: a crucified man could not be the Christ.

We are told by our Gospel sources as they look back on the life of Jesus that he was not recognized, that he was misunderstood essentially by everyone. What they are trying to show is that what Jesus was and what he meant by his miracles and his teachings were far different from the expectations of his disciples, so much so that they seem to have missed the point of his life while he was among them. But it was in this one area especially for which they had no preparation at all in their inherited traditions and doctrines concerning the coming of the messiah, where prior understanding for them was impossible: that he would be rejected, humiliated, and die at the hands of the authorities, and then rise again from the dead. So in the Gospel of John, when Jesus overturns the tables of the money changers in the temple and in the ensuing controversy declares, "Destroy this temple, and in three days I will raise it up" (John 2:19), no one understands that he was speaking of the "temple" of his body. And later when speaking to the crowds, he indicates that he, the Son of Man, will be crucified, and they retort, "We have heard from the law that the Messiah remains forever. How can you say that the Son of Man must be lifted up [i.e., crucified]?" (John 12:34). After Peter rebukes Jesus and is told, "Get behind me, Satan!" (Mark 8:33), we learn later why Peter was so offended by the idea. Jesus states, "Those who are ashamed of me . . ." (Mark 8:38). The fact that the messiah would be crucified was a shame that could not be imagined or tolerated.

But Paul could not deny that this crucified criminal was in fact the Messiah, not after his encounter on the road. Paul had been following the wrong model and living out the wrong story. He had been climbing the social and religious ladder, progressing in his career beyond his contemporaries by hard work and tireless effort. He had been a success so far and had the promises of Abraham and Moses and David to guarantee him further success. He was confident in himself, believing in his own righteousness. He had followed a model that allowed killing in the name of the Lord, and he himself had been persecuting and destroying the growing Church. And then the world changed for him, and the story he was following had to be changed. At some time in Paul's encounter on the road, Jesus became his new master. Now he had a model of a completely different type: Jesus himself had suffered, and now Jesus was showing him how much he must suffer. Suffering was what Saul the persecutor had caused others to do, the outsiders and heretics and enemies. But Paul could do so no longer. Jesus had turned the other cheek—he had allowed the (self-)"righteous" to kill him.

The change in Paul is one of the most significant events in early Christian history, and presented a model for all who came after him to follow. Paul's self-assessment and self-image changed radically after his encounter with Jesus. He had seen himself as full of self-worth, wholly righteous and justified in himself and his tradition; he was high, others were low. He was spiritually rich, and perhaps even relatively well off materially (recall that prosperity was one part of the set of promises to the patriarchs). He expected long life and success. And then he stumbled over the Stumbling Block. It was for him much like meeting with his own death, meeting this dead man now alive from among the dead. His old life was over forever; he himself died and somehow became alive from among the dead. If we look at some of the places in his writings where he may be referring to this experience, we find just such language of personal death and wholly different subsequent life. Twice to the Galatians he describes what appears to be this critical point in his life:

> I have been crucified with Christ; and it is no longer I who live, but it is Christ who lives in me. And the life I now live in the flesh I live by faith in the Son of God, who loved me and gave himself for me. (Gal. 2:19–20)

He had once had occasion to be proud of his lineage, of his circumcision, the depth of the Jewish tradition, and Law that he followed and enforced. But now when encountering other Christians with that former attitude, he counters by saying:

> May I never boast of anything except the cross of our Lord Jesus Christ, by which the world has been crucified to me, and I to the world. (Gal. 6:14)

Paul had to construct a new way to understand himself and the point of his remaining life.

PAUL THE PHILOSOPHER-ATHLETE

The virtue of the hero had traditionally been in the area of military prowess, divided into physical strength and skills, on the one hand, and mental abilities—craftiness in the use of those skills and wisdom in counsel—on the other. These two aspects were exemplified, as we have seen, by the two main characters of the foundational epics of the ancient world, Achilles of the *Iliad* and Odysseus of the *Odyssey*.

War on both local and national levels was a common occurrence, yet few cities had or could afford standing armies. The single most important responsibility of the citizen body was defense of family and city; armies were in the main citizen armies. In times of peace, competitions in athletics were held, especially at religious festivals, as a kind of training ground for the physical and mental abilities useful in wartime. Competitive sports were of military derivation and application and included boxing, wrestling, the pankration (a no-holds-barred combination of boxing and wrestling), foot races of various distances (including a race in full armor), long jump, javelin, discus, and horse and chariot races. Fighting was essentially hand-to-hand combat, and we are told by more than one author that the contests of the athletes developed skills used in warfare: grappling with an enemy, running either to attack or escape, jumping over barriers (especially the ditches used for defense), throwing stones and spears, and of course cavalry skills.

Many of these contests can be found in the texts of Homer, where the very heroes of war and council participate in such sports at the funeral games for the fallen hero Patrocles (*Iliad* 22) or for entertainment, as at the feast of Alkinoos (*Odyssey* 8). The Olympic games, in fact, were continuously held at four-year intervals from 776 B.C. to A.D. 393, when the Christian emperor Theodosius finally banned them as a pagan religious festival; thus organized athletic competitions in Greece predate the writing of the Homeric epics. Plato, in his recommendations for an ideal state, advocates concerning athletics that the city overseers "should devise a series of honorable games with sacrifices, so that there may be certain festival combats copying the real war combats as closely as possible" (*Laws* 829b, GJR). Lucian, in a second-century work attempting to explain the value of athletics, shows their application not only in battle skills for civil defense, but for improving battle qualities of the soul:

> Having devised various kinds of gymnastic exercises and appointing coaches for each one, we teach one person boxing, and another the pankration, so that they might be both accustomed to endure hardships and run to meet blows, and might not turn away out of fear from wounds. (*Anacharsis* 24, GJR)

The normal individual in peacetime most like the ideal hero of epic was the athlete.

Athletic games were held in honor of a god or hero, and the competitions were religious festivals. Biannual or quadrennial games for all of the Greek world were held in Olympia, Delphi, Corinth, Nemea, and Athens. Local games were held in dozens of smaller towns, and after the conquests of Alexander, the institution of the gymnasium and associated athletic competitions became a regular feature of the hellenization of the ancient world. Throughout the East, cities founded on the Greek model or subsumed into the Hellenistic empire built gymnasiums and stadiums. By the second century B.C., Rome began introducing athletic games on the Greek model in Italy and the West. There were essentially no places of note in the Greco-Roman world without knowledge of and participation in the games.

The two aspects of heroic virtue, strength and craftiness, were compared in antiquity, to the detriment of the former. The character Agamemnon, in a play of Sophocles (ca. 496–406 B.C.), tells us:

> It is not the wide-shouldered or broad-backed men who are the most steadfast, but those who think well are victorious everywhere, and likewise a great bull by a small whip on the sides is guided straight on the road. (*Aias* 1250–52, GJR)

The "wisdom" of Agamemnon, the king of the Greeks, is here contrasted with the brute strength of Aias, the largest and strongest of the Greeks, and "the best man of the Argives who came to Troy, except Achilles" (*Aias* 1340–41, GJR). Yet he could not compete for honor with Odysseus and others in council or craft. Even between the two Homeric epics, between the characters Achilles and Odysseus, it is Achilles who is the more tragic because of the raging anger so characteristic of his military prowess. It is this uncontrolled rage that brings his fate down upon him and his companions. The poem opens as a tragedy with this "rage," in the Greek text as its first word: "Sing, O goddess, the rage of Achilles, son of Peleus" (*Iliad* 1.11, GJR). It was raging madness that also eventually caused the death of Aias. Yet it was the craftiness and guile of Odysseus that contributed much to the fall of Troy, that through years of suffering finally brought him home, and that brought about the deaths of those who had wronged his house. So Sophocles is stating a truth through his character Agamemnon long embedded in the heroic tradition: wisdom is superior to military strength.

Athletics also came in for critique among the writers of antiquity. Originally, the games were derived from the exercises of military training, yet, as in modern culture, victorious athletes became local favorites and athletic events the central topics of conversations. Tyrtaeus, an early poet (ca. 650–600 B.C.) of Sparta, contrasts sport with its ancient intent:

I would not make mention of, nor place a man in a poem,
neither for speed of foot nor for skill in wrestling,
not if he had the size and strength of the Cyclopes,
nor if running he beat the Thracian north wind
. . .
not if he had all glories except raging courage. (9.1–9, GJR)

Here the poet contrasts the successes of "mere" athletics with the much more serious application of such training for the soul, to inculcate courage in the face of deadly danger in time of war.

Athletics seemed to emphasize the physical aspects of training, and the contrast we saw above between strength and cunning finds its way into the critique of athletics also. Xenophanes of Colophon (ca. 570–after 480 B.C.) contrasts the wisdom and skill of, for example, righteous lawgivers and governors with those qualities in athletes. The most famous and venerable of the national games were dedicated to Zeus and held at Olympia, and the victors were crowned with a wreath made from wild olive branches. Other national games gave as prizes wreaths of laurel, parsley, celery, bay leaves, or apples, things considered trifles by many detractors. But the poet here shows that victorious athletes received much more of material value upon returning home in triumph; they were all professional athletes. Nevertheless, according to Xenophanes, wisdom is better than mere physical prowess:

If someone should gain a victory by swiftness of feet,
or in the pentathlon, there in the precinct of Zeus
beside the river of Pisa in Olympia, or wrestling
or enduring the painful boxing,
or some terrible contest that they call the pankration,
he would be more glorious for the citizens to behold,
and he would gain the shining front seat in assemblies,
and there would be food at public expense,
and a gift from the city, which would be a treasure for him;
and if with his horses he should gain all these things,
he would not be as worthy as I, for our wisdom is better
than strength of men or horses.
But this is the common opinion though very confused, nor is it right
to judge strength better than good wisdom. (2.1–14, GJR)

That athletes could then, as now, abuse their privileges and strut around proudly offended some of the poets. Euripides writes that "of all the myriads of bad things in Greece, nothing is worse than the race of athletes" (Frag. 282 Nauck, GJR).

One may wonder at the basis for such critique, since the poets and the educated "wise" were almost never among the successful athletes, and athletes seldom among the intelligentsia. But philosophers recognized the value of athletic training. Xenophon (ca. 428–354 B.C.) tells us that Socrates

> himself did not neglect the body, nor did he approve of those who did neglect it. Therefore he rejected that the overeater should over-exercise, but he approved as sufficient workout the amount of exertion the soul received agreeably. For he said that this habit was sufficient for health and did not hinder the care of the soul. (*Memorabilia* 1.2.4, GJR)

Even as caustic and unconventional a character as Diogenes (ca. 400–325 B.C.), from whose shameless behavior the Cynic school of philosophy received its name ("cynic" is from the Greek word for "dog"), valued athletic exercise, since it trained the body to suffer hardship and to require as little as possible. One writer of the third century A.D., Diogenes Laertius, collected sayings of the earlier philosophers and gives the following as Diogenes' opinion of athletic training:

> He used to say that exercise was twofold, the one spiritual and the other bodily; that according to the latter, perceptions arising from continuous exercise provide freedom for the accomplishing of virtue; that the one was incomplete without the other, there being nothing inferior about good health and strength among the proper things for the soul and the body. And he used to provide proofs of how easily one goes from exercise to virtue. (Diogenes Laertius 6.70, GJR)

Three of the most enduring and important schools of philosophy were those of Plato, the Cynics, and Aristotle. Plato's school was called the Academy. Antisthenes, a disciple of Socrates and founder of the Cynic school, used to hold his conversations in the gymnasium of the Fast Hound. And Plato's student Aristotle founded the Lyceum. All three were gymnasiums on the outskirts of Athens. Physical and intellectual training were paired for students from childhood through to maturity.

Philosophers from before the time of Socrates well into the Christian period used the terminology and imagery of the battlefield and athletic competition to illustrate the effort involved in the pursuit of philosophy and virtue. For Heraclitus, "The brave man is not only he who overcomes the enemy, but he who is stronger than pleasures" (214 Diels). The ranking of wisdom above strength in war, and of both above "mere" athletics, produced the inevitable exaltation of the pursuit of philosophy and virtue over and above that of military and athletic prowess. So for Antisthenes, "Virtue is a weapon that cannot be taken away," and "Prudence is a most sure defensive wall, for it cannot be breached or betrayed" (Diogenes Laertius 6.12–13, GJR). Epictetus tells us that

> Circumstances are the things that prove men. Furthermore, whenever a difficult circumstance comes on, remember that God like a gymnastic coach has matched you (in wrestling) with a rough young man. "For what?" someone says. So that you may become an Olympic victor, but apart from sweat, that will not happen. (*Discourses* 1.24.1, GJR)

The struggles of philosophers against their twofold enemies, the passions and drives of the body, on the one hand, and the crass and incorrigible audiences they faced in their public teaching and preaching, on the other, came to be represented in much the same language as the struggles of the classic Homeric heroes and the Olympic athletes. Especially those philosophers who had been persecuted or killed by tyrants and unjust mobs, though their numbers were quite small, came to be seen as heroic figures who had gained for their endurance the prize of immortality. These were, one must recall, the body/soul dualists who believed in the immortality of the soul, as opposed to the vast majority of people who believed there to be no afterlife other than the shades of the dead at the tomb and in Hades.

Paul clearly uses these models to help construct his own new view of himself. He employs the image of the philosophical athlete and warrior to describe himself several times in his letters. In a passage reminiscent of the military metaphors quoted above, he describes his own inner struggle in the battle of the mind and soul for the sake of Christian virtue:

We do not wage war according to human standards; for the weapons of our warfare are not merely human, but they have divine power to destroy strongholds. We destroy arguments and every proud obstacle raised up against the knowledge of God, and we take every thought captive to obey Christ. (2 Cor. 10:3–5)

And in perhaps his most famous use of the metaphor of the athlete, he shows the discipline and exercises in virtue that he had come to use in his attempt to bring his entire life under control for the sake of his mission:

Do you not know that in a race the runners all compete, but only one receives the prize? Run in such a way that you may win it. Athletes exercise self-control in all things; they do it to receive a perishable wreath, but we an imperishable one. So I do not run aimlessly, nor do I box as though beating the air; but I punish my body and enslave it, so that after proclaiming to others I myself should not be disqualified. (1 Cor. 9:24–27)

One should recall here that athletics of this sort were not a part of the old Hebrew tradition. They were a fundamental aspect of Greco-Roman life and were often used as an analogy for the pursuit of philosophical ideals. Paul had been a self-assured persecutor of other Jews whose theological positions were unacceptable to him. He had prided himself on his ancestry and his progress in his religion. Yet he uses a business analogy to describe the change of understanding that came about through his conversion: these earlier things were once like business profits, and "whatever gains I had, these I have come to regard as loss because of Christ" (Phil. 3:7). In spite of the derivation by some scholars of Paul's athletic imagery from the Hellenistic synagogue, Paul himself does not begin to understand himself as a philosopher-athlete and warrior until after his conversion. He was not such a person as a Jew in the synagogue, but only after his encounter with the risen Jesus. These images were respected and easily understood as models for the philosophical struggle of life, a struggle not only against the appetites and temptations of the body, but against such people as the former Saul the Pharisee himself. But Paul's self-understanding and construction of his new life do not stop with respected and easily understood models.

PAUL THE GLADIATOR

The figure of the philosopher-athlete and warrior were positive images honored in Greco-Roman culture, and the true philosopher was admired, if grudgingly, by all. But Jesus had not been admired by all. There were other categories of individual that remained. Paul calls himself a slave of Christ, and it was definitely a shame to be a slave or even to have been born of a slave. Many, if not most, of the early Christians, to the best of our knowledge, were slaves. Nearly two-thirds of people in the Roman world were encumbered by one of the four levels of slavery. But neither Jesus nor Paul had ever been a human slave, and to call oneself a slave of God was no disgrace in either Greek or Jewish culture. Examples abound of such language by both the philosophers and the prophets. Jesus, however, as a free man and by definite obedient choice, had been even worse: he had died the death of a criminal.

Criminals became liable to capital punishment for several different classes of crimes. Martial, Roman poet of the later first century, lists three reasons for execution of a criminal in the arena:

> Finally he received fitting punishment,
> the criminal either stabbing the jugular of his master with a sword,
> or insane, he had despoiled a temple of its hidden gold,
> or had laid cruel torches under you, O Rome. (*Spectacula* 7, GJR)

Murder, sacrilege, and arson are here described as typical crimes deserving capital punishment. Other texts add rebellion and desertion to the enemy. One of the earliest crimes subject to the death penalty, found in the earliest Roman law code, the Twelve Tables dating from the fifth century B.C., was *perduellio*, "treason." In 103 B.C., the Lex Appuleia established *maiestas minuta*, "majesty diminished," as a crime that replaced the earlier but more narrow *perduellio*. Cicero defines it as follows: "To diminish the majesty is to take something away from the dignity or greatness or power of the people or of those to whom the people have given power" (*De Inventione Rhetorica* 2.17.53, GJR). With the rise of empire, *maiestas* was widened to include any attempt on the life or dignity of the emperor or his family. Under Tiberius (r. 14–37), the emperor during whose reign Jesus was crucified, prosecutions for *maiestas* became frequent even on apparently trivial charges. All of the charges listed above except for desertion to the enemy are important for the subsequent history of the Church, as Christians were at one time or another accused and killed for each of them.

Criminals liable to capital punishment died in the main by four methods, though several more "creative" means were utilized to a greater or lesser degree. The most dignified, and that befitting a Roman citizen, was beheading with a single stroke of the sword. As the empire grew, and especially after citizenship was granted to every free person in A.D. 212, the right of execution by the sword was increasingly reserved for the more respected citizens, senators, soldiers, those in service to the emperors, or city council members. All others were subject to the penalties earlier reserved for slaves and noncitizens: crucifixion, rending by wild beasts (*ad bestias*), and burning (*crematio* or *ad flammas*). Executions of criminals were performed in public, typically after flogging or torture, in the most conspicuous places available. Often the forum or the games were chosen as sites for executions. There were few cities with effective police forces, and public humiliation, torture, and execution was, in the minds of the ancients, a necessary deterrent to crime. A speech of the first century informs us that "whenever we crucify criminals, the most frequented highways are chosen, where the greatest number of onlookers can watch, and be persuaded by this warning" (Pseudo-Quintilian *Declamationes Maiores* 274.13). The amphitheaters, popular from the first century B.C. on, were the most favored sites for wild beast shows and hence the execution of criminals *ad bestias*, since the animals could be kept safely and separated from the bystanders.

Nero's persecution of the Christians after the disastrous fire of Rome in A.D. 64 illustrates the "creative" methods used to execute criminals condemned *ad bestias* and *ad flammas*. Tacitus (ca. 55–120), a Roman patrician and historian, describes in his *Annals* the vices of Nero, emperor from 54 to 68. Tacitus despised Nero, a man who "left no vice untried by which he might act more perversely" (15.37). On the night of July 17–18, A.D. 64, a blaze broke out in Rome that raged unchecked from block to block, city quarter to city quarter, eventually burning the imperial palace itself. The fleeing crowds were caught in their own press and often trapped, to the point that many who could escape chose to die in the flames rather than live with the total loss of their families and possessions. The fire burned for six days, destroying much of the city; it killed or left destitute a large proportion of the populace. Nero made several prudent decisions to help those made homeless and destitute and to rebuild the city on a grand scale, but it appeared that the fire had cleared away the center of the city so that he might build a large and lavish new palace for himself.

> But by no human effort, neither by the donations of the emperor nor by appeasements of the gods, did the infamy desist that the fire was believed to have been set by [Nero's] command. Therefore, to erase the rumor, Nero substituted as those responsible, and treated with the most exquisite tortures, those hated for their shameful deeds whom the people called Christians. . . .
>
> First, then, those who confessed were arrested; then on their testimony a huge multitude was convicted, not so much for the crime of arson as for hatred of the human race. And mockery was added to the dying, so that while covered with the skins of beasts they perished by the tearing bites of dogs, or they were affixed to crosses to be torched, and when daylight failed, they were burned as night-lights. Nero offered his gardens for the spectacle, and he sponsored a circus game, mixing among the crowd dressed as a charioteer or standing in his chariot. From this, although these acts were against criminals deserving of extreme penalties, there arose pity, on the grounds that they had been undertaken not for public service but for the cruelty of one man.
> (15.44, GJR)

Criminals were exposed to beasts by various means in the arenas, during shows called "spectacles." They were burned either by the obvious means of being placed in the midst of a burning stack of wood or covered with a pitch-coated garment that was then lighted. In the passage above, Nero provided his own gardens for the "spectacle," which included games and races, along with the execution of Christians as criminals. According to Church tradition, sometime prior to or during this first "official" persecution of Christians, Peter and Paul were executed, Peter by crucifixion and Paul, as a Roman citizen, by the single sword stroke.

The Roman Empire was divided into a series of provinces much like states in a modern country. Provincial governors were appointed from Rome and sent to their provinces to rule for a limited period, often two years or more, and then were replaced by new governors. They had nearly absolute authority in their provinces, and their word could supersede almost any legal right or precedent. A number of governors were rapacious in their abuses, and redress was nearly impossible to obtain. Cicero's successful prosecution (70 B.C.) of the governor of Sicily, Gaius Verres, shows to what remarkable extent the governor acted almost completely without restraint in his province and how he could buy his way out of any difficulties upon return to Rome. Cicero calls him a "man of singular greed, audacity, and wickedness," who is "acquitted by hope in his vast fortune" (*In Verrem* 1.2).

A more just, but again arbitrary, example may be found in the Roman historian Suetonius. Writing about A.D. 120, Suetonius tells us of Galba when he was governor of Spain (60–68), before becoming emperor after Nero's death (68). In one instance,

> a teacher, because he had murdered his pupil by poison after whom he was heir next in line, he [Galba] did away with by crucifixion; and when he invoked the laws and testified that he was a Roman citizen, as if he were going to lighten the penalty by some relief and honor, he ordered that he be moved and placed on a cross much higher than the others and painted white. (*Galba* 9, GJR)

Not even Roman citizenship could protect one from the most humiliating of deaths in the provinces. This point will become quite important in the case of the apostle Paul.

The governor in general was to ensure continued Roman rule against political rebellion, the preservation of the *pax Romana* ("Roman peace"), and enforce basic morality and piety, thus preserving the *pax deorum* ("peace of the gods"), a spiritual contract of symbiosis between the gods and people. If the people preserved piety and the worship of the gods, then the gods would preserve the people; if they neglected their worship or allowed immoral behavior, the wrath of the gods would overturn society.

The preservation of these two kinds of peace became fundamental in the persecution of Christianity, as Christianity was perceived at times as both seditious and immoral, and the Christians for their part adamantly refused to worship the traditional gods of the empire. Pliny's letter to his friend emperor Trajan is one of the most famous accounts of a persecution of Christians to come down to us. He explains in the opening paragraph that "I have never been present at the examinations of Christians," and yet he proceeds by his own creative means. He writes to Trajan to ask advice on how to conduct such trials, and at the time of writing is awaiting his response:

> In the interim, for those who are being brought to me as Christians, this is the method I have followed: I asked them whether they were Christians. If they confessed, I asked a second and third time after threatening them with punishment. Those who persisted I ordered to be led away to execution, for I was in no doubt, whatever it was that they were confessing, that stubbornness and inflexible obstinacy surely ought to be punished. There have been others of like senselessness who, because they were Roman citizens, I have listed to be sent to Rome. (*Epistulae* 10.96, GJR)

Christians are executed for their "stubbornness and inflexible obstinacy," which were not normally capital crimes. Note that, unlike Galba, Pliny sent Roman citizens to Rome for trial. There was no standard treatment and no authority other than that of the governor.

As presented in the New Testament, the case of Jesus is quite difficult to understand if one does not see the authority of the provincial governor as nearly absolute, especially in preserving the *pax Romana*. Why was Jesus condemned and crucified, if, as according to each of the Gospels, he was declared innocent by Pilate, the Roman governor of Palestine? In Luke he is declared innocent by both Pilate and Herod Antipas, the Roman governor of Galilee and Jesus' home territory. In addition, he is declared innocent by one of the two thieves on the cross and again by a Roman centurion standing by witnessing the events. Yet he and his followers were in direct competition with the religious establishment in Jerusalem. The Jewish historian Josephus (ca. 37–100) tells us that John the Baptist had also attracted large crowds and that the same Herod feared that the movement would lead to rebellion; the political danger, according to Josephus, was that the crowds "seemed to do everything by his [John's] counsel" (*Antiquities* 18.117–19). So Herod had John beheaded. This may have been the kind of danger Pilate saw, and concluded, especially after the accusations leveled against Jesus by his Jewish competitors, that this man was a potentially dangerous element. What did the "kingdom of God" mean, anyway? Even though Jesus may have been completely innocent of political sedition and his kingdom entirely spiritual, Pilate had him crucified anyway.

Paul was a Roman citizen according to the book of Acts, although he never addresses the issue in his own writings. Yet in his letters to the Corinthians he makes a shocking statement:

> I think that God has exhibited us apostles as last of all, as though sentenced to death, because we have become a spectacle to the world, to angels and to mortals. . . . We have become like the rubbish of the world, the dregs of all things. (1 Cor. 4:9–13)

The image is taken from the amphitheater and refers to the condemnation of criminals to death.

"Spectacle" is a translation of the Greek word *theatron*, from which we get our word "theater." It normally meant the actual building, a theater or amphitheater, but could be used, as here, in a transferred sense for what was seen, for the shows, in the theaters and amphitheaters of the Roman world. In Latin the word for this transferred use is *spectaculum*, the source of the English word "spectacle." Roman spectacles included four main elements, though only rarely were all the elements present in a single spectacle: *ludi* ("games"), *fabula* ("stories" or plays), the execution of criminals, and *munera* ("offerings" to the dead, the gladiatorial combats). The first two were by far the most common and not at all sinister in intent; they were for healthy competition and entertainment. Cicero, in a philosophical work defining his ideal state, divides the two as follows:

> Now, since public games are divided into theater and circus, let there be established contests between persons in running, boxing, and wrestling, and races for horses to the point of sure victory in the circus; and let the theater resound with song to harps and flutes, as long as they are in moderation as is prescribed by law. (*De Legibus* 2.38, GJR)

The athletic games are the standard type of games we have seen earlier, held in the *circus*, a straight-sided oval especially suited for horse and chariot racing. The Circus Maximus in Rome held over a hundred thousand spectators. In Greek cities the venue would have been the stadium. The theaters were ubiquitous and were the sites of the *fabula*, dramas, plays, comedies, musical performances and public competitions in recitation of Homer and the epics. All cities and many smaller towns had athletic stadiums and theaters.

The site of the *munera*, the gladiatorial combats, was the amphitheater. The most imposing structure in any Roman city of the second century A.D. and later was the amphitheater. Originally *munera* were held in temporary wooden structures built especially for the purpose, and often for the single occasion. By the beginning of the first century B.C. there began to be permanent stone amphitheaters, such as at Pompeii. Vespasian (r. 69–79) began the construction of the Colosseum at Rome, which was dedicated by his son Titus (r. 79–81) in 80. Its capacity was, according to ancient sources, eighty thousand people. After its construction it became the model to be copied everywhere, and city after city built arenas in imitation and emulation. Greek cities had the advantage of large and centrally located theaters, often built centuries earlier, that could be converted into amphitheaters with a minimum of architectural change, with only the addition of walls to keep the animals from the spectators and to hold water for sea battles. North of Italy in Gaul, where constructions from earth were common, Romans built some of the most imposing amphitheaters from brick and earthworks, still visible today.

Munera (singular *munus*) were originally and properly "offerings" to the dead presented at funerals. The first instance of gladiatorial combats being staged at a funeral were three pairs of gladiators who fought to the death at the behest of the sons of Junius Brutus Pera for his funeral in 264 B.C. Tertullian explains sarcastically:

> The elders thought that they were performing a service to the dead by this spectacle. . . . For formerly, since it was believed that the souls of the dead were propitiated with human blood, they used to purchase and sacrifice captives or slaves of low status at funerals. Later it seemed better to overshadow impiety by pleasure. And so, when those purchased had been trained in whatever arms and as they were able—just so they might learn to be killed—then on the appointed day of the funeral rites, they did away with them at the tombs. So they consoled the dead with murders. This is the origin of the *munus*. (*De Spectaculis* 12, GJR)

Tertullian is wrong about it having been a custom to sacrifice humans of lowest status at funerals; there are only a handful of such examples in all of Greek literature, and those are always shocking departures from what was considered pious. He is dependent, no doubt, on the account in Homer of the barbarism of Achilles, who sacrificed twelve Trojan youths on the tomb of his dead friend Patrocles at his funeral. Nevertheless, Tertullian does show the popular rationale for *munera*. These were private affairs, paid for by the families of the deceased, to bring remembrance to the dead and honor to the surviving family. Often included were *venationes*, "hunting spectacles," in which wild animals fought each other or were hunted and killed by professionally trained *bestiarii*, "beast fighters," a special kind of gladiator. These *venationes* survive today in similar arenas in Spain and Mexico as bullfights, though in antiquity nearly every type of animal that could be forced to fight by whips and fire was brought to the arena to fight. Such *munera* were enormously expensive, requiring the construction of a site, the importation from the ends of the empire of wild animals, and the purchase of trained gladiators. Very wealthy families, however, gained no small influence and admiration for such shows and often secured election to high office through their means. With the rise of empire, such *munera* were taken over by the emperor as the only one with sufficient financial means to afford such enormous outlays and the one most interested to keep such publicity and influence in his own hands.

Spectacles that included gladiatorial combats were held rarely, at only two periods in the year. The oldest custom was to hold them at the funerals of powerful individuals, or as commemorative events recalling the life of some notable family member who had recently passed away, but at a time, such as near an election, that would further the political ends of the surviving family members. Under Augustus (r. 27 B.C.–A.D. 14), they came to be held regularly in December at the end of the year at the winter solstice, five days prior to and five days following the Saturnalia on December 17, and in the spring at the Quinquatria, a festival in honor of Minerva (Athena among the Greeks) held March 19–23, marking the end of winter and the birth of the new year. The coincidence with the Christian Christmas and Easter was not lost on the Church. Other types of shows, of games and theatrical performances, musical competitions and recitations were far more common and spread out throughout the remaining months.

Also under Augustus the custom arose to divide the spectacles into three separate and originally distinct elements: *venationes* ("beast hunting") in the morning; the execution of criminals during the midday recess for lunch; and *munera*, the gladiatorial combats, in the afternoon. All three of these divisions are important for the subsequent history of the Church, and the first two more directly for the apostle Paul and the martyrs who were to follow him for the next two and a half centuries.

Suetonius mentions the first two divisions in his account of the emperor Claudius, who was notorious for his love of the arena, especially for the midday executions:

> He was so delighted with the beast fights and those of midday, that he would descend to the spectacle at first light, and at midday, after the people were dismissed for lunch, he would keep his seat. And beyond those so designated (for the show), even for slight and hasty cause he would commit (to the arena) some people from the number of carpenters and even assistants and that kind, if a machine or wooden lift or some other such thing did not function well enough. (*Claudius* 34, GJR)

The arenas were outfitted with various kinds of apparatus that brought animals up from the underground pens by elevators or supplied scenery for dramatic presentations that set the stage for combats or "dramatic" executions. Claudius was apparently not the only emperor to force slaves into the arena to die for such a trivial offense as having built a faulty elevator or ramp. Pliny praises emperor Trajan for having stopped such practice, which was apparently common under his predecessor, Domitian (r. 81–96). In an expanded version of the speech delivered to the Senate as consul in 100, Pliny contrasts Trajan's virtues with Domitian's vices. Domitian had been a fan of the heavily armed gladiator, the *murmillo*, and once had a wealthy citizen, a fan of the Thracian fighters (who fought with lighter Greek-style arms), thrown into the arena for "impiety," because he said that the Thracian was the equal of the *murmillo*, but better than the giver of the games (i.e., Domitian); he was dragged from his seat and thrown to the dogs with a sign reading "A partisan of the Thracians spoke impiously" (Suetonius

Domitian 10). But, Pliny writes, this policy of terror had now changed under the new emperor Trajan:

> Now, how free were the desires of the spectators, how secure their applause. (The charge of) impiety, as it used to be, was cast at no one because he hated a gladiator; no one, made from being a spectator into a spectacle, expiated wretched pleasures by hook and flames. (*Panegyricus* 33, GJR)

The morning shows began early and were the times for animal acts as well as hunts. Trained animals performed much as they do in modern circuses, but also included were the *venationes*, staged fights between ferocious animals of different sorts, and between wild animals and trained *bestiarii*, gladiator animal fighters. Mosaics show animals of different sorts chained together and goaded on to fight by attendants with whips and torches. Martial writes of a rhinoceros who "tossed a heavy bear with his twin horn, like a bull throws straw-men to the stars" (*Spectacula* 22.5–6). The animal later fights a pair of steers, a gazelle, and a wild ox. Lions met tigers, bears fought leopards, elephants rhinoceroses; every kind of animal was brought from the far reaches of the empire to demonstrate the might and extent of Roman power. The mosaics often show several *bestiarii* fighting many different kinds of animals together at the same time, most often successfully, while some are overcome by the animals' ferocity. One *bestiarius*, Carpophorus by name, is applauded by Martial as having killed more than twenty animals in one day (*Spectacula* 27).

It is here that one should recall the statement of Paul to the opponents in his own Corinthian church: "I fought with wild animals at Ephesus" (1 Cor. 15:32). The image is drawn from the morning shows at the arenas held all over the Greco-Roman world. Paul's citizenship would have been no protection against such a fate; we have seen the arbitrary power of the governors in the provinces, and even the emperors in Rome, against citizens. The statement, however, must be interpreted figuratively, for there was (almost) no exit from the arena but death. An especially brave and charismatic fighter might gain freedom by acclamation from the crowd and a grant of clemency from the *editor*, the sponsor of the games, but one can hardly believe that that was Paul's lot. Tertullian was correct to interpret this incident figuratively against the background of the persecutions Paul suffered in the province of Asia, of which Ephesus was the capital city: "We do not want you to be unaware, brothers and sisters, of the affliction we experienced in Asia; for we were so utterly, unbearably crushed that we despaired of life itself" (2 Cor. 1:8).

Between the morning *venationes* and the gladiatorial combats in the afternoon were the public executions of criminals. Those condemned to death were most often killed by crucifixion in public areas, along roadsides or in the forum, but if they happened to receive sentence while games were being held or drawing near, they were reserved for the spectacles. Such "entertainments" were increasingly popular, and the execution of criminals in the arena became a regular feature of the games. Josephus tells us that after the Jewish war (66–70), the victorious Roman general and future emperor Titus distributed most of the captured Jewish prisoners "as presents to the provincial governments to be destroyed in the theaters by sword and wild beasts" (*Bellum Judaicum* 6.418, GJR). Titus spent considerable time in Caesarea Philippi, and while there

> he celebrated his brother's birthday remarkably, having dedicated much of the punishment of the Jews for that honor. For the number of those killed both in the fights against the wild animals and in combat with one another and of those burned to ashes exceeded twenty-five hundred. (Josephus *Bellum Judaicum* 7.37, GJR)

The condemned were thrown to the beasts, or made to fight one another, or burned alive. Mosaics show individuals tied to stakes on carts, which were then wheeled into the arena before attacking beasts. One scene on a lamp shows a woman tied to the back of a bull being mauled by a leopard. Others, such as the Jewish prisoners, were forced to fight the beasts or one another to the death. Seneca, in a strongly worded condemnation of those who enjoyed watching such combats, writes:

> In the morning men are exposed to lions and bears, at midday those who have committed murder are ordered by their own spectators to be exposed to those about to kill them, and the victor is kept on for another slaughter. The (only) exit from the fighting is death. The action is forced along by sword and fire. These things go on while the arena is

empty. "But someone was a thief." So what? Did he kill a man? "He killed a man. Because he killed, he deserves to suffer this." You wretch, what did you merit, that you should watch this? "Kill, beat, burn! Why so timidly does he run towards the sword? Why does he kill with little boldness? Why so unwillingly does he die and is led by blows to his wounds?" (But) they receive mutual stabbings in naked and open chests. "The spectacle is at intermission; meanwhile let men have their throats cut, lest nothing be going on." (*Epistulae* 7, GJR)

Seneca here constructs an imaginary dialogue with the despised spectator, who is the one who clamors for violence. The criminals are forced by torches and whips into fighting with each other without defensive armor, bearing only swords. If one survives, he is forced into another fight, and another, until he is killed. The same is then done to the new victor.

One of the more popular modes of execution was to force some criminal into playing the part of a tragic figure of myth who died in the drama, except that the criminal would actually be killed on stage. Plutarch, Greek philosopher (ca. 50–120) and writer, again criticizes the spectators of such shows:

> Some are no more discerning than children, who see the criminals in the theaters, often crowned, in tunics of gold and sea-purple mantles, dancing the Pyrrhic dance, and admire them and are amazed as though they are blessed, until the moment when they behold them being stabbed and whipped and burning in that flowered and expensive clothing. (*Moralia* 554b *De Sera*, GJR)

A famous Roman slapstick mime current in the first century was called the Laureolus after its main character. It was apparently often performed in the arena because of its horrible ending:

> Just as Prometheus, tied to a Scythian rock,
> fed the incessant bird with his too great breast,
> so Laureolus offered his naked viscera to a Caledonian bear,
> hanging on no false cross.
> His mangled limbs were alive, while the parts dripped,
> and in his whole body was no body at all. (Martial *Spectacula* 7, GJR)

The criminal forced to play Laureolus had committed some capital crime, as the continuation of the poem explains. Tertullian, in his condemnation of paganism, recalls his own former experiences in watching dramas played out by the condemned, where the gods themselves are portrayed as characters or victims, and then someone plays Mercury, the guide of the dead to the underworld, or Pluto, the king of the underworld, to drag off the corpses:

> Obviously you are more religious in the amphitheater seats of the gladiators, where over human blood, over the filth of punishments, your gods dance accordingly the plots and criminals play out the stories, or criminals are punished as the gods themselves. We have often seen castrated the god Attis from Pessinus, or someone cremated alive who had played Hercules. We have laughed also at the sport of the gods at the midday game, where father Pluto, brother of Jove, dragged off what is left of the gladiators with his hammer, where Mercury, with small wings on his baldness, with small fire in his staff, tests by cautery [whether] the breathless bodies are already dead or pretending to be. (*Ad Nationes* 1.10.46, GJR)

People were castrated while playing the god Attis, who was castrated and died in his myth, or burned alive while playing the part of Heracles, who burned himself to death on a pyre.

Paul tells us, "I think that God has exhibited us apostles as last of all, as though sentenced to death, because we have become a spectacle to the world, to angels and to mortals" (1 Cor. 4:9). Paul here likens himself to a condemned criminal, "sentenced to death," who is sent into the arena to be laughed at and killed in a kind of cosmic drama. The *editor* of this spectacle in which Paul finds himself, the one who organizes and pays for everything and gains the credit among the spectators, the one who buys the condemned slaves or captured enemies or criminals for the show and exhibits them in the arena, is God. The spectators are the whole population of the cosmos, human and divine. And, as Jesus says in Luke, "By your endurance you will gain your souls" (Luke 21:19).

We have heard from several critics of the games among the writers of antiquity. Seneca wrote that "Nothing indeed is so damning to good morals than to sit through some spectacle" (*Epistulae* 7), and he was echoed by many church writers. But Romans would never have tolerated such spectacles if they did not find them to be of profit. Pliny tells us that such a show properly held would "incite to beautiful wounds and contempt of death, since even in the persons of slaves and criminals love of praise and desire for victory may be discerned" (*Panegyricus* 33, GJR). The purpose was to steel the spectators for valor in war, and there was a code of valor and endurance among gladiators in the arena. Cicero, writing around 45 B.C., informs us of what the public learned by watching the combats:

> Gladiators, either ruined men or foreigners, what blows they suffer!
> Those who are well trained would rather receive a blow than to avoid it
> like a coward. How often it is shown that they prefer nothing rather
> than to satisfy their masters or the people! Even when done in by
> wounds, they send [messengers] to their masters who ask what they
> wish; if they are satisfied, they prefer themselves to lie down [defeated].
> What mediocre gladiator groans? Who ever changes expression? Who
> not only stands, but even lies down like a coward? Who, when he has
> lain down, when ordered to receive the sword, withdraws his neck?
> (*Tusculan Disputations* 2.41, GJR)

They did not cry out for mercy; they did not cry out at all. They did not shrink from combat or wounds or even death. When defeated, they asked their owners what they wished; if it was for their own deaths, they took the *coup de grâce* bravely.

Sometimes when a gladiator had fought bravely and impressed the crowd, the spectators would call out for *missio*, "release," from the arena and status of gladiator and admission to freedom. Martial commemorates in a poem a remarkable instance of such a moment during the opening series of games at the Colosseum under the emperor Titus in A.D. 80:

> When Priscus was prolonging, when Verus was prolonging the
>   contest,
> And Mars was long equal for both,
> *Missio* often was asked for the men by great clamor.
> But Caesar himself obeyed his own law:
> The law was, after the victory palm was placed, to engage until the
>   finger (was raised).
> But still, he often gave platters (of food) and gifts.
> Nevertheless, an end was found for the equal combat.
> They fought as equals; they yielded (in defeat) as equals.

He sent to both the staff (of freedom); Caesar (sent) to both the
   palms.
This prize innate virtue carried off.
This has happened under no ruler except you, Caesar:
When two fought, and both were victor. (*Spectacula* 29, GJR)

Titus allowed the two gladiators, Priscus and Verus, to fight to an ex-
hausted draw, while the crowd clamored for their release and he sent
food and presents to the spectators. Finally he gave both of them their
liberty, which, Martial writes, they had earned by "innate virtue." The
trained gladiator, once a criminal or enemy or slave, an outcast without
rights, exemplified the Roman virtues of courage and endurance in the
face of death and by employing those virtues could win freedom. After
the experience on the road to Damascus, Paul came to see himself not in
the role of the self-confident, elevated persecutor, but as a condemned
man in the arena, fighting for his soul by faithful endurance; the lessons
of the gladiator were not lost on him.

Chapter 7

MARTYRS AS HEROES

Why did the Romans persecute Christians at all? They did not normally persecute other religions, even foreign religions. They did not even bother the Jews unless the Jews were stirring up some rebellion in Palestine. There does not seem to have been an *a priori* reason for persecution from the Roman side. It may seem obvious in the extreme to say so, but the conflict with the Roman Empire depended entirely in the early period on the Christians throwing down the challenge. Had there been no Christian mission, had Christians not found it necessary to convert others and turn them away from the religions of the empire, there would have been no Roman reaction, no persecution. But there also would have been no subsequent Church. The Christians not only caused their own success by spreading their faith, but also caused a major problem for themselves by forcing the Romans either to stand idly by and watch their traditions be overturned or to react.

And the faith was not spread solely, or for that matter in the main, by "professionals," by apostles and missionaries. Just as every follower of Jesus was required to take up the cross, to join in the example and purpose of the leader, so, we are told (with some exaggeration), "every Christian worker, no matter who," told whoever would listen about the Christian God, though even philosophers found the divine nature hard to explain (Tertullian *Apologeticus* 46.9). The word here translated "worker" (Latin *opifex*) means merely some artisan or laborer or carpenter, an ordinary Christian otherwise untrained in philosophy or rhetoric, not a professional minister. We do not know, for example, who brought the gospel to northern Asia Minor where Pliny encountered his Christians; no record from the first century describes such an apostolic mission. Ordinary Christians, apparently, spread their message like a disease into every corner of the empire.

"Disease," in fact, is part of the description used by the Romans concerned. In Pliny's letter to emperor Trajan, Pliny describes the extent of the infiltration of Christianity into the towns and countryside and his motivation for persecution:

> Not only the cities, but also the villages and rural areas have been invaded by the disease of this superstition; yet this seems able to be stopped and corrected. It is true enough that the temples, until now almost deserted, have begun to be crowded, and the solemn rites, long neglected, are being resumed; and the meat of sacrificial victims is generally available, a buyer for which was to this point only rarely found. From this it is easy to suppose that a multitude of people may be able to be reformed, if there be place for repentance. (*Epistulae* 10.96, GJR)

We find here that Christianity became by the first decade of the second century a major force among the mass of the population. The temples of the traditional gods had become nearly deserted, one evidence of which was the fact that meat was hardly available in the market. A major source of meat came from the temples, where it had first to be sacrificed to one or another of the gods, a portion given to the priests, and then the rest could be sold at market. But at the time of Pliny's persecution, so few people went to the pagan temples any longer that little meat was available. In addition, Christians would not eat food sacrificed to "idols," that is, to the Roman gods represented by statues in temples, and therefore a "buyer for [such food] was to this point only rarely found." Even if such meat did find its way into the market, no one would buy it.

This bit of evidence is more important than it first seems because it comes from a non-Christian Roman governor and persecutor writing to his friend the emperor. He may be exaggerating somewhat the number of Christians in Bithynia to justify his actions in killing them, but he seems to have needed no such justification. These trials were apparently common enough; Pliny himself had simply not been present at any and didn't know firsthand what to do. But he did seem to know that if there were lots of Christians, they needed to be reconverted or killed, and there were lots of Christians in Pliny's province. This fact is of interest because of the number of interpreters who have tried to minimize the influence and appeal of the Christian message, for reasons, one must say, of their own, unsupported by the ancient evidence. Pliny writes in effect that the religion of the Romans had been all but abandoned in favor of Christianity in a far-off province neither Roman nor Greek nor Jewish (though it contained Romans, Greeks, and Jews), a mere eighty years after the death of Jesus. The level of commitment was not particularly heroic for most, since his persecution turns so many back, but without threats of death and actual executions to help them, the Roman gods were losing badly, and much more quickly than generally admitted.

The teaching of the Christian faith itself was to the Romans a disease consisting of "superstition." This derogatory word is used consistently by our sources. Pliny labels it as such. Tacitus calls it a "deadly superstition" (*Annals* 15.44), Suetonius "a new and injurious superstition" (*Nero* 16), and the accuser in the dialogue *Octavius* a "vain and demented superstition" (Minucius Felix *Octavius* 9.1). The Latin term *superstitio* designated in this context an unreasonable religious belief, as opposed to the term *religio*, which designated the proper religious observance employed by the Romans. So we read in various texts of "barbarian superstition," "the superstitions of magicians," and of "fortune-tellers" or "the insane error of superstition," in which there is "worthless fear of the gods," and "the superstitions of imbecilic souls and old women." Cicero tells us that

> not only by philosophers but also by our ancestors, religion (*religio*) was separated from superstition (*superstitio*). . . . So in "superstitious" and "religious" there arose a term for the one of vice and for the other of praise. (*De Natura Deorum* 2.28.72, GJR)

And in a later work: "Just as *religio* ought to be extended, . . . all roots of superstition must be cast out" (*De Divinatione* 2.57.149, GJR). The fact that Christianity was thus classed with the irrational fears found among foreign and despised persons, with "old wives tales" at best, meant that it was not worth understanding; it was, therefore, fatally misunderstood, fatal for thousands of innocent people and eventually fatal for the

gods of Rome and paganism. That Christian ideas were not taken seriously meant that the reasons for commitment to them were grossly
misconstrued.

Why should one take Christians seriously? They were simple and
uneducated people, "idiots," to use the Greek word. What could they
know, and what could they have understood that the Roman government, with all its resources and traditions, did not? And if the commitment of these simpletons could not possibly be, from the Roman view,
to respectable philosophical ideals and religious ethics, to the higher as-
pirations of the soul, because their teachings were mere superstitions,
then it must be that they were attracted to this cult by the baser drives,
by lusts and appetites forbidden to citizens worthy of respect. And so
began one of the saddest chapters of the history of earliest Christianity—according to the many rumors circulated among the Romans,
Christians were really cannibals and incestuous profligates.

Some of the slanders that had been previously leveled at the Jews
were transferred to the Christians because of their early (proper) identification as a sect of Judaism, that is, that they worshiped the head of a
donkey or that they were "haters of the human race." Of the first, there
is even a second-century graffito, scratched into a plaster wall in Rome
by some minimally educated soul (he misspells a word), showing
someone worshiping a crucified man who has the head of a donkey,
with the legend, "Alexamenos worships God." Alexamenos was, obviously, a Christian, otherwise unknown, who had raised the ire of some
devout pagan willing to repeat (in wall scratchings) the common rumors about him and his cult. The "head of an ass" slander was still current two centuries later, but by that time the rumor was added "that
they worship the genitals of their high priest and holy man" (Minucius
Felix *Octavius* 9.4).

The second slander, "haters of the human race," was more deserved
by both Jews and Christians because they would not participate in
pagan rites and ceremonies or even seemingly innocent festivals and
games, because of the association of all such occasions with pagan
gods. Many Jews would not even eat with pagans because of food
taboos. Christians came in for calumny because, even though all foods
for them were thought to be clean in themselves (cf. Mark 7:18–23),
food sacrificed to the Roman gods was forbidden on account of its asso-

ciation with idolatry. This meant, of course, that meat in general was suspect, even when purchased in the marketplace, and meals in temples or during (pagan) religious rites were forbidden entirely—the eating of food sacrificed to idols was sin, for it was participation in idolatry. But Christians were subjected to slanders and accusations much worse than these foolish fabrications, ones that in fact prejudiced the entire case and carried the opinion of the courts against them.

The beliefs of Christians, from the Roman point of view, were mere superstitions, and only rarely did anyone bother to actually read their writings and listen to their arguments in defense. It did happen that one or two notable Roman thinkers actually made an investigation into the doctrinal claims, read some of the documents of the developing New Testament and associated literature, and interviewed those who claimed to be Christians. Their conclusions are revealing. Although the Romans might despise others' rites, the antiquity of those rites commanded a certain amount of respect; such was the case for the Jews, as Judaism was demonstrably old. The Christians, however, were a new sect, just barely invented in the reign of Tiberius and therefore not worthy of esteem. Second, if they had the truth, why couldn't they agree on what it was? They argued among themselves to such an extent that they could not be right in their opinions. Those very few who bothered to look into the Christians' own sources found, in their view, nothing worthy of regard, but also nothing worthy of destruction. Romans did not persecute people for stupidity.

Immorality and treason were other matters. Long before the rise of Christianity, in the early second century B.C., there was discovered in Rome a secret and internal *coniuratio* (literally, a "swearing together"), a term used for a conspiracy or plot against the government. Livy (ca. 59 B.C.–A.D. 17), a Roman historian and older contemporary of Jesus, has given us a long description of the discovery and suppression of the practices of the cult of Dionysus in Rome and Italy known as the Bacchanalia. His account is relatively accurate as we compare it to the inscription of the actual *Senatus Consultum de Bacchanalibus* ("Decree of the Senate Concerning the Bacchanalia") of 186 B.C., the official record of the decision of the Senate to suppress the cult at the time. But his story is of interest in its own right because it was written during the founding decades of the empire and reflects the sensitivities and moral judgments of the Augustan era. His work was used by many later Romans as the standard prose history of Rome. Thus, what in matters of religion was to be suppressed and how it was to be done, according to the manner of the Augustan ideals, may be found in Livy, setting the precedent for later encounters with Christianity. Pliny and his contemporary Roman magistrates seem to have had the same sensitivities and to have been following the same course of action as he describes.

Livy's account begins with a description of the Bacchic cult (Livy 39.8–19). There were "secret and nocturnal rites" that were "initiations" of both men and women, including "washings with pure water." "Men, as if with captive mind, . . . would speak prophecies"; women, even matrons, would likewise act possessed. To these secret activities were added "the pleasures of wine and feasts," and these nocturnal drunken banquets were the occasion for sexual immorality. The accusation that Dionysiac revelries produced immoral behavior was an old one, found even in Euripides (fifth century B.C.). In his play *Bacchae*, the character Teiresias, the blind and aged prophet, answers such criticism by claiming that, although Dionysus does not force a woman to be chaste, a chaste woman would not be corrupted by the mysteries (314–18).

Not so, apparently, in Rome two centuries later. Livy continues: "When wine had inflamed their souls, and night, and males mixed with females," there followed "promiscuous debauchery." The cult produced not only illicit sexual encounters, including homosexuality, but also "false testimonies, false seals (on documents) and wills and evidence," and "poisonings and internal murders," when the outcries of those murdered could not be heard over the din of "shouts and drums and cymbals." There were murders to silence those who might betray the initiates and murders for profit, including the forging of wills and legal documents, and the giving of false testimony in courts. Here is the more sinister origin of the list of crimes the Christians discovered by Pliny were swearing not to commit. They were swearing not to repeat any of the immoralities of the Bacchanalian conspiracy.

"The stain of this evil penetrated from Etruria to Rome like the contagion of a disease" (Livy 39.9.1). The Bacchanalia are described as a disease—exactly the image Pliny later uses to characterize the Christians. When the cult finally came to the attention of the Roman magistrates, they found that its rites had been long present all over Italy, and now that it was in Rome, more than seven thousand people were involved and "daily they became more numerous." Its avowed purpose, according to the magistrates, was to take control of the state itself; it was in fact a real conspiracy. Rome had gods appointed by the ancestors to be worshiped and venerated, not these foreign cults that drove people to immoralities. The Roman gods "because their own divinity was being shamefully contaminated by crimes and lusts, dragged [the Bacchanalia] out of occult shadows to the light . . . so that they would be avenged and suppressed." Informants were paid for bringing any culprits to court or for giving names of initiates. Trials began and names were published of those who fled; if they did not turn up for trial, they were condemned *in absentia*. Assemblies of the initiates were forbidden, along with night meetings, and no celebration of the rites were to be held in secret. Those who had merely been initiated, but had not participated in immoralities or crimes, were jailed. Others received capital punishment; but "more were killed than were thrown into chains." Quintus Naevius, a Roman magistrate about to set out to govern Sardinia, was detained for four months with the investigation, spending some time in Rome but more in the surrounding towns and villages. According to Livy's source, "he condemned as many as two thousand people" (39.41.6). And Lucius Postumius, governor of Tarentum, "took vengeance on great conspiracies of shepherds, and executed with care the remnants of the investigation of the Bacchanalia." Some he himself pronounced guilty, and others were arrested and sent to the Senate at Rome. The Bacchanalia and the progress of its persecution were quite clearly what was in the minds of the Roman magistrates in their persecutions of the Christians.

"Societies that are public are allowed by the laws, but secret societies are illegal." So opens the *Alethes Logos* ("True Story") of Celsus, a pagan enemy of Christianity writing about 178. To Romans like Celsus, Christianity appeared from the outside to be a secret society. We read again and again about the effect that the secrecy of the Christians had on outside observers, for "surely suspicion attaches to secret and nocturnal rites" (Minucius Felix *Octavius* 9.4, GJR). One of the few models available for the early Christians to base their religious practices on was that of the mystery cults. Essentially all cults of antiquity had mysteries, secret doctrines that only the initiates and adepts were allowed to know, and secret rites that were held behind closed doors and out of public view. In fashion typical of many Near Eastern cults, the Jews had an elaborate system barring access to the inner areas of the temple, and rites that no one at all but the very highest orders of priests could even see. So it was with the Egyptian cults and all of the accepted mysteries, of Cybele, Demeter, the Cabiri, and many others. Even the cults of Zeus and the emperor acquired mysteries by the Christian era, although they had been relatively open about their myths and doctrines.

We today in the West are unaccustomed to such secrecy and think that all of Christian doctrine is open to public scrutiny, but we are heir to the ages of the Christian empire when there was no longer need for such concealment and the doctrines became the common property of all. Yet in Eastern Christendom, the tradition of mystery is still practiced: the Eucharist is celebrated behind a screen, out of view of even the church members. Public religion in antiquity was state cult, connected to the government and its program of imperialism and pacification; private religion was mystery cult. So the meetings of the Christians were private and their doctrines reserved for the initiates. Initiation consisted of a period of instruction and then baptism according to the customs of other mystery cults, but the ceremonies, and especially the eucharistic meals, were not for the public. This secrecy led outsiders to speculate rather wildly about what the Christians were doing, and that speculation invented immoralities of the grossest sort.

We have a number of references to the kind of immoralities these early Christians were accused of, and those from quite early. Pliny's letter, written only some eighty years after the crucifixion, already contains what appears to be a reference to the "blood libel," the accusation so common later that Christians were eating the flesh of a murdered baby. He writes that they came together in the evening meeting "for the taking of food, common, however, and harmless." He had expected, quite clearly, that the food they were eating would be something other than common and harmless.

Livy's account of the Bacchanalia does not mention it, but one of the well-known features of the Dionysiac cult was the tasting of the raw flesh of a dismembered animal. This was a ritual reenactment of the rending and eating of the baby Dionysus by the Titans and, spiritually, a ritual that brought, by the symbolic ingestion of the flesh of the god, inspiration and possession by the god Dionysus himself. This possession is what brought forth the prophecies, miracles, and charismatic behaviors that had been part of the cult since its beginnings in ancient Greece. Given the historical context, the fact that Christians understood the Eucharist as sharing in the body and blood of Christ made this type of slander, about the eating of a baby, almost inevitable. In a document defending the Christian faith from the third century, we find a pagan accuser quoted while describing the rumors of this aspect of the Christian cult:

> The stories about initiating neophytes are as detestable as they are notorious: an infant, covered with bread dough so as to deceive the incautious, is placed next to the one who is being initiated into the rites. This infant is killed by the neophyte with blind and hidden wounds, provoked by the surface of bread to deliver, as it were, innocuous blows. From this—how horrid!—thirstily they pour out the blood; from this eagerly they distribute the limbs; with this as sacrifice they make confederacy; with this consciousness of crime they are pledged to mutual silence. (Minucius Felix *Octavius* 9.5, GJR)

Christians objected that it was among the stories of the Greco-Roman and Semitic gods that babies were eaten—children were sacrificed in Palestine and North Africa to Semitic gods, and Romans had stories of Kronos eating his children and the Titans eating Dionysus. Christians never ate babies, but the rumor that they did, because of their association with the Bacchanalia, appears to have arisen in the first century and lasted until the time of Constantine.

The second most common slander was that of sexual immorality, especially incestuous immorality. Christianity was, from the outside, a secret cult with nocturnal meetings that mixed males and females equally, as had the Bacchanalia. Secrecy again played into the creation of slander, and the fact that Christians called each other "brothers" and "sisters" gave rise to the charge of incest:

> By secret signs and insignias they recognize each other and mutually love almost before they recognize. Everywhere indeed among themselves a kind of religion of lusts is joined, and they call each other indiscriminately "brothers" and "sisters," so that even normal defilement might by the intervention of a holy name become incest. (Minucius Felix *Octavius* 9.5, GJR)

This account of the "religion of lusts," ironically, comes from a time when Christianity was more and more emphasizing celibacy, and the first Christian monks were beginning to go out into the desert. Heroic tales were being (composed and) told of the apostles preaching a gospel of celibacy, as may be found in the *Apocryphal Acts of the Apostles,* stemming from the late second and early third centuries. Jesus was apparently celibate, as were Paul and Barnabas and many others. There was a very effective and official ministry carried on by celibate widows in service of the sick and poor. Yet the secrecy of the meetings again left the Christians open to slander.

Another notorious feature of the Bacchanalia were the drunken banquets that provided the occasions for immorality. Bacchus, the Roman equivalent of the god Dionysus, was the god of wine, and in his rites wine was always present. The earliest Christian eucharistic celebrations were also regular meals that included wine, which led occasionally to abuses. There is more than one warning in the New Testament against drunkenness and sexual immorality in the context of the "love feast," the *agapê* meal (cf. 1 Cor. 11:21; Jude 12f.). Here again, pagan imagination and Christian secrecy provided fertile ground for speculation. To the Romans,

> [The Christians'] banqueting is notorious: everyone everywhere talks about it; even our orator from Cirta bears testimony concerning it. To the feast on an appointed day they come together with all their children, sisters, mothers, people of every sex and every age. Then after much feasting, when the banquet is hot and the fervor for incestuous lust burns in the drunkards, a dog that is tied to a lamp, by the cast of a morsel farther than the length of the line with which it is tied, is provoked to rush and jump. So, when the witnessing light is overturned and extinguished, in impudent shadows connections of unspeakable lust roll about through unknown choice, and even if not by deed, nevertheless by consent, all are equally incestuous.
> (Minucius Felix *Octavius* 9.6–7, GJR)

"Everyone everywhere talks about it." The rumors were rife, and old. The "orator from Cirta" was Marcus Cornelius Fronto, born at Cirta in Numidia. He came to Rome and became a politician (consul in 143) and a famous rhetor, serving as teacher in rhetoric to Marcus Aurelius

(r. 161–180) and to his son Commodus. He wrote a famous *Speech Against the Christians*, of which nothing survives except its citation by the author Minucius Felix here in *Octavius*.

That such highly placed Romans could believe and write about this type of immorality for which they had no actual evidence shows how pervasive and influential the rumors were, caused in no small part by Christian secrecy:

> I am passing over many things on purpose, for even these many things are too much, all or most of which the secrecy of this depraved religion declares to be true. For why indeed do they strive with such effort to hide and conceal whatever it is that they worship, when honest things always rejoice in public, and crimes are secrets? Why do they have no altars, no temples, no known images, never speak openly, never congregate freely, unless that which they worship and cover over ought either to cause punishment or shame? (Minucius Felix *Octavius* 10.1–2, GJR)

The secrecy of the Christians had nothing to do with hiding immoralities, but was a perfectly natural aspect of any religious cult in antiquity. There were teachings and doctrines for all to hear and those that only the inner circle could learn. One did not tell everything to everyone. No one expected the Demeter cult to divulge all its secrets publicly; in fact such an act, the telling of the Eleusinian mysteries of Demeter to the uninitiated, was a capital crime in ancient Greece. But there were other reasons for turning speculations about what might be going on into accusations of evil.

There was a political dimension to the Christian movement that is seldom mentioned, but that was of great importance to the Romans. Jesus had been put to death as a criminal in Palestine. In the words of Tacitus, "The founder of this name, Christus, had undergone execution when Tiberius was emperor under the procurator Pontius Pilate" (*Annals* 15.44, GJR). He was no criminal in any moral sense, whatever his detractors might say, but he posed a threat to the Roman view of public order; he was immensely popular, if we accept our New Testament sources, and angered his own Jewish leaders, who ruled a client state under Roman supervision, with his preaching of the spiritual "kingdom of God." The Romans were very sensitive about sedition in the provinces in general and time and again outlawed assemblies of any kind, but the crowds that followed John the Baptist and Jesus were completely out of the question. Once he was accused by the Jewish authorities as a troublemaker, his life was forfeit. And Jewish accusation did not stop there.

We learn from the Roman historian Suetonius that trouble caused by the Jews against the Christians angered the government to such an extent that Claudius (r. 41–54) reacted against them also: "The Jews, who were continually raising a tumult with Chrestus as instigator, he expelled from Rome" (*Claudius* 25, GJR). "Chrestus" is Christ in Roman speech. The Greek word *christos* ("anointed") and the Greek name *Chrestos* ("gentle") were pronounced the same; one could differentiate them only by context (a bit like "for" and "four"). "Chrestus" was an acceptable Latin name derived from Greek, while "christos" would have meant nothing to a Roman. Here the followers of "Chrestus" are (again) at the base of public disturbances requiring official government action. But by the time of Nero (r. 54–68), the situation had gone completely beyond reason: the Christians were blamed for the great fire of Rome (described in Chapter 6). Christianity was viewed as a conspiracy against the government. It had arisen as a sect of Judaism that more than once rebelled against Rome, and it inherited the aura of a religious conspiracy of the Bacchanalia. During the execution of Cyprian, bishop of Carthage, in 258, the Roman governor labels Christians as the "nefarious people of this conspiracy" (*Acta Proconsularia Cypriani* 4.1). How Christianity, or any other cult, could gain this reputation as a religious conspiracy against the government needs some clarification.

People of the ancient world lived under a kind of contract between themselves and the gods, known in Latin as the *pax deorum* ("peace of the gods"). It was the old arrangement that had been in place for thousands of years in many cultures based on the monistic view of the cosmos defined earlier, that everything and everyone had a proper place and function, a set of duties and responsibilities; there was no Devil at war with God, no dualism. Gods were to oversee the workings of the world according to their divine laws, provide rains and crops and protect from disease and foreign invasion, while humans were to obey those laws and provide for the gods by proper rites, sacrifices, and ceremonies. The gods protected and allowed the community to prosper as long as humans provided the gods with a community that supported the gods.

From the human viewpoint, two aspects of behavior were paramount: the religious rites and ceremonies and the maintenance of ethical standards, or in the negative, the avoidance of *miasma* (Greek for "pollution") or *piaculum* (Latin for both a "sin"" and the "propitiatory sacrifice"). In the case of a moral breech, the community as a whole suffered for the sins or pollutions of even an individual. In Israel, the entire nation went into exile for the sins of the king (2 Kings 23:26–7), and God says through the prophet while in exile that his holy name had been profaned (Ezek. 20:39). In Greece, the entire city of Thebes suffered because of the pollution inherent in the fact that Oedipus the king had (innocently) killed his father and married his mother. The crops and animals were afflicted with blight and disease; women were barren; a plague was killing the town's inhabitants. Oedipus had to be expelled from the city (cf. Sophocles *Oedipus Rex* 20–30). In the case of the Bacchanalia of the early second century B.C., the Romans understood the immoralities of the cult as a pollution of the gods. Livy writes of the Roman gods that "their own divinity was being shamefully contaminated by crimes and lusts" (39.16.11). If a community or state tolerated such pollutions, the gods would punish the entire state for the crimes of a portion of its inhabitants. So Tertullian writes that the pagans

> think that the Christians are the cause of every public calamity, every popular misfortune. If the Tiber river floods up to the walls, if the Nile does not flood up to the fields, if the sky stands (without rain), if the earth moves, if there is famine, if there is plague, immediately, "Christians to the lion!" (*Apologeticus* 401–2)

In his typical style, dripping with sarcasm, Tertullian concludes this passage, "So many to one (lion)?" Apparently the final phrase, "Christians to the lion!" (with singular "lion"), was an exact quote. Every public calamity was the fault of the Christians because the Christians (according to rumor) were performing gross immoralities in secret, polluting the land. The gods were punishing everyone as a community: floods, earthquakes, famines, plagues were all their responses to the profanation by the Christians. But that was not all: the Christians most importantly refused to participate in the proper rites, sacrifices, and ceremonies, the worship of the traditional gods on whom the community was founded and on whose favor it depended, including, and especially, their representative on earth, the emperor.

One of the aspects of early Christianity that marked it out from the mass of other cults and religions in the Mediterranean was its sense of the necessity of conversion to obtain salvation. Christianity was not, contrary to much of modern liberal rhetoric, easily able to allow the gods of the Greeks and Romans, or for that matter, the Jews, to save their adherents on their own. These other religions, in fact, did not in general have a concept of salvation of souls in the same sense, and most had no such concept at all. Again, the vast majority of people in the ancient world, to judge from the tomb inscriptions, believed that after death one's body simply died and that if anything lived on, it was only one's shade, a ghostlike entity, that descended to the underworld. There was no fundamental sinfulness and no fiery hell to be saved from, only the present life with its myriad difficulties. Gods granted healing from illness, deliverance from trial and suffering, economic successes, and protection of the community, but they did not grant salvation or eternal life in the Christian sense.

Immortality, such as it was, could be gained according to tradition in two basic ways: through one's children or in the memory of one's community. The first and most basic is explained by Aristotle in his treatise *On the Soul*:

> It is the most natural of acts for living creatures . . . to reproduce another like itself . . . in order that it might share in eternity and the divine in the manner in which it is capable . . . since it is impossible to share in the eternal and divine by continuance [of life].
> (*De Anima* 2.4.415a, GJR)

The other means is explained by Plato, that men and women desire nothing so much as glory "and that deathless fame be established forever" (*Symposium* 208c). So Achilles had made his fatal choice to gain "unwilting fame" (*Iliad* 9.413). But such fame was fleeting, and memory far from eternal. To secure fame and be remembered, capable individuals would strive to accomplish great deeds that would be sung by the bards as memorial and entertainment. If one were wealthy and successful enough, one could employ a professional poet to compose songs as advertisements. Some of the finest poetry to survive antiquity, in fact, is that of Pindar and Bacchylides, who wrote poems (for a fee) celebrating the athletic victories of those who won contests in the great games. Athletes also had statues dedicated recording their names and victories. Great generals put up monuments commemorating their victories. Poets composed songs and writers wrote books. Other means were funerary monuments and paintings in public places recording the deeds and glories of an individual or family. But these things were expensive and restricted to those of wealth and accomplishment. In fact, so much money was lavished on these monuments that laws were often passed limiting size and financial outlay. But most people, the majority by far, neither achieved anything worth remembering, nor had the means to hire bards or set up monuments.

Into this world came the Christians preaching a message of the salvation of souls, of resurrection and eternal life. These things were not entirely new; Christians acknowledged that philosophers had taught many similar things for hundreds of years. Many of the basic doctrines were part of the store of teachings of the common philosophical schools and mystery cults of the day. The stories of the heroes contained many of the features of the gospel and biography of Jesus; he looked like a hero to outsiders. These commonalities made the message seem to an extent familiar and possible, but now the message was for everyone, and especially for the poor. It even threatened and poked fun at the upper classes: to paraphrase Mark 10:25, if you can drive a car through a doughnut, then a rich man can go to heaven. Yet the message contained something else new to the Romans and quite offensive—the necessity for conversion, since the worship of the gods of Rome was the worship of demons.

Christianity had inherited the exclusive monotheism brought west by the Persians and developed in the mix of cultures and sectarian groups that was postexilic Judaism. Among the Jewish sects that accepted the old Zoroastrian claims about the dualism of God and the Devil, about eschatology, the last judgment, and "the world to come," as it was called, were the Pharisees and the Essenes, from whose circles Jesus and the early Jewish Christians had arisen. The Zoroastrians had taught that there was but one true God, and that the gods of the nations were demons. The sect of Judaism in power at the time of Jesus was that of the Sadducees, who ruled the country and administered the temple services under the oversight of the Romans. They were the old traditionalists, like most of the people of the land, who held to the ideals of the Davidic monarchy, a political kingdom, and rejected the developments that had taken place among the Pharisees and Essenes during the later, postexilic Persian and Greek periods. They were "monistic"; they did not believe in the Devil and his coming end or have hopes of resurrection and eternal life, and they rejected "the world to come." This is the sect that saw Jesus as a threat to its political hopes and delivered him over to the Romans. Yet neither did the Sadducees allow the worship of the gods of the nations, for in the Law was written, "You shall have no other gods before me" (Exod. 20:3).

The reasons for the persecution of Christians in the wider Roman Empire at the end of the first century and later, however, and the reasons for the execution of Jesus were not the same; in fact, they were in some respects quite dissimilar. "Treason," understood as fomenting political unrest, would have been the main charge for the Romans, but neither Jesus nor his disciples were persecuted for immorality or accused of atheism. Jesus sent his disciples out to proclaim the news that the kingdom of God was at hand among people who, whatever camp of Judaism they were in, did not allow the worship of gods other than the God of Israel. So he and his disciples did not (have to) preach against idolatry, but instead against a materialistic view of spirituality ("What does it profit if you gain the world and lose your soul?"), against the outward show of religiosity ("Woe to you hypocrites!"), and a political understanding of God's kingdom ("The kingdom of God is within you"). All of these ideas were Greek philosophical ideals, and among the Hellenistic Jews of Palestine and abroad, the Greek concept of monotheism held sway, that there is in fact only one God; in the words of Xenophanes (sixth century B.C.): "That which is wise alone is one; it is unwilling and willing to be called by the name of Zeus" (Frag. 32 Diels). So among enlightened Greeks and Hellenistic Jews who became Christians, the very strong philosophical position was current that "no idol in the world really exists," and that "there is no God but one" (1 Cor. 8:4). But Paul here has to remind the Corinthians that there is more to the story: "What pagans sacrifice, they sacrifice to demons and not to

God. I do not want you to be partners with demons" (1 Cor. 10:20). The Christians went out into the wider world of the Mediterranean area with a doctrine full of the best ethical and spiritual teachings of Semites and Greeks, but with a belief that the gods of the Greeks and Romans were demons and that the worship of those gods was participation in idolatry. If in anything at all, the Romans prided themselves on the strength and depth of their devotion to their ancestral religion; one can hardly imagine an idea more offensive to the Roman soul.

"Three charges are brought against us: atheism, Thyestean feasts, and Oedipean intercourse. . . . It remains for you, then, to examine our . . . loyalty and obedience to you, to your house, and to the Empire" (Athenagoras *Plea* 3). So writes Athenagoras, philosopher and Christian, to emperor Marcus Aurelius about 177 in his defense of the faith. "Thyestean feasts" became the shorthand way among Christian writers of referring to the accusation against them of eating babies: Thyestes, because he had debauched the king's wife, was (unknown to him) fed his own son for dinner. "Oedipean intercourse" referred, of course, to the charges of incest: Oedipus (again unwittingly) had married his mother. "Atheism" pointed to the fact that the Christians did not acknowledge the Roman gods to be real gods. On this point Tertullian's mock dialogue between himself and the Roman accusers is enlightening:

> "You do not worship the gods," you [Romans] say, "and you do not offer sacrifices on behalf of the emperors." We do not sacrifice on behalf of others for the same reason that we do not sacrifice on our own behalf—we do not worship the gods at all. And so we are accosted with the charge of sacrilege and treason. This is the main lawsuit, indeed the entire suit. . . . We have ceased to worship your gods because we do not recognize them as gods. (*Apologeticus* 10.1, GJR)

Here we come to the point of how the Christian religion could be understood as treason. In the passage from Athenagoras above, the fact that Christians were accused for the kinds of things that they were, led to the further questioning of their "loyalty and obedience to you [the emperor], to your house, and to the Empire." Tertullian declares that because the Christians would not worship the Roman gods, they were "accosted with the matter of sacrilege and treason"; they are "public enemies" (2.4). During the year 258, the emperors Valerian and Gallienus commanded that "those who do not practice the Roman religion ought to acknowledge the Roman ceremonies." In Carthage, the bishop Cyprian refused to do so. Galerius Maximus the governor pronounced sentence on him:

> You have gathered to yourself many nefarious people of this conspiracy, and you have set yourself as an enemy of the Roman gods and holy religious rites. . . . And therefore, since you are an author of a most wicked crime and have been caught as leader, you yourself will be proof to these whom you have gathered to yourself in your sin. With your blood discipline will be sanctified. (*Acta Proconsularia Cypriani* 4.1–3, GJR)

The Christians had placed themselves outside the contract between the gods and the community: they were, in the Roman view, grossly immoral, a pollution in the body politic, and they refused to continue the traditional religious rites for either the gods or the emperor. According to the Roman governor quoted just above, these acts were a "conspiracy" consisting of "most wicked crime" and "sin." The Christians were committing treason against the religious and political fabric of the state and were therefore worthy of death.

❧━✦━❧

PLINY FOUND THAT BY PERSECUTION he was able to turn a large number of people back to the traditional worship by giving them a chance, to use his term, for "repentance." Persecution worked; it did cause people to turn away from the new faith. In fact, some of the most difficult problems faced by the Church over the subsequent centuries was what to do with the *lapsi*, those who had "lapsed," had fallen away or denied their faith, when, as so often happened, they wanted to return to the Church after some particular or local persecution was over. Persecutions had already begun by the end of the first century. Some were mob actions, and some were official trials. They were not constant, but usually sporadic and local, prompted by official accusations brought by both Jews and pagans against individuals or by crowds shouting for (more) blood at the arena or after some disaster. Pliny knew of previous "examinations of the Christians," though he had not been present at them, and was in the process of conducting one of his own. He found that some of those he had arrested "said that they were Christians and later renounced it; that they had indeed been, but ceased, some three years ago, some many years ago, not a few even twenty years ago" (*Epistulae* 10.96.6, GJR). I take that to mean that there had already been in Bithynia (at least) three "examinations" some years earlier that had caused these individuals to recant. This coheres rather well with the accounts of persecutions in Asia Minor from the late first century recorded in the book of Revelation and the warnings about official trials ("before governors," Luke 21:12) contained in the Gospels from about the same time period.

What were the Christians doing while persecutions were going on? This question really has two major parts. First, what were they doing in the face of the mechanics of persecution, either to avoid being caught or to aid those who had been caught and were on their way to execution? Second, what were they thinking? What did they believe of themselves? Recall that they were being tortured and crucified, burned, or fed to animals; a few from the upper classes were beheaded. How did they understand their roles as individuals in the larger scheme things? These questions are interrelated, in fact rather closely linked, because what one does in such a critical moment stems very much from what one thinks about oneself and one's place in the larger scheme.

Is persecution and criminal execution a catastrophe or a victory? If it is a defeat, then one will properly do everything possible to avoid it; if a victory, then one may even bring it upon oneself. And here, in the subject of the death of Jesus and the subsequent martyrdoms of so many of his followers, is to be found one of the most remarkable instances of purposeful misunderstanding among scholars and other interpreters. Was the death of Jesus a defeat or a victory? The answer to that question will determine one's frame of reference, one's mode of interpretation. Were the martyrs in general demented or admirable? An inadequate answer (and there certainly was a great debate on what the right or wrong answer was even in antiquity) will fail to understand not only the actions of the martyrs, but also the success of the Christian mission and subsequent rise of the Church.

The Christians were acting like the heroes. Not all of them, of course, but many, and more and more of them as time went on. They learned to be heroes as from the stories of their ancestors, and from other Christians; Christians taught each other and encouraged each other to live and die like heroes. Persecution and false accusation and rumor worked; they turned people away from the new faith and back to the traditional gods and religions. But the behavior of those who died with courage and self-respect, who passed the test with their honor fully intact, made a mockery of the rumors and accusations, and the killing of obviously (otherwise) innocent people sickened the officials involved. Tertullian states, using metaphors from fishing and agriculture, in one of his most famous (and typically sarcastic) passages:

> Whatever your cruelty, the next more exquisite than the last, it profits you nothing: it is greater bait to our school. We become more numerous as often as we are measured by you: the blood of Christians is seed. (*Apologeticus* 50.13, GJR)

The Romans cut up Christians like bait, and only succeeded in attracting more "fish" to become Christians. They sowed Christian blood in the ground, and when they measured the crop, there were more Christians: "the blood of Christians is seed."

In Livy's account of the suppression of the Bacchanalia, one of the reasons given for rooting out the cult was the effect that immoral behavior had on military valor. Recall that there were no guns in antiquity; all warfare was hand-to-hand combat. We have no record of the actual speech given by the Roman governor to the Senate at the beginning of the action against the Bacchic cult, nor did Livy. In fine Latin style and according to convention, he puts into the mouth of the governor a speech that reflects the values of his own times, those of the empire. The Roman consul asks:

> Do you think, citizens, that young men initiated by this rite ought to become soldiers? That arms ought to be committed to these men, drafted from this obscene sanctuary? Will these, overwhelmed by their own and others' disgraceful lewdness, fight with the sword for the chastity of your wives and children? (39.15.13–14, GJR)

Romans and all ancients knew well the effect of immorality on one's character, especially in the most critical times of war, when the citizens had to fight hand to hand and face death with courage or lose everything. This was the justification for the gladiatorial combats, that they schooled the citizenry in contempt of death. And it was here, in the face of death, where Christians were able to show their real strength. The very values that were most important to the Roman character, those of the soldier and athlete and philosopher, were the ones that the Christians demonstrated in their obstinate refusal to worship other gods and in their courage in the face of death. The passage from Tertullian continues:

> Many among you exhort to tolerance of pain and death, like Cicero in his *Tusculans*, like Seneca in his *Fortuita*, like Diogenes, like Pyrrhon, like Callinicus. And yet their words do not find so many disciples as the Christians do by teaching with deeds. That very "obstinacy" that you reproach is a teacher. For who is not aroused by seeing it to inquire what lies at the base of the matter? Who does not, when they have inquired, approve? (*Apologeticus* 50.14–15, GJR)

The Christians were beating the Romans at their own game. Christians were, of course, Romans themselves, and of every other stripe and subset of the empire. Both sides shared the same ideals and culture. The philosophers named were among the most influential of Greece and Rome, who had taught the philosophical basis for the athletic and military ideals of the heroes. And yet it was the Christians, not the philosophers, who were actually able to achieve those ideals and spread them among the common people. Pliny, in his famous letter to Trajan quoted above several times, had sent Christians to their deaths, if for no other reason than that "stubbornness and inflexible obstinacy surely ought to be punished" (*Epistulae* 10.96, GJR). The victims' courage was denigrated as "obstinacy"—what else could it be, if you were killing people for it? Their martyrdoms were denigrated as "suicides"—what else could they be? The Romans could not admit that they were wrong and that these were judicial murders. Yet the onlookers could see through the rhetoric and found themselves drawn to what their culture had taught them to recognize as their own ideals—the Christians were acting like heroes. "When we are killed, we conquer" (Tertullian *Apologeticus* 50.3).

○══◆══○

AT THE END OF THE FIRST CENTURY, the adolescent Christian community found itself in the midst of a very difficult period of rejection and persecution at the hands of both the nonbelieving Jewish community and the pagan and Roman authorities. The pressure and coercion against their new society touched nearly every aspect of life. Believers

lost friends, the love of family members, business and social relationships; they suffered humiliation, mockery, the loss of property, and occasionally beatings and martyrdom. Old religious associations were
lost, both because those left behind spurned the new converts and because the Church rejected the religious ways of the Greco-Roman
world. For the Jewish or gentile convert, the doors to the synagogues
and temples were closed; yet there was always that pressure to return, to
deny the new faith and go back to the religion of one's ancestors, one's
city and people. And that return was made easy, even coerced, by the
Romans themselves. Keeping "the faithful" faithful under such stress,
encouraging one's fellow Christians to heroic behavior in the face of
persecution and possible death, became a major concern of the early
writers and occupies a great deal of our earliest Christian literature.

Sometime in the late first century, roughly contemporaneous with
the Gospel of Luke, an unknown author composed the Letter to the Hebrews, similar enough to the Letters of Paul to have been included
among them and therefore in the New Testament. But the author was
not Paul, as may be readily seen from the great differences in Greek
style and certain differences in theological understanding. A number of
possible authors have been proposed: Apollos, Barnabas, Luke, and others, though there is no way now to know. The book was written after the
beginnings of persecution in earnest, and its purpose is to encourage
Christians who are about to "drift away" (Heb. 2:1) or "turn away" (3:12)
because of persecution to "hold fast to our confession" (4:14). The book
gained its title ("To the Hebrews," though no specific group is named)
from its very sophisticated and creative use of the Old Testament. It is
full of quotations about and references to the sacrificial cult and has led
many to surmise that it was written specifically to Jewish Christians
tempted to return to the synagogue, though it is equally applicable to
Gentiles familiar with Christian teachings based on the Old Testament.
The point here is that although so much of the book is based on the Old
Testament and Jewish modes of interpretation current in the first century, its argument is based on something quite different and now
familiar—Jesus is the (quintessential) hero who secured the means of
salvation for those who would follow him, and Christians are encouraged to do just that, to take up and hold to that role themselves.

Jesus in Hebrews is in many ways similar to Jesus in the Gospel of John—he is an emanation of God incarnated in a human being. Recall that during the centuries between Hesiod's Four Classes of Being in the eighth century B.C. and the end of the first century, the possibilities for how a person might be constituted had become much more complicated. In Hebrews, we find another conception like that of John's "Word of God" incarnated: Jesus is the "radiance of [God's] glory" through whom God made the world (Heb. 1:2–3, GJR), but the human Jesus lives through a life of suffering and death (and ascension), understood very much like that of the classical heroes. God, in order to accomplish redemption for all, has to "perfect the leader of their salvation through suffering" (2:10, GJR), and although he was the Son of God, "he learned obedience through what he suffered" (5:8). This last line contains one of the more common lessons of the heroes: *pathei mathos*, "by suffering comes learning" (Aeschylus *Agamemnon* 177). The reasoning is that since people

> Partake in flesh and blood, he himself likewise shared in the same, in order that through death he might leave powerless the one having the power of death, that is the Devil, and might release those who by fear of death were held in slavery all their lives." (Heb. 2:14–15, GJR)

The word translated "leader" (Greek *archêgos*) in Heb. 2:10 is also used of a chief or founder; it is used of a dead hero who is the protector of his worshipers. In Sophocles' *Oedipus at Colonus*, the inhabitants "boast that the horseman Colonus is their *archêgos* and bear his name" (59–60, GJR), just as Jesus is the *archêgos* of his followers who bear his name. Here he is the leader who dies to overcome death for his followers. In Chapter 6 of this book, in connection with the passage in Matthew, "on this rock I will build my church, and the gates of Hades will not prevail against it" (16:18), Jesus stood as the hero who would descend to Hades' kingdom and open the gates for his followers, as had Heracles and Orpheus and Dionysus, so that they would find the way out of the kingdom of death. In Hebrews, Jesus does the same to Death itself: by dying and then ascending to heaven, he overcomes Death and "leaves powerless the one having the power of death, that is the Devil." The Greek word translated "leave powerless" (*katargeô*) means "to leave

someone unemployed or idle, to make useless or of no effect." The
Devil has no more power after death. Jesus, by suffering death and overcoming it through resurrection, renders the power of death and the
Devil idle and useless. But it was only by passing through death, not by
avoiding it, that he overcame it.

So what of the followers addressed in Hebrews? They are in a world
where many have died as Christians before them; even their own leaders have been executed (13:7). This was a common Roman practice
against the churches, the execution of church leaders to terrify the un-
ranked members. The whole argument of the book is a kind of counter-
point between those who had died through disobedience and those who
died in faith, with the strong encouragement to die (if necessary) for the
confession, looking forward to eternal life, rather than to shrink back
and die anyway, eventually, in disobedience. In fact, we get a whole
chapter of examples of people who had died looking forward to something in the future (Heb. 11). The Christians addressed had once been
earnest; they had formerly

> endured a hard struggle with sufferings, sometimes being publicly ex-
> posed to abuse and persecution, and sometimes being partners with
> those so treated. For you had compassion for those who were in prison,
> and you cheerfully accepted the plundering of your possessions, know-
> ing that you yourselves possessed something better and more lasting.
> (10:32–34)

This community had undergone quite a lot. The term translated
"struggle" is the Greek term *athlêsis*, related to a group of words meaning a "contest" for a prize, used for military, athletic, and philosophical
conflicts. To be "exposed to abuse" is from the term we saw in connection with Paul, when he saw himself as a *theatron*, a "spectacle." Here it
is *theatrizô*, "to be put in the arena." Both the metaphorical and literal
senses of the word are used here: the people addressed in Hebrews had
been "publicly exposed to abuse" because they had assisted those who
had been arrested and literally sent into the arena. They had begun the
"struggle," but, as the writer states, had "need of endurance" (10:36).
The point of the book to which the entire argument leads, with all its
Old Testament examples, its sophistication and intelligent reasoning, is
expressed in a mixture of athletic and military terms:

let us lay aside every encumbrance . . . and let us run with endurance the race that is set before us, looking to Jesus the leader and perfecter of our faith. . . . For consider him who endured such hostility against himself from sinners, so that you may not grow weary or lose heart. (12:1–3, GJR)

This kind of exhortation could have been said (with necessary changes) by any hero in the *Iliad*, encouraging and rousing his men to valor by reference to the examples of their leaders or ancestors. This way of thinking about the "contest" of life, this heroic model, had become common in philosophical and religious language in the intervening centuries. The contest entailed at times both verbal and physical abuse, and sometimes death, but it was worth the price, for it was a contest for a prize. We saw the prize earlier: in a passage from Lucian ridiculing the Christians (as he does with nearly everyone else), he states that "The poor devils have convinced themselves first off that they will be completely immortal and will live forever, on which account they despise death and the majority hand themselves over (into custody) willingly" (*Peregrinus* 13, GJR). That is exactly what the author of Hebrews is trying to convince his readers to believe and do.

A roughly contemporaneous document, *1 Clement*, dated commonly to 96 and written from Rome to the church at Corinth, makes a similar point. The Corinthian church was undergoing a schism, as certain younger members had deposed some older and honored leaders. The author (traditionally thought to be Clement, the third bishop of Rome) writes to warn of the dangers of jealousy and strife and to secure a reconciliation. To do so he cites not only biblical models, but also "from our generation the noble examples" of those he calls "athletes" (Greek *athlêtês*; 5.1). He uses the example of Peter, who "suffered many toils and so having testified [or become a martyr], went to the place of glory due him" (5.4). Paul "indicated the prize of endurance," and "gained the genuine fame of his faith" (5.5–6). The word translated "fame" is the old Greek word we have seen several times, *kleos*, one of the goals of the heroic code and the promise to Achilles, that if he would die at Troy, he would gain unwilting fame. Here Paul gains not merely human, but "genuine" *kleos*. Paul then, "having testified before the rulers, thus departed from the world and was taken up to the holy place, becoming the greatest model of endurance" (5.5.7).

To these men, having lived holy lives, were added a great multitude of chosen ones, who, suffering through jealousy many outrages and tortures, became the most noble examples among us. On account of jealousy, women, persecuted as Danaids and Dirces, suffering terrible and unholy mutilations, attained the sure prize of the faith and received the genuine reward. (6.1–2, GJR)

These are the models of the Christian heroes, both men and women, at the end of the first century. Their numbers were considerable, if Clement is to be believed, and we do not know their names or the specifics of their lives and deaths. They died under torture; some women died in the arenas "as Danaids and Dirces," that is, as we have seen, by being forced to play out the roles of characters who were killed in dramas of the heroes staged in the arenas. In the Greek myths, the Danaids were killed for murdering their husbands; Dirce was tied to the tail of a wild bull by her two stepsons and dragged to death for mistreating their mother. The examples are heroic and the language is heroic. Noteworthy is the final word, "reward." It is the Greek term *geras*, the "prize" given a hero for valor and a measure of one's worth; it was Agamemnon's taking of the *geras* of Achilles that is the beginning of the problem of the *Iliad*. Here the Christian heroes contend for and gain, not the pagan, but the "genuine" *geras*. *Kleos* and *geras*, fame and the prize, the two honors most sought after by the heroes of the epic past, but this time, in the Christian view, the battle was for genuine fame and the real prize. In the words of Tertullian:

The battle for us is that we are called forth to the tribunals so that there at the risk of death we may fight for the truth. . . . The victory holds both the fame of pleasing God and the prize of living for eternity. (*Apologeticus* 50.2, GJR)

Chapter 8

IMITATORS OF CHRIST

There is one aspect of the hero from the list of characteristics I drew in Chapter 3 that interests me most, that of model, example, and forerunner. Why did people follow Jesus? How did the simple people who joined the early Christian movement find the strength to keep on following in the face of rejection by their peers, loss, and sometimes persecution? And especially those who suffered, the martyrs, how did they find the inner resources to endure and "keep the faith," to abuse a phrase? It may be that the martyrs were themselves heroes, as the early Church thought, greater-than-mere-human, somehow planted in the ranks of us, the unmitigatedly average. I think, however, not. It may also be that they were inspired by the Spirit to superhuman strength and endurance, again as the Church claimed. That is true, if we believe their testimonies, but I think that the inspiration had an entrance and stimulus seldom recognized today.

The ancients of Greece had, as I have mentioned, a rather high view of human possibilities: in some ways we ourselves were close to the gods; we ourselves were capable of heroism. Plato (through his character Socrates), in discussing the honor and reverence to be given the heroes who protected the state, tells us:

> We will practice the same observance when any who have been adjudged exceptionally good in the ordinary course of life die of old age or otherwise. (*Republic* 5.469b)

"Any . . . in the ordinary course of life . . ." One should here recall Eumaios, the swineherd of Odysseus. His one claim to fame is his gracious and genuine hospitality offered to a beggar. Socrates says that we may even simply die of old age, one assumes without a virgin birth or high destiny or fatal encounter with the Fates. What inspired the "natural hero," the average person, was the example set by the forerunners. They had fought the same battles and though defeated had somehow won, though killed had somehow survived and become powerful. They were the models and examples who inspired generations of those who heard their stories. So Paul tells us to be "imitators of Christ." I cannot, as the ancients could not, imitate the gods; but Paul could imitate Christ and tell us to imitate himself as he was imitating Christ. That very role of "model to imitate" is the role of the hero, of both the divinely generated and the "normal" variety.

So the heroes were the models, high as ideals, but based in real life and accessible situations. The gods, you recall, are impossible to imitate and difficult at best to deal with in their ambiguity. It might be their will that one loses all one's possessions and one's family, and one's spouse says, "Curse God and die." One can see this negative view of the divinity influencing the depictions of Jesus in the art of the early Middle Ages. Jesus, the Good Shepherd of earliest Christian catacomb art, becomes Christ, the Pantokrator ("Ruler of All"), in the mosaics of churches in the subsequent centuries, stern and distant, even angry and terrifying. Once Jesus enters the upper divine world in the minds of the common people in the late Roman period, they turn away from him to the cult of saints and especially Mary to intercede with the one who was once accessible directly. How does one imitate the medieval image of the Pantokrator?

The difficulty faced by Hesiod in melding the two stories of the Four Ages and the Four Classes of Being is symptomatic of the difficulties faced by the early Church. His poem from the eighth century B.C. is our first evidence of the type of contradictory images and traditions current in the Greco-Roman environment that the early Christians inherited and attempted to combine in constructing their understandings of Jesus. In Hesiod, the Greek idea of the high place of humans in the cosmos competes with the low view of human history; yet the dignity of the heroes remains, and they hold their own to inspire the story with their examples of courage in the face of the contrary forces of fate and the gods. Eventually, however, in Christian tradition, the apocalyptic story of the Four Ages, with its distant and wholly righteous God and its degenerate Iron race of humans, overwhelms the heroes, and they are all but lost.

I have tried to trace the history of an ideal life, a way of being a person, that was the basic model for nearly all people in the Greco-Roman world, the life of the tragic hero, which became the basis for understanding the life of Jesus and the life of the ideal Christian. It was an old and venerable ideal, popularized by the greatest literature produced in antiquity and given at least verbal assent (if not followed in action) by even the most hardened materialists and successful political figures of Rome. Life was in general difficult and short, and most people died early at the height of their powers in the midst of life. So ancient Greeks told stories that valorized such lives, that taught dignity in the face of inevitable suffering and courage and personal righteousness in the face of inimical fate and death. In time among the Greek philosophers, the stories became melded with the dualism of body and soul that led to a view of physical life on earth as a mere shadow of the real life of the immortal soul. In Persia, similar dualistic modes of thought had personified fate into the Devil and his demons, and the human condition was seen as life between two opposing forces of good and evil. In both cultures, the life of the righteous individual was one under assault that required one to call forth the very best qualities of the soul and after death face a judgment and either punishment or reward. These were not Semitic ideas, and originally Israelite religion held a strikingly opposite view of the will of God, with long life and material wealth as rewards for obedience to Law, without judgment after death or substantial afterlife. But wealth and long life were rare for anyone, let alone the righteous, and such a contract in Israel was unable to sustain the realities of military conquest, occupation, and exile by superior nations. Israel was conquered and/or ruled by the Persian, Greek, and Roman empires for most of six centuries before the rise of Christianity, and slowly among a number of the various factions of Judaism that arose during that period, their new ideas began to take hold. It was from among these factions that Jesus and the early Jewish Christians arose. So we see both the dualism of body and soul and that of God and the Devil, and a rather free reinterpretation of the Old Testament and its traditions according to these standards, as constituent parts of the message of Jesus and the early Christian gospel. But as the message reached outside of Palestine and into the larger gentile world, it was the central story of the career of Jesus as hero, the story most familiar to the culture at large, that gave it a hearing, and it was its call for everyone to follow and reap the rewards that the heroes alone had once obtained that gave it such wide appeal.

The bewildering diversity of the early Christian movements has led many to question whether or not Jesus ever intended to start a movement—if he did, why was there no orthodoxy, no common doctrines? A second and related problem is the (now famous) observation that the original message seems to have changed. Jesus, it is said, preached the coming of the kingdom of God, while his followers preached Jesus— the messenger became the message. Yet these are not ancient-world problems but modern ones, problems that arose only after there was such a thing as orthodoxy, and especially after the Reformation, when holding to the proper doctrines of Jesus as the content of the gospel message determined one's salvation.

Not so in the early Church; faithfulness, not the doctrines of the faith, determined one's salvation: "the one who endures to the end will be saved" (Mark 13:13). Jesus had said, "Follow me." He was the leader, and following the life pattern of Jesus the leader until death was what made one Christian and held Christians together. His promise was eternal life, and his basic outlook was based in a dualism of body and soul: "What does it profit if you gain the world and lose your soul?" His presence filled their meetings and his spirit inspired many Christians to imitation in good deeds and courage in the face of persecution. Epictetus, Stoic philosopher of the early second century, noted that two types of people were in the habit of having no fear of death and "considering material things as nothing": insane people and Christians (*Discourses* 4.7.6). Lucian observed much the same in the Christian desire to help those who were jailed during persecutions: "It is amazing the speed they show, whenever some such public action occurs, for in a moment they spare nothing"; for they "have convinced themselves first off that they will be completely immortal and will live forever" (*Peregrinus* 13, GJR). That was the promise and the pattern of the life of Jesus, and that could be seen even by outsiders.

For myself, I admit that I cannot imitate the gods. And even if I could, I would not wish to imitate the miracle workers and snake oil salesmen of both past and present. If in fact these were anything like the Jesus of the early church, we would not have Christianity today. Almost no one in antiquity was so foolish as to follow such people for more than a short time. Health, wealth, and success in the world of money and business and politics were out of reach of the vast majority of people and were understood to be dangers to the health of the soul. We have lost something important. Today we worship the rich and famous, but they seldom do anything worth imitating in the moral and real human sense; they seldom risk their precious posteriors for anything. I think that the reason why the story of Jesus was able to valorize the lives of so many poor and suffering people in the ancient world, why they risked as he had risked, why they imitated him and followed him to the grave, was that in some way that they well understood and we do not, Jesus was their hero.

INDEX

BIBLICAL CITATIONS

OLD TESTAMENT

Genesis 49; 6:2, 130; 6:4, 39; 18:1–2, 109; 18:2, 54; 25:8, 21
Exodus 3:2, 130; 15:11, 23; 20:3, 194; 21:2, 78; 33:23, 109
Numbers 16:33, 21
Deuteronomy 18:15–19, 63; 21:23, 64, 155; 28:20, 22; 30:15, 22; 34:7, 21
Joshua 1:8, 22
Judges 13:6, 130
1 Samuel 15:33, 153
2 Kings 2, 25; 17:7–41, 24–25; 23:25, 25; 23:26-27 25, 27; 23:29, 25
1 Chronicles 29:28, 21;
Job 37:18, 22; 38:7, 122
Psalms 131; 2:7, 74; 18:34, 153; 44:9–26, 25; 137:1, 25; 148:6, 24
Proverbs 8, 112; 10:22, 22
Isaiah 7:14, 74, 117; 45:1, 26, 116; 45:6–7, 26; 53, 63,87
Jeremiah 23:5, 63; 31:29, 25
Ezekiel 18:2, 25–26; 18:25, 25; 20:39, 191; 31:14, 22
Daniel 2, 31, 32; 7:13, 63,130

NEW TESTAMENT

Matthew 1:18, 76; 1:25, 76; 3:7–9, 151; 5:38–39, 62; 5:39, 79; 5:44-45, 79; 8:20, 98; 11:25–27, 149; 11:28–30, 97; 16:18, 11, 142; 19:8, 78; 22:7, 86; 25:31–46, 54; 27:51, 89; 28:19, 70

Mark 3:32, 155; 4:11–12, 148; 4:41, 80; 6:2, 80; 6:3, 76; 7:15, 62; 7:19, 62; 7:18–23, 182; 7:19, 62; 8:15–18, 88; 8:27, 115; 8:27–29, 98; 8:30, 88; 8:33, 156; 8:34, 64; 8:38, 156; 9:43, 55
Luke 1:35, 76; 2:34, 82; 3:23, 90; 6:20, 117; 10:4, 115; 10:18, 84; 11:18, 115; 11:53–54, 86; 13:6–9, 90; 17:20, 116; 19:44, 86; 21:12, 197; 21:19, 176; 24:45, 102
John 1:14, 136; 1:18 (GJR), 72; 1:36, 63; 1:51, 63; 2, 127; 2:4, 136; 2:11, 80; 2:19, 156; 3:3, 11; 3:19, 89; 4:24, 111; 4:54, 80; 5:8, 49; 5:18, 79; 11:3, 12; 12:21–22, 107; 12:23, 108; 14:15, 108; 17:10–13, 108; 17:28, 112; 17:30–31, 82; 17:31, 92, 120–21; 21:20–21, 117; 26:14, 154; 28:6, 108
Romans 1:3–4, 93; 1:4, 120; 2:17–19, 152; 2:20, 152; 3:1–2, 152; 3:25, 63; 9:5 (GJR), 131; 16:25–26, 150
1 Corinthians 2:7 (GJR), 148; 2:8, 85,91; 4:9, 176; 4:9–13, 169; 8:4, 194; 8:5, 93; 9:24–27, 163; 10:4, 63; 10:11, 102; 10:20, 195; 11:21, 188; 11:29–30, 149; 15:33–5, 70, 71; 15:26, 136; 15:32, 173; 15:36, 146; 15:50, 136
2 Corinthians 1:8, 174; 3:6, 62; 4:7, 28; 5:1, 136; 10:3–5, 163; 11:4, 125; 11:20, 152
Galatians 1:10, 153; 1:13–14 (GJR), 153; 2:12, 11; 2:15 (GJR), 105; 2:19–20,